PRETEXTS OF AUTHORITY

*The Rhetoric of Authorship
in the Renaissance Preface*

Pretexts
of Authority

THE RHETORIC OF AUTHORSHIP
IN THE RENAISSANCE PREFACE

KEVIN DUNN

Stanford University Press
Stanford, California

Stanford University Press
Stanford, California
© 1994 by the Board of Trustees
of the Leland Stanford Junior University
Printed in the United States of America

CIP data appear at the end of the book

Stanford University Press publications are
distributed exclusively by Stanford University
Press within the United States, Canada, and
Mexico; they are distributed exclusively by
Cambridge University Press throughout the rest
of the world.

Material from Steven Millhauser,
*Edwin Mullhouse: The Life and Death of an
American Writer 1943–1954 by Jeffrey
Cartwright*, reprinted by permission of
International Creative Management, Inc.
© 1972 by Steven Millhauser

This book is dedicated to my father and the memory of my mother.

Contents

    Renaissance Preface   147

    Notes   157

    Bibliography   181

    Index   195

Preface

I have studied them carefully, those smug adult prefaces. With fat smiles of gratitude, fit thanks are given for services rendered and kindnesses bestowed. Long lists of names are cleverly paraded in order to assure you that the author has excellent connections and a loving heart. Let me say at once that in this instance there are none to thank besides myself. I am not thankful to Dr. and Mrs. Mullhouse for moving away with the remains. I am not thankful to Aunt Gladys for mislaying eleven chapters. I have always done my own typing myself, using both index fingers, and I have never received any encouragement at all from anyone about anything. And so, in conclusion, I feel that grateful thanks are due to my-self, without whose kind encouragement and constant interest I could never have completed my task; to myself, for my valuable assistance in a number of points; to myself, for doing all the dirty work; and above all to myself, whose patience, understanding, and usefulness as a key eye-witness can never be adequately re-paid, and who in a typical burst of scrupulousness wish to point out that the "remains" mentioned above are, of course, literary remains. —Steven Millhauser, *Edwin Mullhouse: The Life and Death of an American Writer 1943–1954 by Jeffrey Cartwright*

Steven Millhauser's parody of the prefatory acknowledgment (placed within his parody of the literary biography) goes to the heart of many of the issues surrounding the practice of prefatory writing. Millhauser's Boswell is the eleven-year-old Jeffrey Cart-wright, who narrates the life of the literary genius Edwin Mull-house, his deceased friend and near contemporary (Jeffrey is, of course, six months older). Jeffrey attacks the inherent subordina-tion of the biographer to his subject and his subject matter most explicitly and resentfully in the preface, deflecting his ire into a statement of self-authorization with an absoluteness possible only in an eleven-year-old. The relevance of Millhauser's parable to the preface lies in the fact that every preface "tells the life story" of its text, with the concomitant subordination to that text implied. Like the biographer, the preface exists nominally only for and because of its subject; like the biographer, it exists ideally in a state of transparence; and like the biographer, it must come both before and after its subject—introducing it from a retrospective vantage point.

Jeffrey detects an irony—that the rhetoric of "adult prefaces" is essentially adolescent, at once "smug" and cringing. If his alternative seems infantile, it nonetheless represents the kind of struggle with the prefatory "relationship" that I will examine in this book. Jeffrey's refusal of the central aim of classical rhetoric—the attempt to capture the audience's goodwill, the *captatio benevolentiae*—is only the logical extreme of a postclassical resistance to authorial self-effacement. The story of Renaissance prefatory rhetoric is a search for forms flexible and large enough to house the ethos of the author, an ethos growing more and more complex with the expanding institution of authorship.

Early modern rhetorical theorists made few contributions to the discussion of the preface, a discussion that had hardly budged since Cicero. Scaliger, for instance, makes only a few passing references to the proem and exordium. In England, Thomas Wilson's *The Arte of Rhetorique* (1560) makes few significant departures from Cicero's dicta, despite the native touch of adding allusions to Robin Hood. Scaliger and Wilson are typical of humanism's reception of prefatory theory. Yet if theory remained static, early modern practice not only took into account but significantly internalized and extended the oratorical prescriptions of ancient theorists. In particular, the resistance to the *captatio benevolentiae* was at its most complex (if not its height) during the early modern period, when the line between the public and the private was being redrawn, and when one system of authority, that of the Church, was fading, while the next great authorizing system, represented by the liberal state and the myth of scientific progress, was not yet fully in place. In this discursive interstice the humanist ideal of authorial individualism emerged, an ideal, however, that was in practice constantly compromised by public discourses that, if weakened or nascent, were still powerful influences toward "corporate" thinking.

That compromised individualism created a system of prefatory rhetoric everywhere heightened by the available possibilities of self-authorization. This practice dramatically reflects the rise of "modernity" where the public and private roles of the author intersect and crucial struggles for authority are fought. These struggles (often part of larger social struggles) give Renaissance prefaces a hermeneutic importance that later prefaces may lack. As Annabel Patterson argues, "In general, late modern criticism has not paid enough attention to the interpretive status of introductory materials in early modern texts." Patterson notes that although the modern reader (and editor) is likely to ignore front matter, this was not the practice in the Renaissance, as evidenced by the Printing Act of 1662, which stipulated that "Titles, Epistles, Prefaces, Proems, Preambles, Introductions, Tables, Dedications" be perused by the licenser along with the body of the text.[1] William Prynne, Patterson reminds us, lost his ears in 1633 over his *parerga*, not his text proper.[2] It is one of the motivating assumptions of this book that we need to recover our lost ear for prefatory rhetoric if we are to comprehend properly questions of authorship and authority in the Renaissance.

Jeffrey Cartwright's exemplum of authorial defiance is undoubtedly liberating and even salubrious, yet it is one that I am unfortunately unable to follow in this Preface. A host of friends, colleagues, and teachers assisted me throughout in the "dirty work" of writing this book. Over more years than I care to recall, I benefited from the advice and encouragement of a long list of helpful readers: John Rogers, Joshua Scodel, Edward Schiffer, Marina Leslie, Susanne Wofford, Elizabeth Heckendorn Cook, Nancy Wright, John Hollander, Edwin Duval, James Shulman, Kevis Goodman, Margaret Ferguson, Liliane Greene, Ian Duncan, Jeffrey Knapp, Lynn Enterline, Ann Fabian, and Jonathan Freedman. Members of the Wesleyan Renaissance Seminar—John Paoletti, Laurie Nussdorfer, Gary Spear, Leonard Tennenhouse, Denise Albanese, and John Klause—read Chapter 2 with critical care.

I should also single out a few people for special thanks. Helen Tartar at Stanford University Press has been as shrewd and humane an editor as an author could hope for. Robert Burdette's meticulous yet sparing hand as a copy editor took much of the anxiety out of preparing the manuscript for press. Timothy Hampton's scrupulous and acute reader's report enabled me to finish the manuscript far earlier and in a far better state than I might have otherwise. Lawrence Manley read the manuscript in many of its various stages, never failing to improve it with his erudition, critical tact, and unflagging generosity. Thomas Greene oversaw the earliest moments of this book as my dissertation adviser and has continued to provide advice, encouragement, and example; his quiet, constant support over the last decade has meant more to me than I can easily express.

My wife, Elizabeth Leavell, and Sarah, Luther, and Pearl have never failed to remind me of the world outside this book and to ensure that it is a good one.

Finally, my dedication is to my first and best teachers, Walter and Ruth Dunn.

K.D.

The following abbreviations are used in the text and the notes. For full citations, see the Bibliography, pp. 181–93.

A & T	René Descartes, *Oeuvres*
CM	John Milton, *Works*
LW	Martin Luther, *Works*
PW	René Descartes, *Philosophical Writings*
WA	Martin Luther, *Werke*
YM	John Milton, *Complete Prose Works*

PRETEXTS OF AUTHORITY

*The Rhetoric of Authorship
in the Renaissance Preface*

1

Prefatory Authority

RENAISSANCE AUTHORSHIP
AND THE EXTRATEXTUAL

In this first chapter I will explore the heightened attention given to the "extratextual" territory of the preface during the early modern period. Before doing so, however, I must briefly map out the terrain onto which the Renaissance inevitably projected itself—classical rhetorical theory. To a large extent, it is the discrepancies between this recuperated and privileged landscape on the one hand and the literary and social terrain writers needed to negotiate on the other that account for the specific shape of not only early modern prefatory writing but early modern ideas of authorship and rhetorical practice.

Classical rhetoric houses in its very presuppositions a decided prejudice against its own project, a prejudice abundantly clear in its theoretical pronouncements about the preface. Ancient theoreticians, while constructing elaborate schemes of prefatory rhetoric, nonetheless voice suspicion about a form whose purpose was arguably to subvert the judgment of the audience. In particular, classical theorizing about forensic rhetoric, with its assumption of a public sphere in which human action is fully intelligible and meaningful, tends to view with suspicion prefatory attempts upon the jury's ability to interpret what ought to be transparent facts. In Book 3 of his *Rhetoric*, Aristotle comments on a tag from Euripides's *Iphigenia Among the Taurians*: " 'Why all this preface?' Introductions are popular with those whose case is weak; it pays them to dwell on anything rather than the actual facts of it. That is why slaves, instead of answering the questions put to them, make indirect replies with long preambles."[1]

The lesson of Aristotle's slave echoes through the history of theoretical pronouncements on the preface: prefatory rhetoric is the rhetoric of the advocate with a bad case, the rhetoric of personal motive. Following Aristotle, Roman theorists distinguished between two kinds of forensic exordia: for "honorable" (*honestum*) cases, the *principium*, which is little more than a statement of the facts of the case, what we would call an introduction; for all other cases, those in which the hostility or suspicion of the audience can be anticipated, the tellingly named *insinuatio*. The speaker who "insinuates" is the speaker with personal motive, the speaker not in honest possession of "the actual facts" or for whom those facts are inconvenient. Such a speaker is a "slave" because, denied access to the transparent public discourse of "facts," he must construct his own "insinuating" narrative to simulate a relationship to his audience that approaches that of the (hypothetically) fully shared story of public fact.

Despite Aristotle's distrust of such narratives in which private interest encroaches on public understanding, he does not shunt aside the exigencies of persuasion, and he constructs the hierarchical classifications upon which subsequent theorists base the strategies of prefatory rhetoric. He outlines four "remedies" (*iatreúmata*)[2] or sources of goodwill that become a standard part of the theory of forensic oratory: the speaker's own ethical self-presentation (*ek tou légontos* / *ab nostra*), his appeal directly to his listeners or judges (*ek tou akroatou* / *ab iudicum persona*), the strength of his case itself (*ek tou prágmatos* / *a causa*), and his presentation of his opponent's ethical weaknesses (*ek tou enantíou* / *ab adversariorum*).[3] Aristotle argues that these "remedies" are "outside the question" and totally unnecessary if the listener is a man of discernment, in which case the oration need include only a perfunctory summary statement so that it does not appear as a body without a head. He does not rest, however, on this simplistic formula where the only variable is the intellectual capacity of the listener. He construes the second variable, the nature of the case, in an equally narrow fashion: the "remedies" of the exordium are to be inherently distrusted since only a bad cause needs them; no matter what the audience, a good cause needs no preface.

It was left to the Romans, who first posited the centrality of the forensic speech for what would become modern prefatory rhetoric, to articulate a full theoretical model of the exordium. For although they inherited something of Aristotle's ambivalence toward rhetoric, their experience in the forum was too important not to inure them to the practical exigencies that rhetoric necessarily involves. The political need for rhetoric under the Republic colors all facets of Roman intellectual life, including the conception of the preface.[4] The public sphere was no less totalizing for the Romans, yet they were always more willing to allow motivated agency into public debate. One's personal business, *negotium*, was part of the public realm, as opposed to one's leisure, *otium*; the public sphere was the place of constant "negotiation" between individuals. This distinction appears in the chiastic relationship between theater and court in the two cultures. Aristotle sees the ideal forensic exordium in terms of the dramatic prologue, as a "plot" summary to orient the listeners (*Rhetoric*, 3.14.8). Terence, on the other hand, constructs his prologues as defense speeches, exulting in the pun on *actor*, which can mean "dramatic player," but also "public speaker," "plaintiff," "defense attorney." In *Heauton Timorumenos*, the Prologue says of the author, "He meant [me] to be a pleader [*oratorem*], not only a speaker [*prologum*] of this part. He has made you the court [*iudicium*] and me the advocate [*actorem*]." The centrality of the courts for Roman life became a legacy for European rhetorical practice.

Not surprisingly, Roman theorists depart markedly from their Greek predecessors in their disposition of the exordium.[5] Cicero, for instance, tells us that there are five kinds of cases: honorable (*honestum*), difficult (*admirabile*), mean (*humile*), ambiguous (*anceps*), and obscure (*obscurum*).[6] This list extends significantly Aristotle's dichotomy of good and bad cases, and the blurring of moral edges it implies creates a freer field for rhetorical exercise. Although the Latin theorists prescribe a different exordium for different kinds of cases, agreeing with Aristotle that the "honorable" case may need only the simplest of openings,[7] they by no means dismiss the more rhetorically and morally complicated exordia, as is clear from their handling of the four sources of goodwill I have noted: oneself, one's opponents, the judges, and the case itself. When one's opponents are obviously negligible or corrupt, the task of the exordium is an easy one, and none of the an cient authorities dwell on these possibilities. Similarly, they waste little time on the question of obtaining the goodwill of the judge through flattery, only exhorting their readers to be subtle in this pursuit. The most important source of goodwill, then, in any but the most open-and-shut case, is oneself, and in fact the central purpose of the forensic exordium is to present the speaker as favorably as possible.

One should not confuse this strategy for oratorical authority, however, with a postclassical sense of the "author" or with an appeal to the persuasive powers of the "subject." The theorists are clear on this point: an effective self-presentation includes a deferential attitude toward the judge or judges, a disinterested stance toward the case, and a low, unornamented style. Quintilian (11.1.6) warns against the excessive use of metaphor, and even Cicero (who resisted the plain style of the Atticists) says in the early *De inventione* that the opening of a speech should be dignified and sententious yet "should contain very little brilliance, vivacity, or finish of style, because these give rise to a suspicion of preparation and excessive ingenuity. As a result of this . . . the speech loses conviction and the speaker, authority" (1.18.25). Putting aside intricate classifications, we have here the core of the forensic exordium. The speaker is to win authority for himself through the appearance of spontaneous eloquence and affected modesty. This appearance is of special importance in an *insinuatio*, which requires a particularly skillful development of the speaker's ethos to distract the judges from the case. Once the audience's goodwill is secured, the orator can then approach the facts of the case gradually.

The topoi that accrue around the *captatio benevolentiae* were established early in antiquity and proved to have remarkable staying power, yet as we shall see, the valence of these topoi shifts significantly in their early modern *Nachleben*. The most important of these conventions can be found in the preface to the *Rhetorica ad Herennium*, a work addressed to a young man named Herennius whom the author wishes to instruct in the rudiments of rhetoric. It begins: "My private affairs [*negotiis familiaribus*] keep me so busy that I can hardly find enough leisure [*otium*] to devote to study, and the little that is vouchsafed to me I have usually preferred to spend on philosophy" (1.1). Topos number one: the author prefers *otium* to *negotium*, a philosophical retirement to the active life of the orator. He continues: "Yet your desire, Gaius Herennius, has spurred me to compose a work on the Theory of Public Speaking, lest you should suppose that in a matter which concerns you I either lacked the will or shirked the labour" (1.1). The second topos proceeds logically from the first: it is only the desire of the dedicatee or audience that has prompted the author to public discourse, and in fact the work maintains a pretense of privacy since it is addressed to only one man, even though the author may have published the work himself. The next step is also a part of the logical progression: "And I have undertaken this project [*negotium*] the more gladly because I knew that you had good grounds in wishing to learn rhetoric, for it is true that copiousness and facility in expression bear abundant fruit, if controlled by proper knowledge and a strict discipline of mind" (1.1).

The worthiness of the speaker's subject, especially as opposed to the relative worthlessness of the speaker himself, would also become a commonplace. In particular, the author of the *Rhetorica* stresses the utility of the subject. He contrasts this utility to the self-indulgent play of his predecessors:

That is why I have omitted to treat those topics which, for the sake of futile self-assertion, Greek writers have adopted. For they, from fear of appearing to know too little, have gone in quest of notions irrelevant to the art, in order that the art might seem more difficult to understand. I, on the other hand, have treated those topics which seemed pertinent to the theory of public speaking.   (1.1)

Thus utility becomes the tool for the clearance of predecessors (in this case, Greek theoreticians) and the justification for the present endeavor. This logical progression of topics—the author's unwillingness, the request of the dedicatee, and the utility of the subject—moves the speaker from the ostensibly valued sphere of private retirement into the world of public affairs that constitutes the significant reality of antiquity.

The commonplaces of classical rhetoric as a whole therefore marginalize, from a modern perspective, the subjectivity of the writer, or more accurately, subordinate it to the "actual facts."[8] The modesty topos is perhaps the most important of these commonplaces. Quintilian makes it clear that the topos takes its power from the inverse relationship between perceived and actual authority: "We shall derive some silent support from representing that we are weak, unprepared, and no match for the powerful talents arrayed against us" (4.1.8). As Quintilian sees, the more effective a speaker's self-abnegation, the more seriously the listener will take his words on a subject, since he has made his own motivation invisible. Quintilian finds a psychological basis for the efficacy of this strategy in the natural defensiveness of the listener, who can more easily afford to trust a weak speaker than a strong one: "For men have a natural prejudice in favour of those who are struggling against difficulties, and a scrupulous judge is always specially ready to listen to an advocate whom he does not suspect to have designs on his integrity" (4.1.9).

Thus classical modesty bases itself on a simple inversion: the less physical, social, or political power one presents oneself as having, the more rhetorical power one has. Modesty does not provide a glimpse of the private voice, the idiom of the writer; rather, it seeks to define the writer as an unmotivated function of the case. As Quintilian puts it, "For thus [through modesty and a good reputation] he will have the good fortune to give the impression not so much that he is a zealous advocate as that he is an absolutely reliable witness" (4.1.7). The most effective speaker is the most transparent speaker, the one through whom the audience can see directly to the facts. As we shall see, it is this assumption of a perfectly intelligible public world, one not needing to be constituted by a series of private articulations, that the writers of the early modern period will challenge again and again as they contemplate the facts of their own cases.[9]

The dilemma of Aristotle's slave thus reflects the primacy of the public sphere in the rhetorical self-presentation of the ancient world. Paul Veyne formulates the public nature of the classical "self" in no uncertain terms, contrasting it with the Christian concept of selfhood:

No ancient, not even the poets, is capable of talking about himself. Nothing is more misleading than the use of "I" in Greco-Roman poetry. . . . He speaks in the name of all and makes no claim that his readers should be interested in his own personal state of mind. To talk about oneself, to throw personal testimony into the balance, to profess that personal conviction must be taken into account provided only that it is sincere is a Christian, indeed an eminently Protestant idea that the ancients never dared to profess.[10]

Much of my account in this book could be seen as the playing out of Veyne's contrast; that is, I ask what happens when early modern writers call upon classical rhetorical forms, forms that were invented to serve as exfoliations of a purely public persona, to handle a self that although by no means a fully individuated and private entity, bore a much more complex relationship to the public sphere.

The shift in prefatory functions in the early Middle Ages already reveals some of this growing complexity. By late antiquity, the rhetorical exordium had been largely shaped by its frequent doubling as an epistle dedicatory, if not totally assimilated to it.[11] This seemingly slight generic shift reflects a transformation in the pattern we have observed in the *Rhetorica ad Herennium*: the unwillingness to give up *otium* becomes an abdication of any public authority; the request of the dedicatee allows the author to shift responsibility to the requester; and the usefulness of the subject now also implies the uselessness of the author. An emblematic instance is the case of *mea mediocritas*, which during this period became the formulaic substitute for *ego*.[12] It is tempting, and not entirely misguided, to connect this abdication of authority and self-belittlement with a general feeling of unworthiness before great predecessors experienced by the authors of late antiquity and the Middle Ages. And yet this almost cringing deference to authority, which so far exceeds classical modesty, can also be seen as a sign of a rift in public discourse—or indeed the dissolution of the public sphere.

The relative importance of prefatory rhetoric during the early modern period is a function of this same interplay between the writer and the public sphere, although that relationship had altered greatly since the early Middle Ages. In his classic account of the development of the bourgeois public sphere, Jürgen Habermas argues that by the late Middle Ages the dichotomy between public and private had come to signify two separate notions. On the one hand, the distinction mapped the division between the common and the particular, between the public "commons" and privately owned lands. Overlaying this economic distinction, on the other hand, was a social and political one in which *public* was a designation of rank, the status of "the public presence of the person of the lord." The public was the arena of representation, but a representation "not for but 'before' the people." Only the public man had a representable public "presence."[13] *Public*, therefore, took on two paradoxically related definitions: that which was possessed by all in common, and that which only "public" figures possessed.

In the seventeenth century, this state of affairs shifted in a complex and nationally varied way as something like the modern sense of "the public sphere" emerged. In France, for instance, the second, social distinction between public and private served as the basis for the locus of public display. Erich Auerbach argues that this public space resided in court, salon, and finally and most significantly the theater. Originally aristocratic, these spaces became more and more permeable to the upper echelons of the bourgeoisie.[14] In England, however, it is the first definition of public and private, as the division between the common and the particular, that became the basis for the public sphere, creating along the way the foundation for the liberal state. From the middle of the sixteenth century onward, there developed a powerful ideology of the "common wealth," an ideology that stressed public utility, the good of the nation over that of private individuals.[15] By the time of the Civil War, this ideology had such a strong hold on the English imagination that it is an apologist for monarchy, Hobbes, who articulates clearly for the first time a theory of representation in the modern sense that implies a public sphere, separate from the state, that rulers represent.

The creation of a bourgeois public sphere brought with it important changes to the concept of authority, political but also literary. For the medieval writer, authority was a textual inheritance, a finite set of authorities who could be adduced and copied but rarely added to. The essential genre for the medieval writer was thus the gloss, the ligature between authority and writer. Whether the gloss was the writer's in the margin of an authorized text or an authority cited to buttress the writer's words, the scene of writing always appeared as an interplay between a preestablished "master text" and the writer's liminal approach to that text. Authority, in other words, was hierarchically determined and inevitably *borrowed*; strategies of what might be called self-authorization were beside the point.

In a curious way, the authorizing strategies of the late seventeenth century recapitulate this situation. The structure of the authorizing hierarchy had largely dissolved, along with the universality of the Roman church and the idea of empire that accompanied it. Yet by the "age of Dryden," strategies of self-authorization, while available, had begun to be held in a certain suspicion. This suspicion, I would argue, is not just the product of familiarity but of a new system of authorization in which the writer takes authority by *representing* his or her audience. This system echoes a characteristic of the public sphere itself, a characteristic Habermas calls its "audience-oriented subjectivity" (28). The paradox of Habermas's phrase is the paradox of "common sense"; the public sphere as conceived at the end of the seventeenth century is an agglutinative entity composed of the private responses of all the citizenry. Timothy Riess describes this movement toward common sense as "the occultation of the enunciating subject *as discursive activity*" and traces its trajectory: "Galileo's *I* becomes Descartes's *we* and the objectivity of 'common speech' from Locke to Lavoisier."[16] The writer's primary rhetorical concern in such a system is to demonstrate that he or she possesses common sense, that he or she represents the audience.

It will be clear from this brief historical sketch that I have omitted the center of the history, the moment between the medieval and Enlightenment models of authority, and that I regard this moment as the space of the fullest exercise of self-authorizing rhetoric in the Western literary tradition before the Romantics. The story of this rhetoric is to a large extent the story of humanism. If humanism quickly made its peace with autocracy and courtly culture, it nonetheless had its origins in the Italian bourgeoisie and took its strength from the growing market for books that was created by the printing press. This double-sided humanism—in service to monarchical and aristocratic interests but at its core part of market culture—thus contains both systems of authorization and representation I described above. Yet if it contains both, it also remains to a certain extent aloof from both, not fully committed to the representations of power or to the diffusion of those representations in the marketplace.[17]

It is this "in-betweenness" of humanism, viewed teleologically, that explains its role as the matrix for the institution of authorship, an institution that in its fullest form is coterminous with humanism. I would thus modify Foucault's famous definition of the author: "Texts, books, and discourses really began to have authors . . . to the extent that authors became subject to punishment, that is, to the extent that discourses could be transgressive."[18] Since both discursive transgression and its punishment antedate the full-blown development of authorship as an institution in the European tradition, I offer a revised version of this formula: texts, books, and discourses begin to need authors at the moment when their transgression itself seeks institutionalization. In other words, it is when the subversive discourse finds itself on the brink of empowerment, of articulating something more than a negative critique of the reigning orthodoxies, that the authority of the author becomes necessary. Thus I would argue that authorship is less the necessary result of what Foucault calls "penal appropriation" than of the more general category of appropriation he discusses as ownership. It is when transgression is itself appropriated as a rhetorical gesture, when it is followed by or becomes part of the authorial claim, that authorship is institutionalized. My argument is that this moment takes place during the Renaissance, and most radically in the Reformation when Luther distinguishes himself from the host of medieval anti-clerical satirists through his ever-growing sense that he needed to present an institutional alternative to the Church.

If the texts I choose to examine in this study are not generally considered central to the humanist tradition, they are nonetheless all engaged in some fashion with the humanist endeavor. That they are marginal to that endeavor reflects my interest in the "edges" of the institution of authorship, its emergence from authoritarian models of textuality, and especially its dispersal into the "representative" voice of common sense. For if in its early incarnation the market for books opened up the possibility of an authorial voice, the highly developed market culture of the seventeenth century and beyond fully commodified that voice. I am thus interested in the moment Peter Stallybrass and Allon White invoke to describe authorship: Ben Jonson, by means of the satire on the sordid market of *Bartholomew Fair*, standing apart from "the social and economic relations which determined his own existence."[19] The moment, in other words, where the writer attempts an ideological separation of himself and his work from the market that created both in order to establish the work as inimitable artifact rather than commodity and himself as author rather than craftsman or chapman.

Foucault claims that "all discourses endowed with the author-function" contain a "plurality of self." But it is "the self that speaks in the preface" (152), to use one of his examples, that is the most quintessentially authored. The "I" that speaks the preface of the early modern book is never merely the writerly "I"; it is first and foremost the essence of the authorial claim. Put otherwise, it is always a rhetorical figure, a gesture with a design on its audience, an attempt at self-authorization. Yet again and again in the texts I examine, the author that emerges, like the subject he shadows, disappears back into his product. This is the paradox of the marketplace: authorship provides value to the textual commodity, but this value grants a currency to the text that draws it from its author. Every preface is also an *envoi*.

A facet of humanism's project that bears directly on the authorial rhetoric of the preface is its sustained engagement with the problem of exemplarity.[20] The rhetoric of example reaches into every corner of Renaissance letters, serving (among other functions) as a ligament to tie the present to antiquity, to assure the humanist and his audience that a transhistorical set of values connect the modern world to the chosen ground of the humanist political and cultural project. As Timothy Hampton has pointed out, this project and its tools of exemplum and exemplar are intimately bound up with the history of subjectivity: "In setting forth the deeds of the exemplar the Renaissance text provides the reader with an image of the self, a model of an ideal soul or personality which mediates between ideals of public virtue and the reader's self-understanding" (19). Perhaps inevitably, this model, drawn from the heroic past, begins to apply pressure on the model of authorial self-presentation.

There can be no doubt that the implied application of exemplarity to the author—a movement of literature into the vacuum left by action as the bases of civic humanism crumbled—could be only tentative at first. If we move ahead to Montaigne, however, the power of this appropriation becomes evident. Montaigne's appropriation takes the form of what Hampton has called the "post-

humanist notion of exemplarity" (139). Having ironized, quali-
fied, and hedged the humanist classical exemplum all but out of
existence, Montaigne returns to exemplarity by instating himself
as exemplar. As he writes in "Of Repentance": "I set forth a humble and inglorious life; that does not matter. You can tie up all
moral philosophy with a common and private life just as well as
with a life of richer stuff. Each man bears the entire form of man's
estate."[21] This strange form of exemplarity requires no exemplary
life, only an open one, so that what is "common" can be factored
out through honest introspection. But it would be a mistake to assume that Montaigne has been able to free himself from the bag-
gage of exemplarity. Even though his claim of a common humanity would seem a modest enough moral claim (if epistemologically
daring), it exposes him to the same kind of scrutiny that he has
turned on classical exemplars. In fact, one suspects that the rhetorical energy Montaigne invests in wriggling out of the very cast
of commonality he has claimed may have a double purpose: first,
to allow him to distinguish himself from those who are truly common; second, to protect him from the subversive implications that
his example implies.

The truism of Montaigne scholarship, that his method regularly entails an initial attack on traditional concepts that is followed
by a retreat behind the skirts of tradition (both moves being empowered by skepticism), is apropos here. In "Of Repentance," his
retreat from his exemplary status is signaled by the very theme of
repentance when Montaigne repents for not repenting:

Let me here excuse what I often say, that I rarely repent and that my conscience is content with itself—not as the conscience of an angel or a horse,
but as the conscience of a man; always adding this refrain, not perfuncto-
rily but in sincere and complete submission: that I speak as an ignorant
inquirer, referring the decision purely and simply to the common and authorized beliefs. I do not teach, I tell.   (612)

Montaigne affirms and denies his exemplary status on the same
basis, his humanity. If his explorations of his humanness make
him somehow an object lesson, the fact that he has neither the stable makeup of a horse nor the transcendent wisdom of an angel
makes that lesson a necessarily contingent one. In fact, the final
sentence, which denies the didactic function of his example, returns us to the opening sentence of the essay, which itself forms

the basis for his exemplum of commonality: "Others form man; I tell of him, and portray a particular one, very ill-formed, whom I should really make very different from what he is if I had to fashion him over again." This subject, that he studies rather than forms, the subject that he "cannot keep . . . still" (610), is exemplary in the very humanness of its giddy instability, yet in need of no repentance since the self that erred is no longer the self that writes.

A similar dynamic operates in Montaigne's engagement with the modesty topos in his preface. On the one hand, no text could embrace modesty more fully; it is absolutely without claims to importance to anyone other than his family and friends, he tells us. On the other hand, the publication of such a document, as Montaigne realizes, is an immodest act, an act that he attempts to literalize by claiming that he would show himself "entire and wholly naked" (2) if society allowed it. By relocating the site in which modesty is a meaningful concept, Montaigne has provided an important marker in the history of private life—one's person, the domestic self, the homebody (as it were), has been elevated in importance to the point that it can now be clothed in rhetorical colors. Montaigne's recourse to the body to ground the ever more elusive authority of the example echoes an omnipresent early modern rhetorical strategy: the individualizing of authority through a "bodily voice."

But he has also marked out the crux of "posthumanist" discourse,[22] and I will thus have cause to return again and again to this moment. His preface begs the question of how to ground and maintain an authorial self built from a set of self-presentational topoi when the origin of those conventions has been eroded. How, in other words, when the system of reading the past that created moral categories and (theoretically) moral human beings has lost its efficacy in compelling belief, can its creation, the author, continue to claim authority? This crisis mimicked, *in parvo*, the one it had itself helped to produce and may in fact have been one of the lingering aftershocks of the earlier crisis.

This book begins as a prehistory of Montaigne's crux; Luther moves through these same issues as he attempts to work out the relation of his private history to the public history he played so large a part in creating. In particular, Montaigne replays Luther's simultaneous attempts to create a subversive discursive space and to seal that space off from potential imitators. On the whole, it might be said that insufficient attention has been paid to what may be regarded as the flipside of *imitatio* theory, that is, discursive practices designed to discourage or to limit imitation by readers, to keep readers as readers and not as writers.[23] Bacon and particularly Descartes (imitating Montaigne) struggle with this same dangerous trace element of humanism, the self-referential exemplum that must now contain its own exemplarity.

The importance of this discursive arrogation of authorial rights is most noticeable in the kind of nonliterary texts I have chosen to examine. Although Jonson's strictures against poetasters show that the cultural import of just anyone writing a poem was on the rise, his were only the first attacks on literary amateurism (attacks that would escalate at the end of the century when literary texts began to serve as a contested site of public authority). The vexed exemplarity of these religious and scientific texts is a marker of their high cultural stakes. I argue that something like a consensus on the question of authorial exemplarity is in place by the end of the seventeenth century, a consensus based on the very idea of consensus, of common sense. Montaigne seems to suggest this possibility in "Of Repentance" without adopting it himself. But by the end of the next century, prefatory rhetoric is dominated by a conflation of two classical appeals: *ab nostra* and *ab iudicum persona*. That is, no longer does an appeal to the judges need to be figured as mere flattery because there is now a bridge between the ethos of the speaker and that of his audience. Concomitantly, the strictures of the earlier conceptions of authorial exemplarity begin to ease: the tentative homology between writer and reader makes efforts to block imitation less pressing.

In Part I, I study the Christian basis for this rhetoric of individualism, first by looking at Saint Paul's abrogation of classical modesty, which he aligns with his rejection of Jewish law. He effects this abrogation and grounds his authority through the same means, his recourse to his suffering body, which both affronts the classical line between private and public and gives Paul a martyr's testimony. I then turn to his Protestant successors and their articulation of what amounts to a subversive individualism. In Luther and Milton, however, this individualism is shifted at the moment of its birth, if it is not altogether stillborn. Luther, under the influence of the humanists, has learned to build self-authorizing personal narrations into his prefatory rhetoric, but at crucial moments this rhetoric slips back into a public voice, thus producing a double narrative of the public and the private without providing the reader a means to construct a hierarchical relation between the two. Milton, at the tail end of the tradition of Renaissance humanism, is even more adept at the use of ethos as a polemical tool. But just as Luther felt the pull of a more medieval corporate voice, Milton registers the force of a new discourse of the public sphere and makes it his ultimate goal in the prose works to show himself "a member incorporate." Thus Milton also adopts a bifurcated self-presentation in which his role as a poet stands for the humanist tradition of self-individuation and his duties as a polemicist for the puritan cause reabsorb him into the "corporate" voice of public discourse.

Part II of the book focuses more fully on the second half of the story told by the Protestant prefaces, that of a new sense of public language emerging in the seventeenth century. I begin with Descartes, who sketches out clearly the deep ambivalence registered by Milton, but especially acute in seventeenth-century scientific writers, between older notions of intellectual activity as the retired musings of the aristocrat and a powerful new definition of that activity as labor, public work for the public good. Descartes was not fully able to accept the ramifications of this downward mobility of the intellectual, but another aristocrat, Bacon, made that ideological jump by committing himself to the institutionalization of the scientific enterprise. This commitment created Bacon as the model and prophet for the discourse of public utility in seventeenth-century Europe. Yet as in so many other matters, it was left to Hobbes to theorize and politicize this discursive movement fully. In Hobbes's *Leviathan*, one can see the lineaments of this new intellectual polity. One can also see in Hobbes a new theory of prefatory rhetoric emerging, a theory more answerable to a new sense that audience is a constitutive part of authority. In Hobbes's view, rhetoric must be *representative* as well as *ethical*—that is, it must demonstrate the author's adherence to common sense rather than merely dramatize his personal quest to enter into canons of textual authority.

I end Part II by discussing a text that could not be less scientific, Dryden's "Preface to the *Fables*." I make this leap between disciplines for two reasons. First, no text shows more clearly how new ideas about the construction of authority are worked out in rhetorical terms. Dryden's "Preface" is nothing if not a manifesto of authorial control of tradition and of a realignment of authority with audience response. Second, the "Preface" shows how the "georgic" ideas of public discourse, which had been percolating in all the disciplines but primarily in the sciences and technologies, had now been fully disseminated. Moreover, I argue that with science having secured its discursive boundaries through the complementary myths of objectivity and public utility, literature became the new site for working out the competing claims of public and private. It is as such a site that literature begins to emerge as an independent category, a place crucial for cultural and political negotiations. Having, however, made such claims for the new rhetorical alignment I have traced into the late stages of the early modern period, I am faced with a final irony that this alignment, which once again privileges the "actual facts" of public discourse, relegates the object of my study, the preface, to a position not unlike the one it held in antiquity—that of a suspect intrusion of personal motive into the already fully intelligible world of the forum.

PART I

"A member incorporate"

PUBLIC AND PRIVATE RHETORIC
IN THE PROTESTANT PREFACE

Self-authorization has always been part of the prefatory project, and the intersection of preface with authorizing strategies is as old as the preface itself. Hesiod provides the archetype for this intersection in the *Theogony*, which opens with a narrative describing the Muses' gift of poetry to him:

And one day they taught Hesiod glorious song while he was shepherding his lambs under holy Helicon, and this word first the goddesses said to me—the Muses of Olympus, daughters of Zeus who holds the aegis: "Shepherds of the wilderness, wretched things of shame, mere bellies, we know how to speak many false things as though they were true; but we know, when we will, to utter true things." So said the ready-voiced daughters of great Zeus, and they plucked and gave me a rod, a shoot of sturdy laurel, a marvellous thing, and breathed into me a divine voice to celebrate things that shall be and things that were aforetime.   (ll.22–34)

Hesiod's narrative provides a useful, if unlikely, starting place for considering the rhetoric of self-presentation in "Protestant prefaces," although one might argue that his portrait of himself before the Muses represents in its most radical form the rhetorical scene of any preface: the ritual humbling ("mere bellies") that the author must endure before he or she can take on power ("a shoot of sturdy laurel") over the audience.

Yet the specific link with the Protestant preface is that Hesiod's apotheosized version of rhetorical self-authorization also teaches us that this scene is not only rhetorical, designed to convince the audience of the author's power, but also exegetical, designed to fashion that power by finding the link to a larger narrative. This exegetical task involves the author's situating himself in relation to earlier representations of the "master text." Hesiod's situating exegesis occurs in the famous words of the Muses—"We know how to speak [*légein*] many false things as though they were true; but we know [*ídmen*], when we will, to utter [*gerúsasthai*] true things"—words that recall Homer's address to the Muses prefacing the Catalogue of Ships:

> For you, who are goddesses, were there, and you know all
>   things,
> and we have heard only the rumour of it and know [*ídmen*]
>   nothing.   (2.485–86)

Hesiod's Muses speak to him directly and introduce the complicated possibility that Homer's confidence in them might have been misplaced. Hesiod's ability to distinguish between those things the Muses "utter" and the things they merely "speak" is a hermeneutic skill that places him closer than his glorious predecessor Homer to the divine text.[1] Moreover, the very adoption of a mythic medium involves allegorical interpretation, of both Homer and the master text, divine Truth.

Hesiod's opening presents, in short, the more acute problems of authority that enter when one injects a personal narrative into a larger, divine text. If his narrative could serve as a model for all prefatory rhetoric, it has special relevance for the writers I will examine in this part. Although his story holds out the possibility of an authorizing hermeneutics, Hesiod veils interpretation with, even construes interpretation as, revelation. He must do so since every hermeneutic, especially if it has revolutionary claims, must have some authorizing fulcrum from which to lift texts into the light of a new mode of reading. This necessity has a special force with Protestant writers. Having denied the stable, hierarchically distributed authority of Rome, they must take their authority directly from God, and establishing this authority becomes the focus of these prefaces. In such a context, the issue of interpretation is a delicate one since it calls attention to the contingency surrounding any knowledge of the divine text. Both Luther and Milton (and Protestant exegetes in general) finesse the problem by adopting the Augustinian principle of *claritas Scripturae*, the principle that Scripture is fundamentally clear in all essential points of doctrine.[2] Such a principle, however, hardly provides an interpretive panacea; one man's *claritas* is another's *obscuritas*. What this conundrum required was a rhetoric of authorship to ground the challenge of the individual to the Church, a rhetoric that could articulate these private challenges in a public parlance.

The most readily available model for such self-authorization was the classical ethical proof, as reinterpreted and reinvigorated by the humanists, but it was a model not without its own problems. Protestant writers found rhetoric, especially the prefatory rhetoric of ethical proof, at once necessary and suspect—necessary because the extraordinary claims they made for their work demanded a validation even beyond that anticipated by classical prefatory rhetoric; suspect because a studied, codified rhetoric strongly implies human agency.[3] Since Luther and Calvin both argued without reservation that man possesses no free will in the performance of any righteous act, they render the very name *author* highly ambiguous. God is the only author of good, the only originator. The writer's attempts at ethical proof always threaten to become both circular—since the only proof of merit is the presence of God's hand, the very thing he had sought to prove in the first place—and presumptuous. Yet, to complete the irony, an author remains the only possibility to break the circularity that authorship itself creates since even the absolute authority of Scripture requires interpretation, a fact that drove both Luther and Calvin to compose many volumes of biblical commentary to replace the accreted glosses of a millennium of papism.

In the works of the earliest reformers, humanism was essential to this project, not so much as a means to resolve the *Teufelskreis* of authorship but as a way of articulating the very terms of this *aporia* of authority. It provided, first, an alternative to medieval hermeneutics, a system of reading that if not based solely on the grammar and rhetoric of the text at hand, was nonetheless firmly *linguistic* in comparison with its medieval predecessors. In addition, although as an evaluative system of reading humanism was perhaps still as dependent on *auctoritas* as its forebears, it invoked a different set of authorities and used them differently. This new way of reading implied a new fashion of writing, and with it a new concept of the author. Humanist attentiveness to language and rhetoric, and its elaborately theorized stress on imitating ancient authors, created a heightened sense of the choices available in expression, choices that could produce an individuated authorial style. Erasmian *copia*, while derived from classical authors, also freed one from overdependence on any one authority through the very abundance of rhetorical possibility.[4]

The humanist influence on reforming rhetoric is evident not just in the scholarship of moderates like Melanchthon but even in the sermons and commentaries of Calvin. In fact, William Bouwsma's recent reevaluation of Calvin centers on the enduring Erasmianism of his work, a continued devotion to the ends of Christian humanism that has been underappreciated by generations of scholars. According to Bouwsma, not only did humanist exegesis play an ongoing role in Calvin's understanding of Scripture, but the ends of persuasive rhetoric spoke powerfully to Calvin's "awareness of the need for accommodation to the times."[5] If a reformer's zeal for the truth tempers this Erasmian sense of accommodation, it nonetheless colors much of his rhetoric. One need look no further than the dedication of the *Institutes of the Christian Religion* (1536) to Francis I. Although ostensibly cast as an epistle dedicatory, this preface is in fact a perfect example of a classical forensic speech, a defense of his work that follows precisely the formula for Ciceronian seven-part oratory. As he himself puts it, "I fear even that too many details have been included, since this preface has already grown almost to the size of a full-scale apology."[6] And it is not merely the structure of the oration but the tone and ethos of the orator that Calvin has learned from the humanists and their models. Throughout the preface he remains moderate, self-effacing, Erasmian in his stance.

Like Calvin, Luther absorbed much of the humanist program of erudition and rhetoric. And yet unlike Calvin, he remains quite outside the ethical and ideological presumptions of Christian humanism. If one contrasts Calvin's preface with Luther's dedication of *The Freedom of a Christian* (1520) to Leo X, one sees how different Luther's demands upon the rhetoric of antiquity were. Cast as an attempt to win Pope Leo's favor, Luther's preface ostensibly separates Leo not only from corrupt advisers but from the moral bankruptcy of the papacy itself, a distinction between man and office unlikely to have mollified Leo. It is not that Luther does not understand full well the topics of the *captatio benevolentiae*; it is merely that he cannot utter them in most contexts without toppling into sarcasm. Luther's description of Rome, for instance, could not have pleased Leo, even though he is thoughtfully excluded from the excoriation: "I have truly despised your see, the Roman Curia, which, however, neither you nor anyone else can deny is more corrupt than any Babylon or Sodom ever was, and which, as far as I can see, is characterized by a completely depraved, hopeless, and notorious godlessness" (*LW* 31, 336). The rhetorical strategy of this sentence is entirely characteristic of the preface, which constantly attempts to include Leo in Luther's outrage, with phrases such as "as you well know" (*LW* 31, 336). Like Folly's artful enfolding of her audience into her *laudatio*, presuming a fellowship of fools, Luther's rhetoric presumes to co-opt its presumably unwilling audience.

But a huge gulf lies between Erasmus's irony and Luther's sarcasm. A genuine sense of community undergirds Erasmus's satire: Erasmus is part of the world of *stultitia*. Although Luther clearly believes that all men exist in the creatural world of sinfulness, his rhetorical stance is always one of self-distinction, of separation from his adversary. Thus the deference of Calvin's apology has no place in Luther's rhetorical universe. Throughout the preface Luther argues from a position of (at the very least) an equal, not hesitating to pose as Leo's savior: "So far have I been from raving against your person that I even hoped I might gain your favor and save you if I should make a strong and stinging assault upon that prison, that veritable hell of yours" (*LW* 31, 338). The ethical proof that Luther employs in this preface, as in so many others, is an extended autobiographical narration, in this case a description of the events that pulled him unwilling and innocent into contention with the papacy. The role that these details play in establishing Luther's counterauthority far exceeds the bounds of ethical proof in classical rhetoric and explains his immodest treatment of Leo.

In fact, it is Luther rather than Calvin who understands, and understands early, the shortcomings as well as the possibilities of humanist rhetoric for the cause of the Reformation. When he squares off against Erasmus in the debate over free will, he foregrounds the question of authorial ethos. In *The Bondage of the Will* (1525), his answer to Erasmus's *Freedom of the Will* (1524), he devotes an inordinate amount of commentary to Erasmus's preface, noting that the preface embraces "practically the whole subject—more almost than the main body of the book that follows" (*LW* 33, 70). Luther recognizes that Erasmus has frontloaded his treatise to place its content under the protective aegis of his ethical proof. It could be argued that the debate centers on a contrast in authorial ethos that is at the same time a contrast of hermeneutic principle, namely, that between Erasmian moderation and Lutheran assertion.

Erasmus attempts to maintain a delicate balance between his independence as author and his irenic instincts toward accepting the status quo through skepticism.[7] His preface shows the strains of this increasingly heavy burden upon Christian humanism. To maintain peace in the Christian polity, the man who had labored for years to produce a definitive edition of the New Testament finds himself forced to argue for the opacity of Scripture in order to protect the need for authority. As appealing as Erasmian moderation appears to a modern audience, it stood little chance against the force of Luther's assertiveness because it required that Luther abide by the same rhetorical rules and forgo the very interpretive freedom that Erasmus himself had helped establish. Luther recognizes immediately his opponent's strategy, his "cleverness in treating the subject with such remarkable and consistent moderation as to make it impossible for me to be angry" (LW 33, 16). Such restraint seems fragile when Luther pronounces the basis for his rhetoric of Christian assertion: "What I am after in this dispute is to me something serious, necessary, and indeed eternal, something of such a kind and such importance that it ought to be asserted and defended to the death, even if the whole world had not only to be thrown into strife and confusion, but actually to return to total chaos and be reduced to nothingness" (LW 33, 50). The urgency of Luther's mission overwhelms any consideration for the public polity of Christendom.

In refusing Erasmus's gambit, Luther connects his insistence on Christian "assertion" with an abandonment of rhetorical modesty. Without questioning or exploring the essence of Erasmus's moderation or Luther's urgency, I want to pursue the structure of this rhetoric of assertion. It has its origin in Saint Paul's reorganization of the classical oratorical persona to correspond more closely to the needs of the Christian evangelist, who required an ethos that could register simultaneously a sense of personal agency (to distinguish that evangelist's specific version of the gospel) and the claim of divine inspiration. The Pauline persona not only stands in a new relationship with the public but also stands in a relationship with a new public, an elect fragment of the population. This atomization of audience gives further impetus to the "privatization" of the Christian orator's voice and lays the foundation for the oppositional rhetoric of the Protestant preface.

2

In Search of a Public Idiom

PAULINE AUTHORITY AND
LUTHERAN AUTHORSHIP

I begin with two moments from Luther's works. The first is the account of his famous appearance before Charles V and the Diet of Worms. The emperor had summoned Luther, already excommunicate, before the Diet of 1521 to interrogate him on his controversial works, and Luther, having received a safe conduct, obeyed the summons. The Lutheran account of the Diet, circulated soon afterward, proceeds in an unexceptional, matter-of-fact fashion in describing the events leading up to the interrogation. When Luther appears before the Diet, however, something quite striking happens. He is asked two simple questions: if he will acknowledge all the books published under his name as his, and if he wishes to recant anything in those books. To the first question, after his lawyer has demanded that the questioners stipulate the actual title of each book, he gives a simple affirmation. But the second question seems to leave him nonplussed, and he asks the Diet for more time to consider his answer. His examiners show understandable surprise that he was not prepared to answer such a direct and easily anticipated question but grant him a day's recess.

The Imperial account leaves little doubt that to most onlookers fear seemed the primary motivation behind Luther's delay: "He began to contrive excuses and to seek an escape" (*LW* 32, 124). Surprisingly, the Lutheran account creates the same suspicion, however obliquely. The narrative relates that on leaving the assembly, "Luther was admonished by various voices to be brave, to act manfully, and not to fear those who can kill the body but cannot kill the soul, but rather revere Him who is able to cast both soul and body into hell" (*LW* 32, 108). Upon his return the next day, Luther does "act manfully," responding to his questioners by uttering the most famous words of his career: "I am bound by the Scriptures I have quoted and my conscience is captive to the Word of God. I cannot and I will not retract anything, since it is neither safe nor right to go against conscience. I cannot do otherwise, here I stand, may God help me, Amen [Ich kan nicht anderst, hie stehe ich, Got helff mir, Amen]" (*LW* 32, 112–13; *WA* 7, 838).

Examined for its historical and even anthropological significance, as it often has been, the defiant climax of this narrative suggests Romantic notions of a heroic conscience resisting authority and structure or, in a modern redaction of these notions, theories of the "self" emerging from the corporate identity of medieval hierarchies.[1] Luther's sudden shift into the vernacular in the final sentence, so characteristic of his prose, here takes on the extraordinary force of subjectivity unleashed. And this stylistic outburst is echoed in the larger grammatical structure of the account. Up to the moment of the reformer's defiance, the narrative is third-person. When Luther takes to his feet to defy his interrogators, however, the point of view switches abruptly to the first-person, as though the very grammar of the account constrained Luther in a straitjacket of objectivity. Accentuating the moment further, the account quickly drops back into third-person narration.

Yet if the third-person frame emphasizes this moment, it also destabilizes it. As compelling as is the drama that can be built around Luther's moment of triumph, it is important not to allow that drama to overshadow the more obscure details that make up the bulk of the narrative. The drama of heroic subjectivity does not illuminate, for instance, the more than momentary hesitation that Luther shows the day before his dramatic defiance of the emperor. He may well have been quite intimidated by his interrogation in front of the Diet of the Holy Roman Empire, but fear does little to explain the failure of the Lutheran account to provide some kind of ameliorating gloss on his delay.

This lack of apologetics is especially puzzling because some of the evidence suggests that Luther was less than petrified by his experience. Within an hour of his initial examination, if we can trust his word on the timing of events, Luther was going about his business as a church organizer, writing a note "from the midst of this turmoil" (*LW* 48, 199) to the humanist Cuspinian to enlist his goodwill. And to Cuspinian, whom he had never met, he adds in a flat tone:

> I appeared at this hour before the Emperor and the Imperial diet. I was questioned as to whether I would want to renounce my books. I answered then that . . . I would tell them my opinion concerning any renunciation the following day, since more opportunity and time for deliberation on this issue has been neither asked nor granted. With Christ's help, however, I shall not in all eternity recant the least particle.   (*LW* 48, 200)

Luther does not write like a man deliberating whether to save his skin or follow his conscience. Heiko Oberman suggests that Luther may have been honestly taken aback by the blunt challenges of his interrogators, misled by the "courteously formulated" summons he had received.[2] I would suggest that despite his excommunication, Luther may also have made a "generic" miscalculation, anticipating that his appearance before the Diet would take the form not of a trial, with its naked display of authority, but of a disputation, like the Leipzig debate with Eck two years before in which the individual tenets of his teaching were subjected to argument and counterargument. In fact, throughout the hearing, Luther attempts to subvert the question of recantation (since he has already confessed to the crime), to turn the inquisition into a debate in which he will accept any argument based on Scripture or "reason." Luther fails to subvert the process, but in doing so discovers that the "genre" of the Inquisition, with its naked opposition between authority and individual, better suits his mission as a reformer than that of the disputation, with its endless adjudications and qualifications.

Yet the nagging question of the Lutheran account's grammatical inconsistency and motivational murkiness remains. The question is ultimately not what was going on in Luther's mind at the Diet but what he was thinking of in publishing and republishing the account. The question, in a word, is one of editorial policy. It has been suggested that the inconsistency of narrative voice in the Lutheran account may reflect the collaborative nature of its composition.[3] Yet the account remained the "authorized" version, and therefore its editorial practice may be examined for what it tells us of the "author." Why, one is entitled to ask, did not Luther or the collective Lutheran author edit out the white noise of doubt and detachment to produce a clearer picture of the "enunciating subject" than that which has been mythologized, in good part because of the selective reading of this very episode?[4]

I will suggest what part Luther himself played in the construction of this mythology, but it is important first to recognize that at the center of the Lutheran account is not the production of "Luther" the subject and author but the Luther who is not fully converted into that product. His moment of standing forth as subject, of breaking through the confusion of controversy, is only momentary. Perhaps the most telling aspects of the account, then, are not the moments when something resembling the modern individuated subject leaps full-blown from the page but precisely those moments when Luther refuses such individuation, as he does by making no retrospective attempt to edit the account to produce a unified point of view and, in the process, a unified picture of an authoritative (and authorial) subject.

Luther's refusal to self-edit brings us to the second, and for my purposes the more important, moment from his works—the opening of his little devotional treatise "Fourteen Consolations," first published in 1520 but reprinted with a preface in 1535. This preface contains his quite conventional lament over the gradual corruption of this work in pirated editions, but it adds an interesting note suggesting that the lack of "self-editing" in the account of Worms has now been raised to the level of a principle: "I have restored the sense of them as well as I could, and I believe they represent the views I held at the beginning. I do not intend to alter or improve the thoughts, as I well might do. In this book I want to give proof of my progress and also please my adversaries [*Antilogistis*] by giving them something on which they can vent their malice" (*LW* 42, 121; *WA* 3: 6, 104).

Luther revises only the errors that have been introduced by unscrupulous and inept publishers who have stolen his work; he makes no effort to update his thoughts to produce a seamless, consistent spiritual self-portrait. In fact, the portrait, the "proof," he wishes to create can emerge only through the contradictions produced by an unstable and contingent self. He ironically embraces the carping of the "Antilogisti" not only because it allows a kind of apotropaic "venting" that would prevent them from attacking his present position but also because it permits him to embrace the contradictions in his life as a manifestation of his spiritual "progress." We can see in retrospect, then, why the Lutheran account of the Diet of Worms remains so unfocused in its point of view and in its account of the reformer's motive. Luther's particular form of self-hagiography is an icon of instability and uncertainty.

The secular prototype of this icon is the familiar one of the humanist author and hero: not just Erasmus's copious orator, saved only by his tenuous hold on decorum from spilling out into an endless ocean of words, but Machiavelli's protean prince and Castiglione's flexible courtier. Above all, Luther looks ahead to Montaigne's wholehearted embrace of his own inconsistencies and foibles. Yet here in the preface to "Fourteen Consolations," Luther finds the means to halt the process without canceling the product of the potentially interminable self-generation of humanist rhetoric through a textualized "Here I stand." The retrospective vantage point of the preface allows Luther to make a stand based on personal authority. He unabashedly admits that the "I" holding the position of authority is a product, the result of an extremely volatile process in which the agent is the Logos and the reagent the Antilogisti. The resulting compound, Luther's "self" and its particular form of personal authority, is an entity constituted by the interplay between the public story of his contradictory career and the idiomatic interpretation he gives of that unrevised story.

As I will show, the model that allows Luther to intervene so decidedly in the conventions of humanist rhetoric is Saint Paul, who himself interrupted the classical tradition of self-presentation. Paul insists on the absolute uniqueness of his apostolic calling while arguing for its full intelligibility to those in the community of the Spirit, a rhetorical task that he accomplishes partially by invoking a "history" for himself, a history that depends on inconsistency. Specifically, it is Paul's simultaneous existence as Saul, an existence that he continues to carry with him in the "thorn in the flesh," that authorizes his apostolic mission by making his miraculous conversion ever present. One can find an incipient version of a similar strategy for authorization in the "unrevised" account of the proceedings at Worms. Rather than representing the triumph of a heroic conscience over the repressive forces of papism, the account describes a consciousness moving between versions of a self,

between third and first person, between an individual fully contingent upon the events and parties that are constructing him and
a willed subjectivity that transcends the historical forces that eddy
about him. Throughout Luther's works, these two versions of self
remain as opposed possibilities for his self-presentation.

In particular, I am interested in how Luther manipulates his
self-portrait through his conception of textual collection, a conception already implicit in the preface to "Fourteen Consolations."
Luther went on, despite his protestations concerning the vanity of
such work, to spend the final years of his life preparing the 1539
edition of his collected German works and the 1545 edition of his
collected Latin works. In those texts he operates under the principle of editing sparingly to create a spiritual autobiography that
demonstrates his struggle for the truth over the course of years. In
contrast, Calvin revised the *Institutes* continuously over a period
of fifteen years, interlarding new material until he could say in a
preface to the 1559 edition, "I was never satisfied until the work
had been arranged in the order now set forth" (3). This teleology
of the book must be set beside Luther's unfolding personal story.
Luther could never be finished in the sense Calvin claims because
what he ultimately presents as significant is not a text but a context, the narrative of a self created by his book but also creating
the meaningful structure for reading that book.

This narrative of progress, a narrative that revels in its inconsistencies, can be definitively distinguished from chaos only
through a second, situating tale, the tale of the hermeneutician
that provides an Archimedean point from which the first narrative
can be budged into coherence. Luther houses this second narrative
in the suitably retrospective structure of his prefaces. There he can
imply his active role in God's plan: by refusing to edit the chaos of
the first narrative, he suggests that his active role was nonetheless
just a role, a scripted part in a divine narrative that he had recited
by rote and prompt. The rhetorical (and theological) need for this
double narrative is so strong that in the last of his great prefaces,
that to the 1545 Latin works, his story bifurcates to include the elements of both personal volition and divine guidance, so that even
in the second narrative Luther feels compelled to represent the two
exigencies that drive his rhetoric: the need for personal authority
and the necessity to ground that authority in a divine will that
negates as it ratifies. Even in this preface, his fullest autobiograph-

ical document, Luther adamantly refuses to settle on a self as a finished, individuated product.

The preface, as interface between audience and text, serves as an important staging ground for the authorization of personal voice in Luther's public idiom. The preface, in effect, plays out the paradox of the prophet: it is seemingly marginal to the authorized text, yet it comes before. Equally important for Luther, it is "preposterous," composed last yet placed first, at once the open, inviting, unprepossessing and underdetermined gesture to the public and at the same time the secretly prepossessing, overdetermined authoritative gesture of the writer who, having finished his work, commences to interpret it for the reader, disguising that interpretation as an inaugural moment. This doubleness makes the preface the logical place for the author to work out proprietary claims to the text, claims that epitomize the attempt to delineate a boundary between public and private, the boundary that defines a culture's definition of authorship. Before examining Luther's contribution to the history of this process, however, I must make a detour within this history, through the works of Saint Paul, who gave Luther a model for transforming classical rhetoric into a system that could accommodate the "private" rhetoric of the prophet.

There are obvious parallels between the rhetorical and pastoral contexts of Paul and Luther, as Luther suggests in his preface to 1 Corinthians (1545). There he explains to the reader the similarity between the proliferation of sects in Paul's time, before an orthodoxy had been established, and the contemporary multiplication of Protestant faiths. It is Paul's experience with rival apostles and the strategies of self-authorization that he develops in the face of these competing authorities that inform much of Luther's rhetoric.[5] Paul, like Luther, bases his authority on his possession of the Spirit, a claim that provides the skilled rhetorician and theologian with rich material to exploit but is nonetheless very difficult to substantiate.[6] The very need for the Spirit as a means of authorization stems from the challenge, by both men, to a public rhetoric of shared meaning. In its place Paul and Luther seek to establish a rhetoric that is personal but at the same time able to exercise authority over a fragmenting public sphere.

As a means of understanding Paul's rhetoric, I would like to look at 2 Corinthians, a text largely given over to the discussion of self-commendation, "foolish boasting." The epistle falls into two sections. Chapters 1–9 address the Corinthians in a conciliatory tone, the context being, as Paul makes clear, the "painful visit" (2.1) he had made to Corinth and the apparently severe letter (2.3–4) that had followed that visit. Paul's authority with the Corinthian church seems to have eroded badly, largely because of "other men's labors" in his field (10.15), but the severe letter must have been a decisive blow in this battle over turf since in the opening chapters Paul works under the assumption that the flock is back within his fold. Scars from the battle and insecurities from the crisis in authority remain apparent in Paul's rhetoric, a rhetoric that combines cajoling and bullying, wheedling and demanding, extolling and criticizing. Yet on the whole he feels confident enough to build a rhetoric of authority on a sense of shared community:

Are we beginning to commend ourselves again? Or do we need, as some do, letters of recommendation to you, or from you? You yourselves are our letter of recommendation, written on your hearts, to be known and read by all men; and you show that you are a letter from Christ delivered by us, written not with ink but with the Spirit of the living God, not on tablets of stone but on tablets of human hearts. (3.1–3)

Paul recognizes here the ethical difficulty of self-commendation and figures the solution as a letter of recommendation. His sly "to you, or from you" encloses the audience in a spiritual union and accomplishes its end by tautological fiat. Paul says in essence, "I have God's authority because I have God's Spirit."

This tautology maintains a real rhetorical force, however, because Paul is able to identify his audience with the very rhetoric he employs upon them: "You yourselves are our letter of recommendation." In the traditional terms of classical rhetoric, this moment is simply an example of what happens when an orator has a "good case": the motive for self-authorization falls away; rhetoric becomes transparent; and orator and audience exist in the closed system of Aristotle's "actual facts." Yet Paul's tautology transcends the situation envisaged by classical theorists in the "good case." Rather than the erasure of rhetoric and the effacement of the orator's ethos implied by the rules for properly conducting a "good case," we have a community of Spirit between orator and audience in which the *effect* of rhetoric on the audience is coterminous with the *ends* of the case, where merely to move the audience is to prove the orator's possession of the Spirit and to instill that Spirit in the audience.

In such a structure, the orator does not disappear, he is transformed into a prophet of "boldness":

> Since we have such a hope [for a "splendor" surpassing that of the Law], we are very bold, not like Moses, who put a veil over his face so that the Israelites might not see the end of the fading splendor. . . . Therefore, having this ministry by the mercy of God, we do not lose heart. We have renounced disgraceful, underhanded ways; we refuse to practice cunning or to tamper with God's word, but by the open statement of the truth we would commend ourselves to every man's conscience in the sight of God. (3.12–13; 4.1–2)

Paul understands his new bold self-commendation as a revocation of the rhetoric of the Old Testament, but it is equally an abrogation of the laws of classical rhetoric, and preeminently of the modesty topos with its rhetoric of antirhetoric. Paul, the hellenized Roman Jew, always uses his multiple cultural languages dialectically rather than merely syncretically. That is, Pauline Christianity could have arisen only as a result of a *mutual* opposition of Judaism and romanized Hellenism in which the revelation of Scripture challenged the public reason of forum and agora, and the voice of the classical rhetor tore through the veil of the Torah's monovocal authority.[7] Both prophetic rituals and oratorical indirection are for Paul examples of "cunning" and obfuscation to which the Christian apostle need not resort. Both draw a veil over the face of the speaker to hide the individualism of the enunciator behind a fiction of "splendor," the splendor of disembodied authority. To that veil Paul opposes the apostle's possession of the Spirit, which, since it can be shared by the audience, need not occlude the apostle himself.

This new Pauline rhetoric, however, cannot always rest within its closed system of perfect community. Paul cannot always preach to the converted, and he needs strategies to handle situations in which he has a "bad case," when he cannot assume that the audience is already a "letter of recommendation." In fact, as schematically neat as his rhetoric of the Spirit appears in the passages I have quoted, when the "actual facts" were in dispute, as more often than not they were, this rhetoric faces problems of authorization more acute than any anticipated by classical rhetoric. To examine the strategies Paul employs to handle these problems, one must turn to the second part of 2 Corinthians, chapters 10–13. The tone of these chapters departs so sharply from that of the preceding ones that they have been held to be a separate, though authentically Pauline, text interpolated by a later editor.[8] While any extended ethical defense is difficult to contain formally and therefore may only appear to be a textual intrusion, these chapters seem to address a context radically different from that of the opening chapters and may even be the severe letter Paul alludes to in chapter 2.

In this heightened, more fully rhetorical context where motive cannot be readily dispersed into the audience itself, Paul must resort to a more paradoxical understanding of "commendation." Constructing what might be regarded as an extended preface, Paul employs all the maneuvers of a classical ethical defense to win the audience, repeatedly using the language of the courtroom, yet at the crucial moment he asks, "Have you been thinking all along that we have been defending ourselves before you? It is in the sight of God that we have been speaking in Christ, and all for your upbuilding" (12.19). Paul pulls the rug from beneath centuries of rhetorical tradition, legitimizing his extended self-advocacy by denying its very existence. Self-advocacy, he implies, no longer poses the problem it had for secular orators since ultimately it is not himself that he advocates. The modesty topos is a meaningless gesture, part of an outmoded system of secular *gloria*. "In Christ Jesus, then," Paul writes, "I have reason to be proud of my work for God" (Rom 15.17). Pride, for one invested with the Spirit, is not only not a sin; it is a glorification of God. " 'Let him who boasts, boast of the Lord.' For it is not the man who commends himself that is accepted, but the man whom the Lord commends" (2 Cor 10.17–18).

In the face of opposition, however, the apostolic boast "in Christ Jesus" becomes difficult to distinguish from the veil of Moses, a seizure of authority through a gesture that would seem to occlude the speaker's humanity and individuality. The paradoxical subjectivity of the prophet, simultaneously the voice and the mask, stands behind Paul's famous paradox of the Christian fool: "I repeat, let no one think me foolish; but even if you do, accept me as a fool, so that I too may boast a little. (What I am saying I say not with the Lord's authority but as a fool, in this boastful confidence; since many boast of worldly things, I too will boast.) For you gladly bear with fools, being wise yourselves!" (11.16–19). Boasting, the ultimate validation of the self, becomes for Paul the source of self-abnegation, the medium for "visions and revelations of the Lord" (12.1).

A clue to the origin of this paradox lies in the charge the Corinthians have brought against Paul and his response to that charge. Recounting the accusation, Paul writes, "For they say, 'His letters are weighty and strong, but his bodily presence is weak, and his speech of no account' " (10.10). When he paraphrases their words in his reply, however, he alters their range of signification in order to find strength in weakness: "Even if I am unskilled [*idiótes*] in speaking [*lógoi*], I am not in knowledge [*gnósei*]; in every way we have made this plain to you in all things" (11.6). Not only has Paul translated the classical antithesis between rhetoric and philosophy into a Christian one between preaching and the possession of gnosis, but as George Kennedy has pointed out, he does so through the highly charged term *idiótes*, which means not only "unskilled person" but as the etymology of *idiom* would suggest, "layman," "private person."[9] In other words, Paul is saying "I may be a private man in the field of oratory, but in the seemingly closed and ineffable world of gnosis I possess a skill that grants me a public efficacy." And he expects the Corinthians to be able to read the signs of that skill, even in his weakness.

"Forced" by the Corinthians' criticisms, Paul takes his means of self-authorization from a transgressive fusing of the public and private spheres in the form of self-commendation. This self-commendation grants the lack of public power, traditionally conceived, but finds that power in the private spheres of inspiration and the body. The transgressiveness of this breach in conventional boundaries between public and private is the basis for a new rhetorical ethos and a concomitantly new idea of the author. Horace on his Sabine farm has much to say about life in the forum, and Cicero on the rostrum can always appeal to the life of retirement as authorizing alternative—he would be in the countryside if the needs of Rome did not compel him to lead a public life. But Paul sees that autobiographical detail is absolutely inseparable from his task as an apostle and that his "apostolic self" (to borrow a phrase from Schütz) cannot be defined in the traditional terms of the public man or entirely divorced from the public duty it is called upon to address.

The ultimate transgression, but also the ultimate grounding, of this apostolic self is its recourse to a narrative of physical suffering, the weakened body for which the Corinthians upbraid him. Paul follows the passage on foolish boasting with his famous litany of the hardships he has endured as a missionary. The ostensible point he is making can be cloaked in the traditional rhetoric of modesty since his persecution would seem to demonstrate his weakness. Paul is thus the first practitioner of the "cultural *humilitas*" that Auerbach finds characteristic of early Christian rhetoric with its "insistence on Christ's corporeality" and the "humility of the Incarnation": "If I must boast, I will boast of the things that show my weakness" (11.30).[10] But if the paradoxical nature of this boast were not enough to alert one that Paul has left the confines of classical theory, the content of his boast would do so.

By invoking the actual lashings and stonings he has undergone, Paul creates for the first time a rhetoric of martyrdom, a rhetoric in which *showing*, the exhibition of the "personal," establishes the speaker's public credentials. Describing the rhetoric of the courtier, Kenneth Burke points out how martyrdom functions as rhetoric:

Note that in this way of bearing witness, the courtier's relation to his social superior is as martyr to God, as writer to public, as actor to audience. . . . Mortifications *must* be witnessed; they are evidence, presented to an invisible divine audience. Martyrdom (bearing witness) is so essentially rhetorical, it even gets its name from the law courts. However, it is vanity when addressed not to the Absolute Witness, but to human onlookers. (222)

Although Burke is correct to make the connection between martyr and witness, it is the fundamentally nonrhetorical *appearance* of witnessing that Paul relies on. As Quintilian noted, the skillful advocate will leave the jury with the impression that he speaks with the transparent, motiveless "reliability of a witness" (*testis fidem*; 4.1.7). Paul's body provides him with the *testis fides* to persuade not God but the Corinthians of his superiority to his rival apostles. While acknowledging the element of boasting, Paul is nonetheless determined that his mortification take on a voice that can grant him authority with the recalcitrant church in Corinth.

Paul's recourse to his body is an important moment in the history of the author's relation to his text. To borrow Elaine Scarry's phrase, it is the "sheer material factualness" of his body that Paul draws upon as the ultimate ground for his apostolic authority, the basis for his claim that he is to be believed.[11] His "thorn in the flesh" (12.7) reverses the trope of Moses's veil; it is in the revealed body of the apostle rather than through the obscured face of the prophet that God speaks. While sending the thorn to humble Paul, God nonetheless tells him, "My grace is sufficient for you, for my power is made perfect in weakness" (12.9). The possession of a body, made visible by suffering, becomes both the proof of God's grace and the guarantee of a personal unveiled authority. Relevant here is Scarry's description of the transformation of Jewish culture by the notions of the Incarnation and the Passion. Rather than locating voice (and therefore authority) in God alone and the body (and therefore sentience) in man alone, as the Old Testament does, suddenly the New Testament gives the experience of a body to God and the voice of authority to a man. "The altered relation in the Christian scripture between the body of the believer and the object of belief subverts [the] severed relation between pain and power, assuring that sentience and authority reside at a single location and thus cannot be achieved at each other's expense" (219). Paul's use of his suffering *in imitatione Christi* as a means of taking on authority, is a preeminent example of the process Scarry describes.[12] Suffering is no longer a sign of disobedience, of alienation from power, but at least potentially a source of power, implying as it does the "certainty" of sentience.

By making public a nonetheless privatized body, Paul forges a link between autobiography and authority, providing himself with the distinguishing marks of the martyr.[13] Paul's thorn in the flesh is thus distinct from that other important instance from antiquity of the body as rhetorical witness—Coriolanus's display of his wounds to the plebeians. Writing a generation after the death of Paul, Plutarch still portrays the classical conception of the body. Coriolanus's wounds are publicly owned signs on a body that is a fully public ethical proof; his worthiness for office can be read in a corporeal history of the Republic's battles. Paul's shadowy thorn on the other hand serves as an ethical proof precisely because it is shadowy, a private affliction suffered for the sake of a public ministry. The effect of the Christianization of the body can be clearly seen in Shakespeare's redaction of Plutarch. Plutarch reports no resistance from Coriolanus to the electoral rite; Shakespeare's Coriolanus is mortified by the invasion of his body, finally allowing the plebs to see his wounds with the comment "I have wounds to show you, which shall be yours in private" (2.3).[14]

I conclude this section with a final observation on Paul's "thorn in the flesh." My argument has been that this thorn represents the transgressive and subversive intrusion of the body into two realms of authoritative rhetoric, classical and Hebraic, and that this intrusion allows Paul to create his own authority. This new authority, however, partakes of many of the features of the authorities Paul had abrogated: in the infamous illusiveness of the thorn in the flesh itself, Paul reconstitutes the veil of Moses that he had rejected. The shadowy metaphor of the thorn veils the actual body, investing Paul with power by mystifying the locus of his authority. The revelation of the body had served to abrogate authority, but the veiling of the body in abstraction leads directly to the unveiling of power. In the final chapter of 2 Corinthians, Paul reveals that the weakness on which he had based his authority has been fully converted into strength:

I warned those who sinned before . . . and I warn them now while absent . . . that if I come again I will not spare them—since you desire proof that Christ is speaking in me. He is not weak in dealing with you, but is powerful in you. For he was crucified in weakness, but lives by the power of God. For we are weak in him, but in dealing with you we shall live with him by the power of God.   (13.2–4)

Although it is quite unclear how Paul will demonstrate this power, it is evident that he is threatening to provide the Corinthians with the proof of authority they had been seeking, proof that Paul suggests will come in the form of a direct exercise of power.[15] Wresting authority from its traditional locus is never enough for the prophet; he must also prevent his example from replicating endlessly among potential contenders for his authority.

Yet even if Paul seems to have come full circle here, to have reimmersed himself in structure and the authority of voice, he has done so with a difference. Taking on power through an imitation of Christ's suffering opens up a new rhetoric of *private* self-authorization in which the challenge is to adjudicate between a public discourse of "actual facts" and a "personal" narrative demonstrating access to the "Spirit." It is this new rhetoric that Luther rediscovers, practices, and refines.

While Luther's body has been the focus of much attention from historians, critics, and psychoanalysts, it is the metaphoric corpus of the 1545 collected Latin works that provides Luther with the same rhetorical ammunition as Paul's suffering body. Here Luther puts forward his creatural proof of his authority, his credentials as a prophet. For Paul's suffering body, Luther substitutes his unedited self-presentation, vulnerable to Antilogisti, granting him a weakness that he can convert to strength. In particular I am interested in examining the preface to the 1545 works as the place of struggle where Luther attempts to maintain both his own contingent authorial individuality and the absolute authority of God and Scripture.

The danger of authorial presumption is evident in an earlier preface, that to the 1522 translation of the New Testament, where Luther ruminates on the tendentious nature of the preface for his project of bringing the clarity of Scripture to "the ordinary man":

> It would be right and proper for this book to go forth without any prefaces or extraneous names attached and simply have its own say under its own name. However many unfounded interpretations and prefaces have scattered the thought of Christians to a point where no one any longer knows what is gospel or law, New Testament or Old. Necessity demands, therefore, that there should be a notice or preface, by which the ordinary man can be rescued from his former delusions, set on the right track, and taught what he is to look for in this book.   (*LW* 35, 357)

Luther would seem to side with Aristotle, positing a "right and proper" realm in which the "actual facts" of Scripture could exist in a state of perfect lucidity, unclouded by human rhetoric and hermeneutics. In this realm, the preface joins gloss and commentary as textual metaphors for "slavish" papist embellishments on the simplicity of God's Word. Without centuries of Roman obfuscation, the Bible would have needed no prefatory mediation, not even the "preface" of Luther's works themselves.

Yet it is clear that Luther imagines such a state of pristine, gloss-free Scripture as existing only in the distant past if at all. As we have seen, he was deeply aware of competing interpretive discourses surrounding Scripture, even in Paul's time. Thus for Luther, in the discursively fallen world the Word cannot exist without intervening preface, and he must tackle head-on the problem that his translation and commentaries are also additions to Scripture, additions that threaten to "scatter" further rather than unify Christian thought. While Luther never specifically articulates a means by which his prefaces can be distinguished from their "scattering" cousins or the merely marginal gloss, his later work builds a framework within which his unifying authority can be recognized, if not verified.[16] This framework, as mentioned earlier, consists of a double narrative. The first part is told by the collection of his works into a "corpus" analogous to Paul's suffering body. Here, by historicizing himself, Luther presents himself as a text written by God. Yet through the contours and irregularities of his evolving ideas, through error itself, Luther produces a body of thought that, even if subject to a larger authority, shows itself as individuated and therefore "authored." The picture of Luther's development as a reformer, and only the whole picture, can represent the personal (and theological) truth. Thus the 1539 edition of his German works and especially the 1545 Latin works become for Luther as much a spiritual autobiography as a theological *summa*, a portrait as fitful and chaotic as life itself yet one that can show the reader, through the welter of contradictions, the progressive enlightenment of the reformer.

Within such a conception of the *opera omnia*, the second part of Luther's double narrative, the preface, plays the part of a contextualizing agent for material that Luther refuses to revise. Although much of his writing admits autobiographical detail, his own sense of the historical inviolability of each text within the collection prevents him from achieving anything like the autobiographer's overview in any particular text. It is in the prefaces, cut loose from historical specificity, that Luther can give such an overview. Although prefaces had often contained autobiographical material before Luther, no previous author shares Luther's systematic conception of prefatory work as the compilation of autobiographical segments.

One could argue that Luther is only articulating and giving structure to something that is inherent in all prefaces. Contrasting the introduction and the preface, Derrida argues that while introductions form part of the logic of the book, addressing the "architectonic problems" of the work, "the Prefaces . . . are multiplied from edition to edition and take into account a more empirical historicity; they obey an occasional necessity" (17). The narrative daisy chain of prefaces that Derrida describes, however, contains for Luther not just "a more empirical history" but "a more transcendent history." The "occasional necessity" compels Luther to interpret his life from a perspective that transcends both the words of his collected works and the actions of his career as reformer. Luther has thus realized the tremendous power on the one hand of the automythography inherent in collecting his writings and on the other the rhetorical vantage point offered by the prefatory autobiography that allows him to comment on his life and works almost as if they were not his own. This double narrative of preface and work allows Luther to have his cake and eat it too, to show himself the unwitting servant of God's plan and a prophet who has come to an understanding of his role in that plan, an understanding that serves as the basis for his ministry. He can thereby represent himself as simultaneously responsible agent and mere tool, thus solving the rhetorical quandary of the Protestant writer.

If Luther views the preface as the site for staking out authorial boundaries, the lines between words as personal property and as textual public domain, this site is nonetheless difficult, uncleared terrain. Even by 1539, in the preface to the first part of his German works, he continues to state his horror at supplementing Scripture and extends these statements even to the notion of "collection": "I shudder to think of the example I am giving, for I am well aware how little the church has been profited since they have begun to collect many books and large libraries, in addition to and besides the Holy Scriptures" (*LW* 34, 283). Although he is collecting his own corpus, he cannot help seeing it as part of the larger, corpulent body of the Church. Unlike his translation of the

Bible, Luther's works as a whole do not seem to him necessarily a warranted supplement to Scripture, and he seems uneasy in distinguishing them from other compilations.

In the 1545 preface, however, published just a year before his death, Luther has developed a new sense of confidence in his project of collection. Even the modesty of the traditional exordial topics with which he begins is colored by this sense of purpose:

> For a long time I strenuously resisted those who wanted my books, or more correctly my confused lucubrations, published. I did not want the labors of the ancients to be buried by my new works and the reader kept from reading them. Then, too, by God's grace a great many systematic books now exist, among which the *Loci communes* of Philip excel. . . . But my books, as it happened, yes, as the lack of order in which the events transpired made it necessary, are accordingly crude and disordered chaos [*rude et indigestum chaos*], which is now not easy to arrange even for me.   (*LW* 34, 327; *WA* 1: 54, 179)

Luther's "modest" self-deprecation of his collection in the face of the "systematic" work of Melanchthon describes what he actually thinks to be most significant about his writing, the sign of his special calling. His work is not systematic because it is so thoroughly implicated in history, "made necessary" by the events in God's larger system. History has created the shape of his collection of writings, and it is a shape over which he himself has only a tenuous control.

Yet there is more than a touch of *superbia* in Luther's allusion to the Ovidian description of the chaos that preceded creation: "Chaos-rudis indigestaque moles."[17] If his life and work are merely chaotic matter, this matter is nonetheless the material out of which the editorial demiurge can create a divinely inspired narrative. Not surprisingly, then, when Luther repeats the time-tried "piracy" topos, his version shows a more than conventional interest in warding off the claims of others to his work. His importuners warn him that should he not edit his works while alive, after his death will come editors "wholly ignorant of the causes and the time of the events . . . and so out of one confusion many would arise" (*LW* 34, 328).

As he had with his New Testament, Luther here defends not the text but the control of the context.[18] That is, Luther sees his works not as static pieces of disputation but as the product of "causes and the time." He must therefore exert his proprietary interest in the interstices of the hermeneutician: the marginalia, the *parerga*. And publication becomes a means to contain the significance of his discourse; by publishing the confusion together with its authorized interpretation, he limits the dispersal of his work's meaning. Luther is by no means convinced that the "multiple confusions" his work might elicit (and in fact had elicited) could be reduced to order on the model of his own life. I will return to the problem of exemplarity and the proliferation of interpretation, but it is worth noting now that Luther ends his discussion of his decision to publish the collection with an appeal to secular authority: Prince John Frederick commanded the publication.[19]

The *narratio* of this preface plays out the dialectical process through which Luther can claim a proprietary interest in his own text while still presenting that text as divinely authorized.[20] The modesty of earlier prefaces still appears, but it is now subordinated to a larger automythographical scheme. Luther compares his early years as a monk to Paul's role in persecuting Christians, but his conversion experience, like Paul's, authorizes his ministry, so that his past as a "Saul" is a matter not of shame but of glory. The 1545 works tell the story of his intellectual and spiritual life, and it is a story whose mythic value for self-authorization far outweighs the danger of misleading the Christian reader or, for that matter, leaving himself open to the criticisms of the Antilogisti: "You will, therefore, sincere reader, ascribe this error, or, as they slander, contradiction to the time and my inexperience" (*LW* 34, 328). It is essential to Luther that we read his papist early years as "error" rather than "contradiction" because the latter term threatens to construe his life as a logical construct, and he wishes to be understood as a continuously significant, if variable, narrative. Luther does not "contradict" himself because his "errors" are extended temporally into a narrative of progress; it is the inconsistency of his thought over time that represents his experience on the road to Damascus. Later writers will use this instability of self as a means of absolving themselves from responsibility for their words,[21] but Luther makes this inconsistency the source of his authority and has no desire to shirk responsibility—except insofar as he fits into a larger plan: "At first I was all alone and certainly very inept and unskilled in conducting such great affairs. For I got into these turmoils by accident and not by will or intention. I call upon God himself as witness" (*LW* 34, 328).

Luther then proceeds with his "outer" narration of these "accidents" beyond his "intention," the story of how his challenge of indulgence sales led ultimately to his challenge of papal authority. Luther's stance throughout this narration is a complex one. Clearly, God has intended him to play this part in history; at the same time, he admits the horrible results of the schism and attempts to exculpate himself. He represents himself as a man pressed again and again to confront forces he would rather let lie. This alternation in tone from triumph to regret and back is evident in his attack on Albrecht of Brandenburg, who authorized Tetzel's sale of indulgences:

> The entire guilt belongs to the one at Mainz, whose smartness and cleverness fooled him, with which he wanted to suppress my doctrine and have his money, acquired by the indulgences, saved. Now counsels are sought in vain; in vain efforts are made. The Lord has awakened and stands to judge the people. Though they could kill us, they still do not have what they want, yes, have less than they have, while we live in safety. This some of them who are not entirely of a dull nose smell quite enough.   (*LW* 34, 336)

The somewhat confusing compression of causality here, and the shifts in attitude and tone, can undoubtedly be ascribed to a real ambivalence. We know from Luther's reaction to the Peasants' Revolt that he was capable of remorse for the political consequences of his writing (even if it is the consequences of the remorse that we find distasteful). But there is also a rhetorical strategy behind this confusion. Luther obscures the whole question of authority by making it unclear who "authored" the facts in question. Although the purpose of the narrative would seem to be at least partly to explain his role in creating the Reformation, at the same time, as we have seen, Luther's story serves to demonstrate God's control of events. The narration is also, however, an apology for the author's having shown himself in history, a kind of extension of prefatory shame into the field of historical event. Insofar as it is an apology, Luther wishes to deny not only his own agency but also God's; the "guilt" is Albrecht's, and Tetzel is the "primary author of this tragedy" (*LW* 34, 335).

It is not difficult to understand the apparent ambiguity of human and divine responsibility in terms of Luther's theology, particularly his debate with Erasmus on free will where Luther argues that a man may be predestined yet still guilty. Nor is it difficult to comprehend how Luther's vision of history as simultaneously bloody tragedy and triumphant epic stems directly from this double set of causes and "responsibilities." For my purposes, however, the essential matter is how Luther translates this vision of history rhetorically. The strategy is similar to Paul's; Luther hypostatizes authority as a series of "authors": Leo X, Albrecht, Tetzel, Eck. The Catholic hierarchy becomes for Luther what Judaizing Christians and pneumatic apostles were for Paul—agents that force his hand, compel him to take up his role in history. But Luther offers a more dialectical picture of his confrontation with history than Paul, showing the reader the process of his implication into the events of the Reformation, thereby dramatizing the merging of his authority into a larger authority.[22]

Luther's most intriguing strategy for historicizing his authority and presenting that history as dialectical lies in the doubleness of the *narratio* itself. After providing an etiological myth for his development as a reformer, he proceeds to supply a second myth, the "inner" narration, a version of the "tower experience," in which he came to understand "by the mercy of God" "the passive righteousness with which merciful God justifies us by faith," an understanding reached only through a violent assault on scriptural obscurity: "Nevertheless, I beat importunately upon Paul at that place [Rom 1.17]" (*LW* 34, 337). As in the earlier *narratio*, Luther juxtaposes without comment language of passive acceptance and the most strenuous exercise of personal will, yet the relationship between the two narratives is not easy to ascertain. Luther begins this second narration with a simple temporal transition: "Meanwhile [*Interim*], I had already during that year [1518–19] returned to interpret the Psalter anew" (*LW* 34, 336; *WA* 1: 54, 185).[23] In other words, Luther would seem to place the "conversion experience" *after* the indulgence controversy and his implication into history.

Scholars have repeatedly, and perhaps correctly, attempted to move this experience back, usually to 1513–15, during the time of Luther's first set of lectures on the Psalms.[24] Luther's actual placement, however, is significant since it either makes his dialectical implication the cause of his interpretive insight or, to follow a more empirical theory of causality, dissociates the two experiences altogether. And in fact Luther gives the reader no handles other than temporal sequence for understanding the relation of these two narrations. Even "temporal sequence" may be too strong a connection between the two narratives; although "meanwhile" (*interim*) might be taken to imply an action begun after the wrangle with Tetzel, it literally signifies a temporal concurrence in which neither of the two narratives has any necessary priority. In effect, the juxtaposed narratives serve once more to obscure the actual locus of Luther's authority by suggesting a confused network of causality, of public indictment and private inspiration, in which he has become enmeshed.

Like the account of the Diet of Worms, where one is left unable to decide between corporate and individuated versions of Luther's self, this doubling of explanatory schemata leaves the reader at an impasse. As tempting as it would be to see the second narrative *emerging* from the first—and to see Luther's heroic individualism emerging along with it from out of the faceless constructs of the Middle Ages—Luther gives us no firm footing for deciding between his two narratives. The "inner" narration of the 1545 preface will not solve the mystery of the "trial" at Worms by giving voice to the mysterious silence between the two days of Luther's interrogation and providing the reader with a self-constituting subjectivity that evolved alongside the public conscience of the antithetical resister.

Perhaps the best that can be said is that these narratives do not stand either as alternatives for Luther or as a temporal and causal sequence, but as mutually enabling stories. His meticulous manipulation of his confusion and enlightenment, his pointed refusal to provide a real causal or even temporal link between his two narratives, demonstrates that the subject *Luther*, whatever its origin and makeup, can claim authority only through recourse to both its public and its private faces. Luther's textualized version of this self figures the public self as unedited collection and the subjective self as the prefatory hermeneutics upon this collection. While the second narrative, the story of the preface, might seem the telos of the collection and the chaos of life itself, in another sense it remains at the level of a commentary, meaningless without the unstable and polysemous story of Luther's unedited life and works.

It is possible, however, to glimpse a larger motive behind this doubled representation in the conclusion of the preface: "To this point, to the year 1520 and 21, the indulgence matter proceeded. Upon that followed the sacramentarian and Anabaptist affairs. Regarding these a preface shall be written to other tomes, if I live" (*LW* 34, 338). Luther's ongoing prefatory project of self-definition, like his career, came to be designed not just to assert a personal authority against the Catholic church but finally to occlude the source of that authority as a means of protecting it against those who, like the Anabaptists, attempt to imitate it. That is, by implicating his "inner" narrative into the public narrative of history, Luther shores up his authority against those who would see him as an exemplum that could be infinitely replicated. Luther preserves the uniqueness of his experience and establishes the institutional authority of his reformed church by refusing to edit out the white noise of history, finding in that static the ethical proof of his peculiar election to lead the reinstituting of Christ's real church.

This strategy is essentially Pauline. Luther exhibits his confused (but not contradictory) corpus and the narrative of his implication into history much as Paul displays his body: as a public testimonial to God's hand, which writes in suffering. But this public document, open not only to salubrious reading but also to scattering imitation, must be reviled, its exemplary powers contained. Luther's means for constraining the exemplary implications of his life and works is the Olympian height of the hermeneutician he claims in his preface, and the palimpsest of the second narrative obscures a story that might otherwise suggest that we might all read a prophetic trajectory into the chaos of our lives. Thus Luther found in Paul's rhetoric the means for challenging an authorized discourse while closing off similar challenges to his own authority. He was not ultimately successful in closing off these challenges, but in the attempt he created a distinctly early modern rhetoric of self-presentation.

In this rhetoric, "author" and "subject" become closely allied entities, for subjectivity comes into being as an act of rhetorical closure, of claiming for oneself an inimitable authority, publicly intelligible yet distinct from traditional models of authority and at the same time unavailable for reduplication. The Lutheran self, then—and the cultural resonance of this self can be felt in an author as different as Montaigne—shows itself in nearly simultaneous revolution and reaction, establishing itself as authoritative but blocking off any attempt to read it as exemplary. Luther wants to roll up the road to Damascus behind him, to reveal his corpus in preemptive commentary, thus maintaining his "idiom" while insisting upon the public import of his story.

3

Humanist Individualism and the Puritan Polity in Milton's Antiprelatical Tracts

More than a century separates the careers of Luther and John Milton, yet despite the passage of time and a vastly different cultural context, Milton stands as a true heir to Luther's rhetorical legacy. More than any writer between them, Milton broods on the difficult calibrations to be made by the private prophetic voice in achieving public ends. If it is ultimately the differences between the rhetorical attitudes of the two men that prove most interesting, it is the similarities with which I will begin.

Like Luther, Milton found prefatory conventions a suitable site for exploring the relationship between the public and private faces of authorship. His first extant prose work, the *First Prolusion*, begins with an epideictic digression on the very subject of exordial rhetoric:

> All of the most distinguished teachers of rhetoric far and wide have left behind the opinion . . . [that] the exordium ought to be occupied with securing the goodwill of the listeners. . . . But if such is the fact . . . to what desperate straits am I reduced this day! I, who at the very beginning of my speech [*in ipso Orationis Limine*] fear lest I may advance something not at all worthy of orators and lest I should have deviated unavoidably from the primary and principal duty of a speaker; indeed, how can I expect your goodwill, when, in this great assembly, I perceive almost as many persons hostile to me as I behold with my eyes? Hence it is that I seem to come as an orator to those who are inexorable. (*CM* 12, 118–21)

Milton addresses the issue that will occupy so much of his later prose work, the *officium oratoris*. Although Milton understands this duty in terms entirely conventional to the classical preface, he also converts the topos into a sophisticated ploy for the entry into the text ("Orationis Limine") by a neophyte orator, a strategy that, as we shall see, continues to resonate throughout his prose works. Moreover, the seeds are already present for his mature conception of "office" as an opposition between a rhetorical duty to please one's audience and a philosophical duty to bring them a necessary but unwanted truth, as if he were a Hebrew prophet (or a Luther) placed in the Roman forum. By the time of *The Doctrine and Discipline of Divorce* (1644), Milton has developed this opposition into a characteristic portrait of himself as the "sole advocate of a discount'nanc't truth" (*YM* 2, 224). He refines the satiric stance of the *First Prolusion* by incorporating it into the larger stances of solitary prophet-poet and youthful usurper (stances, however, that he anticipates in the *Sixth Prolusion*'s picture of himself as Orpheus), but the basic dialectic remains: a lonely voice in the wilderness facing its ultimate responsibility to address the Christian *res publica*.

This stance leads Milton, like Luther, to reject or qualify what had been the two mainstays of the classical preface, the modesty topos and the *captatio benevolentiae*. By 1655, Milton's sense of his own election had made any pretense of modesty seem a slight to God's plan. In response to an attack on his prefatory self-defense in the *Defensio secunda* (1654), Milton replies:

> It is a singular favour of the divinity towards me, that I, above others, was chosen out to defend the cause of liberty, which had been maintained with such dauntless valour; and this favour I must affirm I acknowledged; nor can the time ever come when it will cease to be my duty to acknowledge it; and that I took hence, which in my judgment can hardly be imputed to me as a fault, the noble matter of my exordium [*praeclaram . . . exordiendi materiam*].   (CM 9, 86–87)

Once *officium* and *beneficium* are firmly identified with each other, modesty becomes an empty rhetorical form. Once Milton has made this identification, he can announce, in words reminiscent of Montaigne, that he himself is the "noble matter" of his preface.

The *captatio benevolentiae* is already under implicit attack in the passage I have quoted from the *First Prolusion*. By creating artificial differences with his audience, Milton constructs the figure of an orator working against uneven odds for whom the achievement of the audience's benevolence is a scant possibility. One could still construe this early example of Milton's attack on the *captatio* as a cleverly troped version of the traditional topos of the weak (and therefore rhetorically trustworthy) speaker. Yet if this topos stands behind much of Milton's oratorical self-presentation, it has been redefined as a defiant pronouncement of authorial independence and distinction. As he argues in the *Pro se defensio* (1655), "I am not at liberty . . . to imitate the common practice of writers, with whom it is usual to premise something in commendation of their work with a view to procure a favorable hearing" (*CM* 9, 4–5).

My argument bears on the history of a paradox inherent in this sentence, a paradox in the prefatory rhetoric that Milton creates in the course of his career as a prose writer. While abandoning the ostensible self-effacement of the modesty topos and the slavish attempts to capture his reader's approval, Milton figures these abandonments not as liberation from conventions that fetter the author's freedom but as a rhetorical self-renunciation, the jettisoning of the copious persona of the humanist orator with all its comfortingly stable self-presentational topoi. If one feels the continuing presence of this persona, in its elaborate denial if nowhere else, Milton nonetheless continues to chip away at the humanist "self" through a series of renunciations that reveal a new rhetorical persona, one more responsive to his need for a *public* authority. This authority, constituted very differently from the hierarchical one against which Luther worked, is nonetheless constructed communally. And for the protean, theatrical, "aristocratic" authorial self of Erasmus and Montaigne, Milton substitutes a stable, writerly, publicly responsive self.[1]

Milton forges his persona in the antiprelatical works of the early 1640s, two of which, *The Reason of Church-Government* and *An Apology Against a Pamphlet*, will serve as the focus for this chapter. Milton's vehicle for creating his public authority is his concept of *officium*, which he actively develops even before it has been literalized and institutionalized in his appointment as Latin Secretary in 1649. This "office" is dramatized in a form of autobiography and ethical proof very different from that of the Puritan writers with whom he is quite often associated. Miltonic autobiography is based not on personal revelation but on personal renunciation, on his establishment of a subjective repleteness that he will invoke and then refuse to articulate. I will argue that in *The Reason of Church-Government* Milton uses his role as poet to represent his turn to prose as a kind of moral, ethical, and literary *recusatio*, a refusal to linger in the leisured and self-indulgent pursuit of poetry, and that this refusal establishes his credentials as public spokesman. By emphasizing that Milton's poetical persona is a form of *recusatio*, I hope to counteract what seems to me the universal tendency, even in critics who have devoted their entire careers to Milton's prose, to view the prose as teleologically pointed toward *Paradise Lost* and the other late poems. I then go on to consider *An Apology Against a Pamphlet* in which Milton has internalized this rhetorical ploy, transforming it into a new understanding of authorship as a public institution.

The Reason of Church-Government was Milton's fourth tract in the antiprelatical controversy, following the flurry of anonymous works from 1641–42—*Of Reformation, Of Prelatical Episcopy*, and *Animadversions*. Significantly, *Church-Government* alone among all the antiprelatical tracts bears Milton's name on the title page and thus stands as the starting point of my argument, since he must establish himself as author before beginning any renunciation. Although still relatively unknown, Milton breaks the circle of anonymity created by the war of invective and comes forward to present a lengthy ethical proof, concentrated mostly in the famous "digression" of the preface to the second book. In fact, the inordinate length of the prefatory segments in this tract stems from what Joseph Anthony Wittreich calls Milton's "particular stress upon ethical proof." Wittreich notes that Milton "distorts the formal proportions of the classical oration not only as a gesture of rebellion but in order to enable the oration to carry the heavy weight of the ethical proof he offers."[2] Milton strains to keep personal digression within its classically prescribed boundaries, so that the deformation of oratorical form manifests itself in the inordinate length of the preface to Book 2 and in the very division of the prefatory work into two segments. In later works Milton will feel free to introduce such digressions without making structural adjustments. In *Church-Government*, however, he retains the classical alignment of ethical proof and exordium. Not having yet established a congruity between his prophetic, oratorical persona and the work of the Reformation, he must continue to separate the self-presentation of the preface from the "content" of reform.

The first preface to *Church-Government*, although contained within classical boundaries and less "digressive" than the preface to Book 2, lays the groundwork for Milton's alignment of his "office" with the Puritan cause. The preface contains little specifically autobiographical material, but it creates a set of analogies through which Milton and his opponents are transumed into a larger historical and theological drama. These *figurae* serve as the basis for the later digression and allow an obscure young poet to present his entrance into a controversy as a meaningful recapitulation and enactment of Protestant history.[3] Two sets of opposed figural alignments begin to emerge by implication in this preface: Milton-Christ-gospel versus prelates-Moses-law.[4] The effect of Milton's figural alignment of his persona with antiprelacy widens the rhetorical possibilities of this contrast between the old law and the new law of the gospel. Milton begins his brief autobiographical statement with a very specific reference to the signs of grace: "And if any man incline to thinke I undertake a taske too difficult for my yeares, I trust through the supreme inlightning assistance farre otherwise; for my yeares, be they few or many, what imports it? so they bring reason, let that be lookt on" (*YM* 1, 749). Milton was thirty-three when *Church-Government* was published, an age that hardly seems to justify such a proleptic defense.[5] Portraying oneself as an inexperienced youth has some obvious rhetorical advantages; it reduces the audience's expectations and as a corollary demonstrates the virtuosity of the young orator, creating obstacles, as in the *First Prolusion*, that he can then surmount in a kind of Burkean "self-interference."[6]

But Milton may have had even more specific reasons to adopt his stance as young orator. The dichotomy of young versus old echoes not only the kind of polemical relation Milton sets up between the presbyterians and the party of the bishops but also a more pervasive Protestant schema for conceptualizing history. In this scheme, Protestantism is not the young offshoot of Catholicism but the old stock off of which a corrupt branch had grown. In the words of Thomas Cartwright, an Elizabethan Puritan, "This [presbyterian Puritanism] is no innovation but a renovation, and the doctrine not new but renewed, no stranger but born in Sion."[7] In *Church-Government*, Milton extends this paradox by identifying the Old Testament with the tradition that is actually younger than the forces that would "innovate." Since the gospel is the "end" of law, since the law presupposes its fulfillment in the gospel, since the gospel subsumes the history of the law and extends beyond it into the future, then the gospel is in a sense temporally prior. Milton sets forth his rationale for this usurpation of antiquity in his answer to his opponents' invocation of the Old Testament as an authority and model for the priesthood. He wishes to be satisfied, he says, "how then the ripe age of the Gospell should be put to schoole againe, and learn to governe her selfe from the infancy of the Law, the stronger to imitate the weaker, the freeman to follow the captive, the learned to be lesson'd by the rude, will be a hard undertaking to evince from any of those principles which either art or inspiration hath written" (*YM* 1, 763). Milton suggests that the first figural cluster I have noted transumes the second. In *An Apology Against a Pamphlet*, alluding to 1 Corinthians 13.11, Milton declares that while the law offers the "childish enticements" of "earthly rewards," "the Gospell is our manhood" (*YM* 1, 950).

   This familial-rhetorical-historical configuration is essential to the thematics of *Church-Government* as a whole since Milton will set about earning the birthright for the younger son presbyterianism as well as for his youthful orator. Having placed himself under the gospel (in both the theological and figural senses of *under*), Milton feels compelled for rhetorical reasons to reject the law and to reject it with a severity unusual even among Protestant thinkers. The form this rejection takes is an attack on imitation:

If any thing done by the Apostles may be drawne howsoever to a likenesse of something Mosaicall, if it cannot be prov'd that it was done of purpose in imitation, as having the right thereof grounded in nature, and not in ceremony or type, it will little availe the matter. . . . That which is thus morall, besides what we fetch from those unwritten lawes and Ideas which nature hath ingraven in us, the Gospell, as stands with her dignity most, lectures to us from her own authentick hand-writing, and command, not copies out from the borrow'd manuscript of a subservient scrowl, by way of imitating.   (*YM* 1, 763–64)

   What was implied in the preface is here made explicit: Moses is a precedent, but a precedent to be transcended. And not only is the gospel not an imitation of the law, the law itself is a "borrow'd manuscript of a subservient scrowl."[8] Milton's picture of imitation is not humanist *imitatio* but the mindless, monkish copying that carries each manuscript further from the "authentick hand-writing" of God's word. Such copying privileges letter over spirit, and Milton argues that spiritual morality cannot imitate the law or even "morality, which ever was the same thing. This very word of patterning or imitating excludes Episcopacy from the solid and grave Ethical law, and betraies it to be a meere childe of ceremony" (*YM* 1, 765). By positing the derivative nature of Old Testament law and its imitators, Milton creates a clear criterion by which to judge the relative authority of the two polemical camps. Any appeal to Old Testament precedent without reference to the gospel automatically marks the speaker as a "childe of ceremony." This criterion provides yet another insight into the age of Milton the orator. For just as the lateness of the gospel is converted through its place as the logical "end" of the law into the law's "original," so Milton's youth becomes a weakness converted into strength, a sign of independence from "patterning or imitating" that gives him precedence over his opponents.

The figural self-portrait that Milton paints in the preface to Book 1 fits perfectly the context of controversy out of which it arose. Milton silently but surely aligns himself with the "young" movement of English presbyterianism and the hermeneutic power of the gospel's simple message. He also succeeds in forcefully conveying the paradox that each element in this triple analogy is prior to its nominally older counterpart and therefore possessed of greater authority. The preface to Book 2, however, dissolves much of the solidity behind this edifice of analogy. While Milton continues to think in terms of *figurae*, the disjunction between the roles he feels called upon to play begins to take on as much rhetorical force as analogy had in the opening preface. When Milton turns to the actual "story" of his ethical proof, a profound dissonance arises between his two vocations as poet and prophet, interfering with the precise identification of self and task that he implies earlier. But it is in this disjunction, I will argue, that Milton's new form of ethical proof can emerge.

Milton delays stepping forward in the first person for several pages of the preface to Book 2; when he does, it is once again in the persona of the youthful prophet:

For me I have determin'd to lay up as the best treasure, and solace of a good old age, if God voutsafe it me, the honest liberty of free speech from my youth, where I shall think it available in so dear a concernment as the Churches good. For if I be either by disposition, or what other cause too inquisitive, or suspitious of my self and mine own doings, who can help it? (YM 1, 804)

He resolves to cut short his "suspitious" scrutiny of his motivations so that he does not become paralyzed. He thus translates prophetic license into "the honest liberty of free speech from my youth," co-opting the prophetic tradition of the Old Testament into his stance as youthful proponent of the gospel.[9] And with this subtle abrogation of the figural schema of Book 1 comes the first hint of Milton's strategy of personal *recusatio*. He portrays a "self" replete with "doing" that is worthy of inquisition, but he suggests that there may be a danger in a too "suspitious" scrutiny of this self should it transcend the "concernment" of the "Churches good." He must therefore suspend if not fully deny this self until the work at hand has been accomplished.

Milton's explanation of his compulsion to take up the pen in the Puritan cause represents the closest parallel in his prose to the autobiographical writings that would shortly become a characteristically Puritan mode.[10] His motivation is that "I foresee what stories I should heare within my selfe, all my life after, of discourage and reproach" (YM 1, 804) should he not take up God's cause. Yet the remarkable aspect of Milton's personal narration is the extent to which it *diverges* from what might be considered the Puritan norm. For Milton, this inner voice of guilt amounts to a calling, a calling based on his ability to "foresee"—a word Milton insists on through repetition—the implications of inaction. The foresight that he claims, however, is prophetic only in its ability to produce a calling to God's work, since Milton foresees different, equally unacceptable scenarios, depending on the success of the Puritan reformation.[11] Entirely absent is the essentially Augustinian narrative of conversion with its agonizings over the question of conversional "proof," agonizings that inevitably center on meticulous investigations of the subject's interiority. In *Church-Gov-*

ernment, and in Milton's prose as a whole, such a narration of a "self" never emerges.

If Milton found conversional narrative, with its naked exposition of subjectivity, an inhospitable medium, he nonetheless needed a "story" to validate his text. The model he turned to in shaping his self-presentation is of classical rather than Christian origin, the dichotomy between *otium* and *negotium*. This opposition between leisure and "unleisure" has two generic sources, both of great importance to Milton. The first comes from pastoral and georgic poetry. The opening phrase of the preface—"How happy were it for this frail . . . life of man"—suggests one form of this generic tradition, the *beatus ille*. The contrary-to-fact condition of the first sentence, though less cynical than the perspective of Horace's Alfius, places Milton firmly in the world, where "business" will always demand its due.[12] Michael O'Loughlin has demonstrated eloquently and at length how the poetic motifs of *otium* and *negotium* could be translated into Christian categories, tracing the competition between contemplative and active Christianity in terms of pastoral and georgic.[13] This schema is convenient since, as we shall see, Milton conceives of his "call" in poetic categories.

The other source of this dichotomy is the preface itself. Cicero returns to this dialectic again and again in his philosophical and theoretical works,[14] but the topos can be seen in perhaps its simplest form in a passage from the pseudo-Ciceronian *Rhetorica ad Herennium*, quoted in Chapter 1:

My private affairs [*negotiis familiaribus*] keep me so busy that I can hardly find enough leisure [*otium*] to devote to study, and the little that is vouchsafed to me I have usually preferred to spend on philosophy. Yet your desire, Gaius Herrenius, has spurred me to compose a work on the Theory of Public Speaking, lest you should suppose that in a matter which concerns you I either lacked the will or shirked the labour.   (1.1)

The author is called from leisured activities to perform a public task, and the unwillingness with which he abandons the elevated pursuit of philosophy increases his authority in the public realm he enters.

The dialectic between these two sets of values as they appear in *Church-Government* forms the core of Milton's ethical self-presentation. Poetry has replaced philosophy as the leisured pursuit, but the essential shape of the dichotomy has remained intact. Milton would seem to grant the point that his work as presbyterian apologist must and ought to supplant poetic *otium*. His conscience upbraids him,

> Yet ease and leasure was given thee for thy retired thoughts out of the sweat of other men. Thou hadst the diligence, the parts, the language of a man, if a vain subject were to be adorn'd or beautifi'd, but when the cause of God and his Church was to be pleaded, for which purpose that tongue was given thee which thou hast, God listen'd if he could heare thy voice among his zealous servants, but thou wert domb as a beast; from hence forward be that which thine own brutish silence hath made thee. (*YM* 1, 804–5)

Even if the passage seems to admit the possibility that "leasure" could be employed to speak for God, such employment is always on the point of being assimilated to the "sweat" of manual labor. For the Christian, pastoral leisure always threatens to become "brutish," a solipsistic escape from one's duties in the City of God that is proper only to beasts. Even though it draws on the antique privileging of the public sphere, Milton's idea of intellectual labor inverts the classical alignment of true humanity with leisure and "brutishness" with labor. Such an inversion is a pointed rejection of humanist and aristocratic categories for understanding intellectual endeavors.

Milton, however, was no Winstanley, and the persona of the humanist author continues to hover about his pronouncements on his office. The inversion of classical notions of labor, although reflecting a growing sentiment among Puritan thinkers, must be understood primarily in terms of the rhetorical goals of self-authorization. Milton clearly still values the quiet life of *studium* and poetry, and he stresses his abandonment of *otium* only to prove that "neither envy nor gall hath enterd me upon this controversy, but the enforcement of conscience only, and a preventive fear least the omitting of this duty should be against me when I would store up to my self the good provision of peacefull hours" (*YM* 1, 806). He seems to privilege "peaceful hours" over the "duty" of addressing this "wayward subject against prelatry." The authority of his jeremiad lies in the very seductiveness of the leisure that the burdened prophet agrees to forgo. The renunciation empowers the prophet, turning his apology for "green yeers" into a statement of strength, the strength of the "liberty of free speech." For Milton makes it clear that to abandon poetry is to abandon the things of value "to my self," and to abandon the self is to take on the voice of the public good.

Milton's ethical proof thus relies on the rhetorical maneuvering between a poet's life of leisure and the prophet's renunciation of that life. The wide variety of critical responses to Milton's prophetic vocation is largely due to the somewhat serpentine nature of that maneuvering. John Huntley articulates the prevailing view of Milton's two "offices" of poet and prophet when he argues that "because the author is trustworthy in other respects (being cultivated, poetical, and above petty vanity) his comments on ecclesiastical administration must also be significant." A thinker as different as Christopher Hill nonetheless argues in a similar vein that "in the Utopian enthusiasm of the early forties, Milton began to envisage the possibility of a reconstructed society in which the true poet could step forward as the acknowledged legislator of mankind. That is the point of the prayer at the end of *Of Reformation*, and of the autobiographical passage in *The Reason of Church Government*."[15] In the view of Huntley, Hill, and many others, then, Milton invokes his poetic office as a straightforward ethical proof: "Because I am a good poet, I am therefore a reliable, possibly even a divinely inspired, prophet."

My own understanding is that for Milton there is a necessary disjunction between the two vocations, a discontinuity that is the basis for the particular kind of ethical proof he employs here, one that depends on the distinction between *otium* and *negotium*. Milton's words are quite specific:

> To him ["the elegant & learned reader"] it will be no new thing though I tell him that if I hunted after praise by the ostentation of wit and learning, I should not write thus out of mine own season, when I have neither yet compleated to my minde the full circle of my private studies, although I complain not of any insufficiency to the matter in hand, or were I ready to my wishes, it were a folly to commit any thing elaborately compos'd to the carelesse and interrupted listening of these tumultuous times. (*YM* 1, 807)

This statement, repeated in various forms throughout the preface, does not depend on the analogy of good poet and truthful orator except insofar as the analogy must be established to be repudiated. Milton is forced to write "out of season" by "these tumultuous times," and this replacement of private desire with public duty is proof that the tract is not motivated by the quest for personal fame.[16]

There are clear filiations between this ethical proof through renunciation and the emphasis on the appearance of disinterest in classical ethical proof. Yet Milton's elaborate, schematic use of the figure of the poet is more than a proof of moral character, just as it is more than a statement of regret for abandoning poetry. Rather, poetry stands as a figure for the private, the otiose, the self-indulgent. Thus the famous "left hand" passage: "Lastly, I should not chuse this manner of writing wherin knowing my self inferior to my self, led by the genial power of nature to another task, I have the use, as I may account it, but of my left hand" (*YM* 1, 808). Since it is unlikely that Milton's reader would have seen the work of his right hand, poetry itself cannot be the primary focus of this passage. As John Guillory has noted, in the antiprelatical tracts, Milton consistently works to create "a sense of authority *prior* to any actual achievement as a writer."[17]

This rhetorical goal explains why Milton uses an ethical proof that depends on disjunction rather than analogy. By setting aside poetry at the same time that he foregrounds it, he convinces the reader to accept his poetic vocation without inviting a challenge to that vocation as part of his credentials. He buttresses this simultaneous elevation and (temporary) rejection of poetry through the often-noted contractual nature of the digression, "covenanting" with the reader, trading present trust for future poetry: "Neither doe I think it shame to covnant with any knowing reader, that for some few yeers yet I may go on trust with him toward the payment of what I am now indebted" (*YM* 1, 820).[18] The potential reader of *Church-Government*, however, Puritan or Anglican, would have had much less interest in an unknown poet's future verse than in his credentials for speaking on the controversy at hand. Joan Webber rightly sees the entire digression as a form of *praeteriteo*, "promising poetic excellence in the future in language that offers a sample of it now" (198). Yet it is a mistake to see that future poetic excellence as the major thrust of the *praeteriteo*, a mistake originating in the assumption that *Paradise Lost* is the telos of both Milton's right and his left hand. When Milton "covenants" with the reader, trading present trust for future poetry, it is the present trust that would have concerned his reader, and it is the attempt to win that trust that deserves further scrutiny.

In the rhetorical present of Milton's figure, the choice of "my self inferior to my self" means relinquishing a "better" self. The nature of this self and its relation to the empowering trope of renunciation becomes clearer as Milton progresses:

> For although a Poet soaring in the high region of his fancies with his garland and singing robes about him might without apology speak more of himself then I mean to do, yet for me sitting here below in the cool element of prose, a mortall thing among many readers of no Empyreall conceit, to venture and divulge unusual things of my selfe, I shall petition to the gentler sort, it may not be envy to me.   (*YM* 1, 808)

Even though his poetry can hardly be held out as a preeminent example of lyric utterance, an outpouring of "private" fancies, Milton here identifies his public *officium* with the abandonment of poetry, a poetry of *otium* and, significantly, autobiography. Yet he simultaneously casts off his "singing robes" and holds on to them in appealing to the poetic audience, the "gentler sort" of reader, to allow him to speak of himself, if not entirely "without apology" then nonetheless with openness. Meanwhile, he asks the "many readers of no Empyreall conceit" to accept the fact that a renunciation has taken place and that the poet has descended into the "cool element of prose." The force of Milton's *praeteriteo* therefore lies in its very literalness; he does in fact pass over poetry while at the same time giving it value as a counter in his ethical proof.

It is now possible to reappraise the famous passage of "autobiography." What is striking about this passage, which I will not analyze at length here, is its lack of real autobiographical content, by modern standards and even by the standards emerging rapidly in Milton's time. His poetic ambitions are related to the reader in terms of self-described circuitousness: "Perhaps I might seem too profuse to give any certain account of what the mind at home in the spacious circuits of her musing hath liberty to propose to her self, though of highest hope and hardest attempting" (*YM* 1, 812–13). Again and again, what we might regard as the "subject" Milton emerges only in the form of public constructs: the canned poetic biography of the Virgilian generic *rota*, the literary histories of imitation theory, and above all, the laureate identification of poet with his homeland. One searches in vain, despite the powerful sense of Milton's vocation, for the least trace of Montaigne's bodily voice with its peculiar self-authorization, or even the soul-searching of Puritan journals. Instead, Milton regards even his appearance in controversial prose as "an abortive and foredated discovery" (*YM* 1, 820) and gives a version of a self that is not only highly public but almost completely deferred.

A new authorial self, built out of its own absence, can be postulated from Milton's discourse of the body, articulated throughout his prose works. As we have seen, for Paul and Luther, the possession of a body or of a *corpus operum* served as a guarantee of a personal, individuated authority, the martyr's testimony. Milton, in contrast, spills much of the ink he spent on prose defending himself from the "bodily" charges of licentiousness. Such a defense became especially necessary after the scandal-provoking *Doctrine and Discipline of Divorce* (1643), but he had already devoted a large part of his apologetics in *An Apology Against a Pamphlet* to the question of his sexual conduct. This shift from Luther's use of the body suggests in part the change in sexual mores and the decorum of controversial writing during the Renaissance, but Milton's cloaking of his body also has a specific significance in his work.

For Milton, the significant body is always the public body. This body often takes the negative form of the "over-bodying" of the soul Milton finds in the public ritual fostered by prelacy (*YM* 1, 522), but it can also appear as *Areopagitica*'s "lovely form" of "virgin Truth" (*YM* 2, 549), the highest form of public incorporation, the object of all Christian discourse. Such a schema has little place for Paul's corporeal testimony and Luther's conception of *opera omnia* as an autobiographical *corpus*. Not surprisingly, although Milton might lament the *sparagmos* of Truth, he remains unconvinced by the sufferings of individual martyrs. In *Of Reformation*, writing of Cranmer, Ridley, and Latimer, he turns the words of Paul himself against the authority of a martyr's testimony:

But it will be said, These men were *Martyrs*: What then? Though every true Christian will be a *Martyr* when he is called to it; not presently does it follow that every one suffering for Religion, is without exception. Saint *Paul* writes, that *A man may give his Body to be burnt*, (meaning for Religion) *and yet not have Charitie*: He is not therfore above all possibility of erring, because hee burnes for some Points of Truth. (*YM* 1, 533)[19]

One cannot substitute one's own body for the body of Truth, partially because the body of Truth has itself been dismembered, but also because Milton denies the synecdochic relationship between these two bodies. If in *Church-Government* Milton constitutes himself as subject only to withhold that subject from the reader, it is because the significant subject is what Milton will call the "member incorporate."

This phrase comes from what is perhaps the most autobiographical of Milton's early prose works, and the one most permeated by prefatory rhetoric, *An Apology Against a Pamphlet Call'd A Modest Confutation of the Animadversions upon the Remonstrant against Smectymnuus*, published shortly after *Church-Government* in 1642. The *Apology Against a Pamphlet* is no longer a proleptic self-justification; the battle has been joined, and its itinerary can be traced back through its name. Although he prefers to date the war back to "the Remonstrant's" (probably Joseph Hall's) attack on the five Puritan divines whose initials form the anagrammatic "Smectymnuus," Milton had joined the battle uninvited, and in fact unknown, by his adversary with his *Animadversions Upon the Remonstrants Defence, Against Smectymnuus*.[20]

Although contained within the traditional boundaries of classical rhetoric, the preface of the *Animadversions* is of interest in its own right since its subject is the modification of the *captatio benevolentiae*. Milton cites biblical authority for his questioning of this mainstay of prefatory rhetoric: "No man can serve two masters" (Matt 6:24), and serving God must not be compromised in order to please man. Nevertheless, he does make some concessions to the necessity of rhetoric, and he designates the preface as the locus of any such compromise:

Although it be a certaine truth that they who undertake a Religious Cause need not care to be Men-pleasers; yet because the satisfaction of tender and mild consciences is far different from that which is call'd Men-pleasing, to satisfie such, I shall adresse my selfe in few words to give notice before hand of something in this booke, which to some men perhaps may seeme offensive, that when I have render'd a lawfull reason of what is done, I may trust to have sav'd the labour of defending or excusing hereafter.   (YM 1, 662)

Milton may profess a desire to save himself "the labour of defending," yet it will be this very labor, necessitated by the attacks of the Confutant, that guarantees him a place as a part of an authorizing public body and that drives the rhetoric of *An Apology*.

The distinguishing structural feature of the *Apology*, its prefatory gigantism, springs from this "labor of defending." The preface to the *Animadversions* represents an important clue to the construction of the later work since Milton seems to consider the *Apology* an extension not of the *Animadversions* per se, but of its preface: "To beginne therefore an Apology for those animadversions which I writ against the Remonstrant in defence of *Smectymnus*, since the Preface, which was purposely set before them, is not thought apologeticall anough; it will be best to acquaint ye, Readers, before other things, what the meaning was to write them in that manner which I did" (YM 1, 871). Since Milton devotes roughly a third of the tract to personal apologetics before beginning the formal confutation of his opponent's arguments and equates such apologetical material with the preface, the prefatory portion of the *Apology* can be seen to occupy an unprecedented share of the text. This prefatory bloating has its proximal cause in the dispute itself, but it also represents Milton's increasing tendency to conflate exordium and narration into a new kind of preface. The formal interface between preface and self-portrait is that blurry line between exordium and narration—the place where the "facts of the case" take over from the more conventionalized rhetorical self-presentation of the opening.[21] Classical theorists give frequent precedents for such a mingling of these two oratorical segments, but the *narratio* is still not considered part of ethical proof.[22] For Milton, however, the "facts of the case" now include, at unprecedented length, his self-presentation, as if he had fully taken to heart Quintilian's dictum "I prefer to follow the authority of the greatest orators, and hold that whatever concerns the pleader is relevant to the case" (4.1.12).[23] The facts of the case are indistinguishable from the person of the orator. To apologize is never to leave the preface; to "apologize against" is to legitimize this extended prefatory moment and free it from prefatory shame.

The appearance of an adversary has ensured that the apology no longer need be defensive but may be aggressive as well.

The *Apology* grounds itself upon this conflation of orator and case, a conflation justified by the context of invective: "But when I discern'd his intent was not so much to smite at me, as through me to render odious the truth which I had written . . . I conceav'd my selfe to be now not as mine own person, but as a member incorporate into that truth whereof I was perswaded" (*YM* 1, 871). Milton's new sense of himself as a "member incorporate" results in his rejection not of ethical proof but the commonplace that limited prefatory rhetoric even as it generated it, the modesty topos. His starting place is a defense of his abandonment of moderation; he refuses to be "a cold neuter in the cause of the Church" (*YM* 1, 868),[24] and as authority for his manly stance, he alludes to the biblical injunction against "lukewarmnesse" (Rev 3.16).[25] To show rhetorical moderation in a matter of such import is no different from showing undue and disingenuous modesty—it separates the self from the cause. Zeal, which becomes Milton's foremost virtue in this tract, is nothing more than the perfect identification of self with God's work.

Milton's opening sentences enmesh the reader in God's will, demonstrating a major thesis of the work, that moderation is anything but self-abnegation:

> If, Readers, to that same great difficulty of well doing what we certainly know, were not added in most men as great a carelessenes of knowing what they, and others ought to do, we had bin long ere this, no doubt but all of us much farther on our way to some degree of peace and happinesse in this kingdome. But since our sinfull neglect of practising that which we know to be undoubtedly true and good, hath brought forth among us, through Gods just anger so great a difficulty now to know that which otherwise might be soone learnt, and hath divided us by a controversie of great importance indeed, but of no hard solution, which is the more our punishment, I resolv'd (of what small moment soever I might be thought) to stand on that side where I saw both the plain autority of Scripture leading, and the reason of justice and equity perswading. (*YM* 1, 868)

These roundabout periods are typical of Milton's openings, but here they demonstrate something very specific. Milton's modesty has been reduced to a parenthesis (and is soon to disappear altogether). More important, their sinuous logic makes it very difficult

for the reader to extricate divine will from Milton's personal volition. The first sentence, for instance, seems to state that the de-
pravity of "most men" adds problems of knowing to natural problems of doing. The second sentence, however, states explicitly that
problems of knowing are divine punishment for our failure to do
well. Moreover, despite the divine punishment, Milton sees no
problem with basing a personal resolution on *claritas Scripturae*
("the plain autority of Scripture"). Joan Webber has documented
the way Milton manipulates style to show that he is God's "instrument" (196), and here this manipulation has the specific purpose of demonstrating divine authority for his rejection of "moderation."[26] The speaker is so deeply implicated in the cause of the
presbyters that such moderation does not present itself as a viable
possibility.

Milton, aided immeasurably by the *Modest Confutation*'s attack, has worked out the problem that vexed—and inspired—him
in *Church-Government*, the relation of his vocation to his cause.
The *Modest Confutation*'s personal invective enrolled him among
the Puritan saints; by acknowledging him, his attacker guaranteed
him a legitimate role in the controversy, so that he no longer needed autobiography to grant him the authority to speak. But the situation is complicated by the fact that Milton cannot be entirely
sure of the identity of his attacker, an important figuration for his
rhetorical self-definition. "I have not doubted," he says, "to single
forth more then once, such of them as were thought the chiefe and
most nominated opposers on the other side" (*YM* 1, 869). Because
the *Modest Confutation* was printed anonymously, Milton was
forced to rely on the "nominations" of others, and although he
sometimes seems to assume that Joseph Hall was its author, at
other times he attributes it to a younger man ("this young queasi-
nesse"; *YM* 1, 894). Elsewhere he hedges his bet more clearly, and
admits that his knowledge is hearsay. He says his attacker has
abused him "in revenge of his Remonstrant, if they be not both
one person, or as I am told, Father and Son" (*YM* 1, 897).[27]

Given the importance Milton places on the youthful poet in
Church-Government, one can see that his ignorance of his opponent's identity allows him an advantageous flexibility in figuring
his own rhetorical identity. At the beginning of the tract, Milton
does not hesitate to proceed as if the Confutant were Bishop Hall

himself (without, of course, actually naming him). The concomitant stance of Milton himself is much like that of *Church-Government*:

Knowing that if heretofore all ages have receav'd with favour and good acceptance the earliest industry of him that hath beene hopefull, it were but hard measure now, if the freedome of any timely spirit should be opprest meerely by the big and blunted fame of his elder adversary; and that his sufficiency must be now sentenc't, not by pondering the reason he shewes, but by calculating the yeares he brings. (*YM* 1, 869)

It might be more accurate to speak here of a dialectical step beyond *Church-Government*. The rhetorical gains of Milton's "earliest industry" now seem to be the foundation on which he will build. That is, Milton's claim to be a "timely spirit" exhibits a confidence beyond that of one "that hath been hopefull," and having tried "his elder adversary," he has already found him wanting and his fame "blunted" (by none other than Milton in his *Animadversions*).

It is in the issue of "nominations" that a paradox basic to *An Apology* arises—and it is a paradox with an important historical dimension. The more Milton feels himself to be a "member incorporate" of the presbyterian movement, the more urgent the process of "nominations" becomes. A decade later, for instance, after he had become the spokesman for the Commonwealth as Latin Secretary, Milton would insist against all good evidence that Alexander More was the author of attacks against him in *Clamor Regis*.[28] In one sense, the paradox is simply resolved: since he requires the attacks of others to gain his "incorporate" authority, Milton needs to name his attackers to grant them their own kind of authority, to validate the gravity of their attacks. Yet the real paradox is that in requiring their attacks he also requires their "nominations." Here is the paradox of the marketplace, which Milton reduplicates as author: by conveying an object to the market as a commodity, one makes it at once a "common" good, capable of being purveyed to any taker, and yet for that reason all the more in need of proprietary boundaries if it is to serve as a profit-producing commodity.[29] The more "incorporate" Milton's voice—the more it purports to serve as the common parlance—the more it needs the designations of ownership to grant it authority as a product. The suppression of the subject, which we saw in

Church-Government, is therefore not consubstantial with the disappearance of the author. On the contrary, it signals the fuller creation of an authorial system in which proprietary rights to texts are granted by a market that requires recognition from the authors it creates. This recognition takes the form of "nominations," a system of labeling in which a subject earns its authority by agreeing to see itself as representative rather than unique.

The subject thus reemerges under competitive pressures from the Confutant as a representative entity. Milton realizes that the task of self-presentation will run afoul of traditional expectations of modesty and that silence might have been the best defense had he not discovered that his opponent wished "to render odious the truth" for which he stands. Under the pressure of the Confutant's attacks, he is "forc't to proceed from the unfained and diligent inquiry of mine owne conscience at home (for better way I know not, Readers) to give a more true account of my selfe abroad then this modest Confuter, as he calls himselfe, hath given of me" (*YM* I, 869–70). The Confutant's invitation to move the discourse from "abroad" to "home" enables Milton to cast his defense as a scrupulous self-examination and therefore escape the charge of mere self-praise.

More important, this turn inward enables Milton to make the connection between inwardness and the written word, the only index the reader possesses to judge this inward character in a nameless debate. This connection lies behind Milton's famous version of the ancient dictum that a good orator must be a good man:[30] "He who would not be frustrate of his hope to write well hereafter in laudable things, ought him selfe to bee a true Poem, that is, a composition, and patterne of the best and honourablest things" (*YM* I, 890). As we have seen, in *Church-Government,* "pattern" was the mark of "ceremony" (*YM* I, 765). For the "nominated" and "incorporated" Milton, however, pattern has been resuscitated as a moral and ontological category. To be "a true Poem" is to be a construct of public morality and aesthetic taste, so that poem and prose alike do not so much display Milton's inwardness as his inwardness displays a "pattern" that can be construed as a kind of poem. And it is in the integrity of this pattern that his inwardness can be judged. Milton therefore no longer needs to rely solely on the contractual invocation of writing well "hereafter," and he turns the connection between style and ethical authority to coin by discrediting the Confutant's prose. Style provides a kind of on-site verification for the ethical credentials of the orator, a process that works through the identification of self with text—or substitution of text for self.

Milton's transformation of religious debate into literary criticism is thus a cornerstone of his ideas of authorship.[31] His recurrent analogy between the Confutant's Senecanism and Anglican abuses of power is well-known: "For certainly this tormenter of semicolons is as good at dismembring and slitting sentences, as his grave Fathers the Prelates have bin at stigmatizing & slitting noses" (*YM* 1, 894).[32] The prelatical party tortures both dissenters and syntax because both acts are part of its "composition." The defects in "patterne" that Milton castigates in his opponents include abuses of prefatory self-presentation. One need look no further than the title, he argues, to find the insinuating falsehoods of the modesty topos:

And because he pretends to be a great conjector at other men by their writings, I will not faile to give ye, Readers, a present taste of him from his own title; hung out like a toling signe-post to call passengers, not simply *a confutation* but *a modest confutation* with a laudatory of it selfe obtruded in the very first word. Whereas a modest title should only informe the buyer what the book containes without furder insinuation, this officious epithet so hastily assuming the modesty wch others are to judge of by reading, not the author to anticipate to himselfe by forestalling, is a strong presumption that his modesty set there to sale in the frontispice, is not much addicted to blush. A surer signe of his lost shame he could not have given, then seeking thus unseasonably to prepossesse men of his modesty. (*YM* 1, 875–76)

There is nothing more immodest, he claims, than an attempt to show oneself modest, to hang a "signe-post" announcing one's modesty. Milton is not just exposing a rhetorical infelicity in the Confutant's title; his description of the ideal relationship between writer and reader circumvents the entire province traditionally assigned to rhetoric. He asks the reader to judge the text and its author with no mediation, as if the author could be himself without "forestalling" himself.

Like the preface, rhetoric seems to have a hazy spatial and temporal relation to "content." It was common in the Renaissance (as it is now) to think of rhetoric as ornament coming *after* the "matter." But from the perspective of the reader, what is added after almost necessarily stands before (or in front of) the textual core. Thus Milton's attitude can be seen as either a reactionary (and impossible) desire to present pure *res* for the reader or a plea for a more integral conception of rhetoric as simultaneous with (if not constitutive of) matter. Milton is thus doing more here than criticizing the Confutant's title; he is blowing the whistle on the rhetorical practice of nearly two millennia, reasking Aristotle's question. For although (as Swift would demonstrate) Milton is undoubtedly right in questioning the rhetorical wisdom of including the word *modest* in a title, much of traditional prefatory rhetoric has no other purpose for an author than "unseasonably to prepossesse men of his modesty." Why, one might ask, does Milton feel he can announce with no personal risk that the emperor has no clothes?

The answer lies in the fact that Milton conceives of his text as radically different from that of the Confutant. His specific point of differentiation resides in the inconsistency of inside and outside in the Confutant's work, an inconsistency he does not share because he is for all practical (rhetorical) purposes identical to his mission. The implications of this belief not only obviate the need for the modesty topos—since the self has been swallowed by the cause, modesty, like moderation, has no real meaning—they also explain the obscure exordial boundaries in much of Milton's prose. Whether one sees the purpose of the exordium as ethical proof or as *captatio benevolentiae*, the preface can no longer be conceived as a unit discrete from the text. The true author is not added to the text; he is himself a "true Poem" to be read. As he puts it, "For doubtlesse that indeed according to art is most eloquent, which returnes and approaches neerest to nature from whence it came; and they express nature best, who in their lives least wander from her safe leading. . . . So that how he should be truly eloquent who is not withall a good man, I see not" (*YM* 1, 874). Moreover, it is no longer necessary to win the goodwill of the audience since the worthiness of the cause will be self-evident to the judicious reader. Milton thus arrogates to himself and his work a hermeneutic principle directly analogous if not identical to the principle of *claritas Scripturae*. It is this principle that enables him

to return to Aristotle's rhetorical Eden, where the preface is unnecessary. In his version of this state of paradise, however, the
preface loses itself not by being lopped off but by merging with the
text.

Milton figures this new kind of rhetorical "integrity" in his per-
sistent use of the clothing metaphor, a metaphor that recurs
throughout the antiprelatical tracts:

With me it fares now, as with him whose outward garment hath bin in-
jur'd and ill bedighted; for having no other shift, what helpe but to turn
the inside outwards, especially if the lining be of the same, or, as it is
sometimes, much better. So if my name and outward demeanour be not
evident anough to defend me, I must make tryall, if the discovery of my
inmost thoughts can.   (*YM* 1, 888–89)

The metaphor aids him in asserting his rhetorical integrity in two
ways. First, it stresses once again that he bares his soul only under
compulsion; only the besmirching of his garment could lead him
to break his silence. Second, he has "no other shift"; in reversing
his garment, he remains the same, despite the fine lining. Thus he
possesses a consistency between inner and outer that the Confutant with his superadded "Frontispice" lacks. Milton's oration has
integrity in the root sense, and in a sense perhaps unavailable before.[33] This integrity has its own danger, as Milton realizes. Of
coming forward with "the summe of my thoughts," he says, "I am
not ignorant how hazardous it will be to do this under the nose of
the envious, as it were in skirmish to change the compact order,
and instead of outward actions to bring inmost thoughts into
front" (*YM* 1, 888). And yet the danger is limited, given the com-
pactness of Milton's ranks where, as we have seen, front and rear,
inner and outer, stand close upon each other.

Milton contrasts the integrity of his rhetorical self-presentation
to the Confutant's unintegrated frontispiece and to the prelatical
party's dependence on marginalia, a dependence he had already
commented upon in *Church-Government* where the prelates "club
quotations with men whose learning and beleif lies in marginal
stuffings" (*YM* 1, 821–22). In the *Apology*, he frequently refers to
the Confutant's glosses as a kind of waterway, separated from text
itself but necessary to it: "For what with putting his fancy to the
tiptoe in this description of himselfe, and what with adventuring
presently to stand upon his own legs without the crutches of his

margent, which is the sluce most commonly, that feeds the drouth of his text" (*YM* 1, 910). And again: "Nor yet content with the wonted room of his margent, but he must cut out large docks and creeks into his text to unlade the foolish frigate of his unseasonable autorities" (*YM* 1, 921–22). The latter quotation not only admirably describes the appearance of a page dredged open by marginal commentary but also perfectly evokes the alienation of self from text that Milton finds in the Confutant. The author appears as a middleman, trying to import truth into his text by opening up channels in it through which he can "unlade the foolish frigate of his unseasonable autorities." The criticism of the "unseasonable" importation of authorities into an argument implies a theory of decorum in which any use of authority not subordinated to both the logic and the ethos of a writer's argument is a misuse of authority. For Milton, the integrity of the author, the consistency with which he can align "office" and persona, rather than the forcefulness with which he can ally himself to previous texts stands as the proof of his claims.

Milton's new understanding of ethos can be measured by the distance between the prefatory rhetoric employed in *Church-Government* and in the *Apology*. In the latter work, Milton is no longer content to isolate his persona within neat prefatory boundaries or to claim the pamphlet as the work of his left hand, lest he occupy the same marginal space to which he relegated his prelatical opponents. Along the way, he redefines for himself the rules of prefatory self-presentation, abandoning the modesty topos as appropriate only for the alienated "frontispiece." The product of this redefinition may be seen in the confident, almost rhapsodic self-portraits of the *Pro se defensio* and the *Defensio secunda* in which ethical proof seems able to encapsulate a defense of Puritanism as a whole. To quote once more Milton's defense of his prefatory technique in the *Defensio secunda*, "It is a singular favour of the divinity towards me, that I, above others, was chosen out to defend the cause of liberty . . . and this favour I must affirm I acknowledged; nor can the time ever come when it will cease to be my duty to acknowledge it; and that I took hence, which in my judgment can hardly be imputed to me as a fault, the noble matter of my exordium" (*CM* 9, 86–87). What began in effect as a rhetorical ploy, a manipulation of ethos that nonetheless remained within the boundaries of classical ethical proof, has become a new understanding of authorial subjectivity and, arguably, subjectivity itself.

This paean to the self, however, is also a manifesto of a bounded self and a publicly constituted author, the self as textual "matter," the author as "chosen" to perform his "duty." In Milton one can see the dissolution of one system of authority, based on a privileged hierarchy of texts (and individuals), and the beginnings of a new system, based on a publicly constructed discourse of common sense (and a publicly constructed commonwealth). If he has reintegrated the public and private selves Luther found it necessary to divide, he has done so by dissolving Montaigne's free-floating author in his discourse of *officium*. Thus Milton, the great master of the humanist tradition, stands as a sentinel for an emerging posthumanist discourse in which "pattern" might be said to replace modesty as authorizing strategy. Milton grounds this pattern in his "incorporation" into the Puritan cause. I would suggest that the metaphor behind incorporation is fortuitous but not serendipitous; Milton defines his rhetorical persona through the competition of the marketplace of ideas but shelters himself through a corporate identity from the potential dangers faced by a solitary contender and the charge that he had a monopolistic personal stake in his discourse. The market, which had helped distribute humanist ideas, also compromised the construction of authorship included in those ideas. In the next two chapters, I will trace the struggle of seventeenth-century scientific writers to create in their prefatory rhetoric an institutional form of a new discourse of public utility that was more answerable to the market.

PART II

Prefatory Method in the New Science

It might, indeed, be of ill Consequence to the Publick, as well as unprofitable to private Persons, to alienate so much Ground from Pasturage, and the Plow. . . . But why may not a whole Estate be thrown into a kind of Garden by frequent Plantations, that may turn as much to the Profit, as the Pleasure of the Owner . . . ? Fields of Corn make a pleasant Prospect, and if the Walks were a little taken care of that lie between them . . . and the several Rows of Hedges set off by Trees and Flowers, that the soil was capable of receiving, a Man might make a pretty Landskip of his own Possessions.   —Addison, *The Spectator*

The urgency with which Luther, and particularly Milton, address the need for a public supplementation to the humanist rhetoric of authorship replays itself in the discourses of science that were emerging in the seventeenth century. The subjects of this section, Descartes, Bacon, Hobbes, and Sprat, worked patiently to disarticulate these discourses from those of not just academic Aristotelianism and theology but humanism itself. The ideology of authorial individualism, so important in allowing scientists to assert their authority against that of the Church and that of Aristotle, also stood squarely athwart the enabling twofold myth of the New Science—its public utility and its epistemological objectivity. Operating under this myth, the scientist could assert himself as a means of challenging the ogres of scholasticism, but the field being cleared of villains, he needed to abandon the field himself to the disinterested, impersonal, and publicly beneficial pursuit of the "facts" of nature. As it had with the writers of Protestant tracts, the preface proves to be a crucial stage for acting out questions of individual agency versus supraindividual forces, now no longer the hand of God but the objective reality of nature and its sociopolitical correlative, common sense.

The epigraph from Addison comes from late in the history of this myth's development (although it is still with us). In the middle of the sixteenth century, Ramus was espousing a new pragmatic didacticism in an attempt to revivify the political humanism of the Quattrocento. His efforts to produce competent bureaucrats presumed a sphere of common intelligibility and political accessibility, and his homogenizing of the humanist canon reflects this same drive toward a public utility.[1] At the same time in England, "Commonwealthmen" were beginning to exert influence on governmental and mercantile policy, stressing, as their name indicates, social and national interests over those of the individual.[2] But the idea of public utility as the overriding consideration in both governmental policy and intellectual endeavor spread primarily through the efforts of scientific thinkers like those I will discuss in this chapter. Bacon and his followers, and in France men such as Théophraste Renaudot, spread their gospel of socially pragmatic research and even legislation, and with it emerged its epistemological foundation in common sense.[3]

Addison's essay shows the extent to which the myth was culturally (and generically) disseminated by the end of the seventeenth century. His musings, however, also make explicit what might be seen as the generic models underlying a struggle between humanist and scientific ideas of authority and authorship. His criticism of the waste of expansive pleasure gardens is a criticism of an aristocratic pastoralism, and he formulates that critique in the language of georgic, the mode of public use, in an essay, now the genre of public opinion rather than private meditation. Yet he combines elements of both pastoral and georgic into a new compromise discourse of public individualism, a paradox that takes its resolution from Locke's theoretical sanctification of property as the logical result of a man's owning his own labor. Addison finds the labor that legitimizes ownership in the landscape he is surveying, thus creating a Horatian amalgam of pleasure and utility in the land itself.

Addison's landscape is the place toward which the figures and texts I discuss in the next three chapters lean, a place where the rhetoric of individualism is secured without the sacrifice of a framing discourse, namely, that of public utility and common sense. I discuss Descartes before Bacon, although Bacon preceded him, because Descartes figures the split between pastoral and georgic models much more sharply than his predecessor, and Bacon comes closer to being able to imagine what that georgic model—which would become the basis for modern science—might entail both rhetorically and politically. Bacon understood science and learning as institution and therefore became, questions of epistemology aside, the true progenitor of scientific method as we know it. After examining the relation between authorship and the public sphere in works by Hobbes and Sprat, I conclude Part II by leaving science altogether to look at the cultural dispersion of this same concern in a literary work, Dryden's "Preface to the *Fables*."

4

"A great city is a great solitude"

DESCARTES'S URBAN PASTORAL

Touchstone. Truly, shepherd, in respect of itself, it is a good life;
but in respect that it is a shepherd's life, it is naught. In respect
that it is solitary, I like it very well; but in respect that it is private, it is a very vild life. Now in respect it is in the fields, it
pleaseth me well; but in respect it is not in the court, it is tedious.
As it is a spare life (look you) it fits my humor well; but as there is
no more plenty in it, it goes much against my stomach. Hast any
philosophy in thee, shepherd?   —*As You Like It*

In 1637, Descartes published his *Discours de la Méthode* together with three technical treatises that the title page describes as
"des essais de cete Méthode" (*A & T* 6, xiii). The *Discourse* as a
whole, therefore, serves as a philosophical preface to these tracts
since it supplies the framework of a formal method that they then
fill with content. In a letter of March 1637 to Mersenne, Descartes
makes this point very specifically, going so far as to label the *Discourse* a "preface": "But I didn't understand very well what your
objection was concerning the title. For I didn't entitle it *Treatise
on Method* but rather *Discourse on Method*, which is the same as
Preface or Reflection Concerning Method, in order to show that I
had no intention of teaching, but only to talk about it" (*A & T* 1,
349).[1]

In fact, the *Discourse* provides an epitomized introduction to
Descartes's work as a whole, an idea he puts forward in the preface to the *Principles of Philosophy*: "The first part of these essays
was a *Discourse on the Method of rightly conducting one's reason
and seeking the truth in the sciences*, where I summarized the prin-

cipal rules of logic and of an imperfect moral code which we may follow provisionally while we do not yet know a better one" (*PW* I, 186–87). Descartes goes on to suggest that his oeuvre is a series of interlocking texts, each serving as a preface to the next, each preparing the mind of the reader for the next step in his philosophy. Viewing the *Discourse* in retrospect, then, he reveals yet another sense in which the work functions as a preface, namely, as an anticipatory précis of the *Meditations*. And the *Meditations* are in fact an exfoliation of the cogito narration of the *Discourse*, a narration liberally sprinkled with the rhetoric of abbreviation, as if it were anticipating the fuller treatment of the *Meditations*.

The *Principles* therefore provide a formal basis for considering the *Discourse* as prefatory in conception, and the *Principles* also point toward the basis for the drama of exemplarity played out in the work on method. The preface to the *Principles*, entitled "Author's letter to the translator of the book which may here serve as a preface" (*PW* I, 179), is Descartes's contribution to Abbé Claude Picot's 1647 French translation of a work he had published in Latin three years earlier. The "Author's letter" is largely concerned with the question of reception, and Descartes is acutely aware throughout of the irony created by simultaneously presenting a public text and "coming before" it to overlay a private reading on it. He plays out this irony through the person of the translator, who comes to represent the public face of his text. Descartes presents himself modestly, almost apologetic for his incursion into another man's text:

> But although it would seem to be up to me to produce this preface because I ought to know these things better than anyone else, all I can persuade myself to do here is to summarize the principal points which I think such a preface should deal with. I leave it to your discretion to pass on to the public as many of them as you consider to be pertinent.   (*PW* I, 179)

The preface hovers on the edge of the envoi: Descartes flirts with bidding his "little book" to be gone. But the figure of the translator, the one who would "carry across" the book to the public, allows Descartes to reintrude himself and reassert the Janus-like nature of his text that retains a private face. Such a picture of textuality carries with it the ready possibility that the private face will be badly translated, misrepresented in the process of publication, and near the end of the preface Descartes pleads with his readers "never to attribute to me any opinion they do not find explicitly stated in my writings" (*PW* 1, 189).

In this chapter I will argue for the centrality of this double-faced representation of self in the *Discourse on Method*: the conflicting pull between public and private created by the redefinition of the two concepts during the seventeenth century. Descartes draws heavily on the growing cult of retirement to ground his identification of the autonomous self with the aristocratic detachment from the increasingly vital public sphere of the urban marketplace. This private self, with its roots in the humanist individualism of Montaigne, proves effective in producing an originary authority for Descartes's thoroughgoing revision of Aristotelian method. This authoritative voice, however, offers little help in establishing the new science as a nonproprietary, public discourse. Descartes must therefore explore, however tentatively, the representation of self as exemplum, as a replicable model for future scientists.

The resulting ambivalence—which, I will argue, is one of class as much as rhetorical approach—leaves indelible traces on Descartes's prefatory method. In an emblematic moment from the preface to the *Principles*, he plays the interpreter as well as the author. His desire to play two roles, to be both inside and outside the text, finds its echo in the instructions he gives the reader: "I should like the reader first of all to go quickly through the whole book like a novel, without straining his attention too much or stopping at the difficulties which may be encountered" (*PW* 1, 185). This analogy with the novel, which may seem a casual one in relation to the *Principles*, exemplifies a tendency of Descartes to represent much of his work as "fable." By insisting that his reader view his work as an instructive fiction, he can advance autobiography as *exemplum*. Yet at the same time he pulls back from his own exemplary claims. As he said in the letter to Mersenne quoted above, he entitled his work a discourse (or preface) to show that he "had no intention of teaching." At once a private tale and a public model, Descartes's text hovers between genres but also between different constructions of authority that these genres imply. I will concentrate on one story in the complex of fables that makes up the *Discourse on Method*—his retirement to Amsterdam, a sto-

ry that straddles two authorial models. But I must first pause briefly over the function that storytelling in general plays for Descartes
in the *Discourse*.

I have spoken of several texts for which Descartes considered
the *Discourse* a kind of preface, but to introduce the prefatory fable of the *Discourse*, I need to mention a final one, *Le Monde, ou
Traité de la Lumière*, which Descartes epitomizes in Part V of his
work on method. Descartes suppressed *Le Monde* after the condemnation of Galileo in 1632 and never published it. His summary of its contents in the *Discourse* thus becomes the example (judiciously chosen not to offend the authorities) of the content his
method could generate. In Descartes's sense of his oeuvre, then, *Le
Monde* serves as both the origin and the telos for the chain of
"prefaces" I described earlier. Its suppression necessitates the elaborately rhetorical set of exercises for approaching the philosophical core of his thought.

Crucial for my purposes, therefore, is the fact that the famous
"fable" or "*histoire*" of the *Discourse* is a substitution for an earlier, less well-known fable in the suppressed text. In the middle of
that tract, while discoursing on "the number of elements and their
qualities," Descartes suddenly changes his method of presentation:
"But in order to make this long discourse less boring for you, I
want to clothe part of it in the guise of a fable, in the course of
which I hope the truth will not fail to become sufficiently clear,
and will be no less pleasing to see than if I were to set it forth
wholly naked" (*PW* 1, 90). Descartes flirts here with Montaigne's
suggestion of a "naked" text, a possibility that he comes closer to
realizing in the autobiographical fable of the *Discourse*.[2] Of equal
importance, however, is Descartes's complication of the traditional notion of rhetoric as a covering of the truth designed to make it
more palatable. Descartes "clothes" the rest of the discourse in
this fable of a new, hypothetical world where no physical phe-
nomena exist that cannot be imagined. This parallel world is a scientist's utopia in which no confusing accidents stand in the way of
understanding the wholly intelligible "laws of Nature." Moreover,
the fable enters the text at the precise moment that Descartes must
broach the sensitive topic of cosmology. Rhetorically (one might
even say politically), this hypothetical world enables Descartes to

analyze a "new" nature unencumbered by Aristotelian science or Church dogma: he is this world's original interpreter as well as its creator. The fable reveals, stripping away encrustations of tradition, even as it clothes.

Descartes only enhances this paradox when he exchanges his fable of utopian cosmology for one of autobiographical epistemology. For although the fable of the *Discourse* shares with that of *Le Monde* the rhetorical purpose of clearance (Aristotle and the philosophy of the schools are banned early from Descartes's intellectual autobiography), the new fable is more than a new, safer version of the utopian legend of *Le Monde*. It is more "protective," more rhetorical and less philosophical, at the same time that it depends even less on any obvious literary accoutrements. As Jean-Luc Nancy points out, the fable of the *Discourse* "has even abandoned the fiction of the feint of being a simple ornament, like that covering the fable of *Le Monde*";[3] it has none of the literary trappings of the genre. Rather, as Nancy also notes, it is a fable only insofar as it is *exemplary*. What puzzles Nancy is the manner in which Descartes describes or circumscribes the exemplarity of his story:

But I am presenting this work only as a history [*histoire*] or, if you prefer, a fable in which, among certain examples worthy of imitation, you will perhaps also find many others that it would be right not to follow; and so I hope it will be useful for some without being harmful to any, and that everyone will be grateful to me for my frankness [*gré de ma franchise*]. (*PW* 1, 112; *A & T* 6, 4)

Nancy concludes that the fable actually exemplifies only the author's "frankness." As a "fable of fidelity" (646), the *Discourse* must always fail in its avowed purpose since the exemplum must always "withdraw to its original" (647) before it can fulfill its didactic end. Put another way, to follow Descartes's example of clearance and self-origination, a reader must either include Descartes in his own clearance and therefore distrust the exemplum or allow Descartes to enter fully into his fictional projection as example, thereby eroding the purity of the frankness and the basis for positing the cogito as an unalloyed "simple."

A fable that presents more than one exemplum and that refuses to indicate which of these is truly exemplary, or exemplary for a specific audience, is indeed a strange fable. As David Simpson puts it, "Where the *Discourse* is so elusive is in its presentation of a private voice which seems to stand in a plurality of possible relationships to its social or public context."[4] It is possible to view this elusiveness as not merely endemic to exemplarity but as specifically grounded in Descartes's particular relationship with his project and his audience. That is, with the experience of Luther behind us, we can examine the particular problems of exemplarity for an author confronting both a coercive authority and an audience that is at once potentially receptive and potentially unruly. The "self" of the *Discourse* is elusive because it is a self presented to a public sphere that is itself fragmented, unable to present the narrator with an unambiguous route to establishing a social identity.

A clue to the private ambivalence and public ambiguity of the *Discourse* lies in Descartes's word *franchise*, which is rendered correctly by "frankness" but which like "frankness" needs historical excavation. John D. Lyons, reminding us that the *Discourse* appeared anonymously and therefore could be making only attenuated claims for the author's sincerity, writes, "In such a context the older sense of the term *franchise* seems to impose itself—a limit on sovereign authority."[5] *Franchise* is the liberty or freedom of the landed and "enfranchised" "franklin," the *franc bourgeois*. Descartes is therefore claiming the liberty to speak freely within the realm of inquiry governed by the authority of the schools, but more specifically he is obliquely grounding that freedom on the claims of class—a class, as we shall see, toward which he had ambivalent feelings.

This ambivalence is legible in the contrast between the beginnings of the *Discourse* and the *Meditations*. "Good sense is the best distributed thing in the world" (*PW* 1, 111). Thus Descartes opens the *Discourse*, without a formal preface, giving only a short abstract of the argument. The importance of his beginning in French, with "good sense" that is well "distributed," can be judged only by jumping ahead to the prefatory matter of the *Meditations*. There Descartes divides his address to his readers into an epistle dedicatory to the faculty of the Sorbonne and a preface *ad lectorem*. Lest, however, one think that this division separates an "elite" from a "vulgar" audience, Descartes makes his conception of audience clear in his preface to the reader: "I briefly touched on the topics of God and the human mind in my *Discourse on* . . .

Method. . . . I thought it would not be helpful to give a full account of it in a book written in French and designed to be read by all and sundry, in case weaker intellects might believe that they ought to set out on the same path" (*PW* 2, 6–7). The practical problem behind the exemplary fable of the *Discourse* is here made clear: if the vulgar tongue and a common audience have their uses in combating the authority of academy and church, they also place Descartes in company for which he has more than a little contempt. He thus uses Latin in the *Meditations* as a kind of winnowing to rescue the didactic possibilities of his narrative for an audience perhaps adept enough to follow his method. What Descartes seems to construct, in effect, is a series of concentric circles with himself at the center and the illiterate masses at the extremes, outside the final circle—the professors of the Sorbonne falling somewhere in between.

As we shall see, this "hierarchy" has important ramifications for Descartes in defining the public and private spheres. But Descartes complicates this schema through his multiple trips down the "road" of metaphysical and methodical inquiry. For not only does he address the "feebler minds" in French in the *Discourse*, he also attacks the very audience he will address in the *Meditations*. In formal terms, one can say that although Descartes could manage the topics of the epistle dedicatory with its elitist assumption that a small audience guarantees a private discourse, he could equally well manage the topics of a "To the Reader" preface in which the same small audience figures as the authority that he must clear away. At every turn in the *Discourse*, Descartes, like Montaigne, valorizes the "natural reason" of the common man rather than learning; this, he tells us, is why he chose to write in French: "And if I am writing in French, my native language, rather than Latin, the language of my teachers, it is because I expect that those who use only their natural reason in all its purity will be better judges of my opinions than those who give credence only to the writings of the ancients" (*PW* 1, 151).

I will turn first to the question of how Descartes articulates and adjudicates between these two stances of aristocratic sage and populist intellectual revolutionary. For although written in French with the avowed purpose of clearing away authorities, the *Discourse* contains both of these stances. Having established the relation between these two motives in the *Discourse*, I will reimplicate them in the context of exemplarity that bears so importantly on Descartes's understanding of prefatory rhetoric.

In March 1629 Descartes, citing the lack of privacy allowed him by the social life of Paris, removed himself to Amsterdam where, he tells the reader of the *Discourse on Method*, "amidst this great mass of busy people who are more concerned with their own affairs than curious about those of others, I have been able to lead a life as solitary and withdrawn as if I were in the most remote desert, while lacking none of the comforts found in the most populous cities" (*PW* 1, 126). Despite this neat formulation, he seems quickly to have grown tired enough of the "crowded throng" to move to a smaller town across the Zuider Zee. As one of Descartes's biographers has pointed out, "In spite of his remarks on Amsterdam, he evidently preferred a country life, or else to live in the outskirts of a town."[6] And not only was his urban retirement more suburban, even rural, than urban; his letters from this period, liberally peppered with requests for friends to visit him, show that his dedication to a life of solitude was more figurative than real.[7]

But if Descartes led a life that was neither solitary nor urban, his actual choice of abode serves only to underscore the importance of his residential fable with its conceptually tidy paradox. Having more philosophy in him than even Touchstone, Descartes attempts to take the conflicting sentiments of his time toward a number of dichotomies—city and country, civic engagement and retirement, labor and *otium*—and turn contradiction into a paradox that could describe his philosophical project. It is the content of that fictional paradox that I wish to explore, remembering, however, Descartes's *real* address, an address that registers his difficulty with the spatial and ideological construct that he articulates through his narrative of urban retirement. Like Touchstone in his assault on the shepherd's sensibilities, Descartes is performing an ideological operation upon the landscape, assigning social functions to spatial configurations. Unlike Touchstone, however, he is also questioning traditional dichotomies and attempting tentatively to bridge them. The compromise implied by his yoking of the discourses of retirement and civic engagement, and his uneasiness with his compromise, stand very close to the center of his concerns in the *Discourse on Method* and his philosophical work as a whole.

Descartes's urban retreat is situated in an old literary neighborhood. The topos he adapts in praise of urban anonymity is at least as old as Strabo, who quotes an unknown "comic poet": "Eremía megále 'stìn he megále pólis," (The great city is a great desert).[8] In its original context, the proverb comments on urban blight at a time when many Hellenistic cities had become depopulated, and the pun on the Peloponnesian city of Megalopolis betrays the tone of the phrase. Guarino renders the tag accurately: "Megalopolis idest ampla civitas ampla fit desolatio."[9] The phrase was canonized, however, by Erasmus in his *Adagia* in the form "Magna civitas, magna solitudo" (A great city is a great solitude).[10] The ambiguity of the Latin translation of *eremía*, *solitudo*, which can mean both "solitude" and "a place of solitude," "a desert," opened up the social and psychological context in which the Renaissance understood the tag. Bacon assumes this context when he explicates the topos: "*Magna civitas, magna solitudo*, because in a great town friends are scattered; so that there is not that fellowship, for the most part, which is in less neighbourhoods."[11] The strictly demographic content of the original has turned into a lament over the lonely anonymity of the contemporary city. Descartes's adaptation of the phrase retains this interpretation of *solitudo* but gives the commonplace a positive valence by grafting it onto the discourse of retirement, the *beatus ille* topos, thereby making the city the ideal location for the philosophical eremite.[12]

Descartes gives his fullest exposition of the "lonely crowd" in a letter of 1631 to Jean de Balzac, a letter that provides much of the context for the motif as it appears in the *Discourse on Method*. Balzac had already built a literary reputation on his letters, many of which debate the time-honored opposition between a contemplative country retirement and an active public life. In his letter, which predates the *Discourse* by six years, Descartes explains why he prefers Amsterdam as a place of retirement to the rural retreat his friend praises:[13]

However perfect a house in the country might be, it always lacks countless comforts that are only found in towns; and even the very solitude one hopes for there is never found to be entirely perfect. . . . Whereas in this great city where I am, containing not a single man except me who doesn't pursue a career in trade, everyone is so attentive to his own profit that I could live here my entire life without ever being seen by anyone. I take walks every day amidst the confusion of a great multitude, with as much liberty and repose as you could experience along your footpaths, and I consider the men that I see here no differently than the trees I would encounter in your forests, or the animals that pasture there. Even the noise of their bustle does not interrupt my reveries any more than would that of some brook. If I sometimes reflect on their activities, I receive the same pleasure that you would in seeing your peasants cultivate your fields; because I see that all their labor serves to adorn the place where I reside, and to ensure that I lack for nothing here. *(A & T* 1, 203–4)

Descartes develops at length (I have quoted selectively) the topos that has such important implications for the work on method he would soon compose. He shows that remarkable ability, often commented upon in the poets of the period, to assimilate what would properly be the stuff of georgic, manual labor, into the pastoral ideal.[14] The picture of Balzac at his ease, watching his peasants cultivate his fields, is a case in point: the labor central to that enjoyment is present, but marginalized as part of the landscape.[15]

Descartes's transposition of this picture onto an urban canvas, even though presented in a playful fashion, cannot dispel the stress lines gathering around the pastoral ideal. His "reveries" among men who are indistinguishable from trees and farm animals not only reflect back ironically upon Balzac's homogenized landscape but also problematize his own attempts to see his work as the fruit of aristocratic leisure. The bustling burghers of Amsterdam will not readily metamorphose into happy swains, even though Descartes goes on to make the somewhat strained argument that they are serving him by importing the commodities he needs for his comfort.[16] The "busyness" of the bourgeoisie played a central role in the changing attitude toward labor, and in fact Descartes's urban solitude does not provide repose at all but a means to make uninterrupted intellectual labor possible. He would seem to be moving unwittingly, or at least reluctantly, toward Bacon's georgic conception of scientist as aristocratic laborer in the fields of public welfare.[17]

Descartes's implied solution to the problem of aristocratic labor seems to be simple contiguity: through his adjacency to the Dutch merchants he can associate his philosophical researches with labor and the pursuit of the public good. Like Milton with his labors of prose, Descartes would seem to be abandoning the humanist discourse of leisure. Yet the effect of his analogy between Amsterdam and Balzac's country estate is not so much to ratify his intellectual activity as labor as to identify it with the pastoral pipings of the aristocracy and thus deny its status as labor altogether. Descartes's social ambivalence therefore generates his paradox of the urban pastoral, a paradox that produces an internal commuting in the *Discourse* between the values of urbanized georgic, with its stress on labor for the public good, and the rural values of aristocratic leisure.[18]

Before tracing the itinerary of this commute, I should clarify the source of the ambivalence. Auerbach, in his study of the seventeenth-century French "public," describes Descartes as a *grande robe* who also seemed to possess a noble title.[19] By this time, the *grande bourgeoisie* had all but ceased to perform its function as the bureaucratic class, and its mercantile role lay even further in the past. "Like those of many other periods and countries," says Auerbach, "these bourgeois were characterized by a desire to escape from their class and to stabilize their wealth. . . . Spreading side by side with prosperity, humanism and its ideal of *otium cum dignitate* also encouraged the flight of the bourgeois from their class" (171–72). Richard Sennett, following up on the implications of Auerbach's research, notes that if the *grande bourgeoisie* of *la ville* was successfully shaking off its connection to its mercantile origins and merging for all practical purposes with *la cour*, it was at the same time creating a new sense of the word *public*. No longer did the word connote only the "public weal"; it also came to stand in opposition to the "private" as the "special region of sociability."[20] No longer could the aristocrat, with his ethic of voluntary public service, consider public action as consubstantial with his own actions. For the French aristocrat of the mid-seventeenth century, whether a member of the *noblesse de la robe* or the *noblesse de l'épée*, public action connoted a kind of display, defined by his appearance first in the fashionable salons and then somewhat later in the theater. It was this "public" that Descartes was fleeing when he left Paris. Having tried and failed to maintain secret lodgings in that city, he felt obliged to seek a place where he could quietly pursue his work.[21] At the same time, as the letter to

Balzac shows, Descartes was attracted, however condescendingly, to the bourgeois activity of Amsterdam, which offered the kind of anonymous public space to which we have become accustomed.

Amsterdam thus becomes a means for Descartes to gather up and bind together two representations of the same social unease: nostalgia for the intimate social structure of the aristocratic coterie on the one hand and on the other the desire to absent himself from the dynamic urban scene that was replacing this intimate structure. The flight to Amsterdam, then, is both toward and away from his bourgeois origins. He desires to reduce the class that produced him to a picturesque backdrop against which he can perform his laborless toils. By moving his eremite back home, but home to a city that remains foreign, Descartes creates a suburban compromise within the city limits in which the subject contributes his labor to the common good but remains socially alienated by retaining his private plot of ground. But the business of the burgher contaminates the busyness of the philosopher, and unlike the aristocrat donning the shepherd's weeds for a courtly entertainment, Descartes the *grande robe* can in fact disappear all too easily into the georgic landscape of Amsterdam. It is not surprising, then, that Descartes devotes much of the *Discourse on Method* to avoiding such an assimilation, to retaining a distinct, private voice even as he pursues his georgic vocation of public utility.[22]

Descartes's social and philosophical ambivalence is woven into the basic stuff of the *Discourse on Method*'s metaphoric fabric. In his famous meditation in the "stove-heated room," he implies that just as a centrally planned city is to be preferred to one that has grown up organically, so his system is superior to traditional philosophy because it is free from the inconsistencies of accretion. The analogy argues in effect for the public utility of a private method:

Again, ancient cities which have gradually grown from mere villages into large towns are usually ill-proportioned, compared with those orderly towns which planners lay out as they fancy on level ground. Looking at the buildings of the former individually, you will often find as much art in them, if not more, than in those of the latter; but in view of their arrangement—a tall one here, a small one there—and the way they make the streets crooked and irregular, you would say it is chance, rather than the will of men using reason, that placed them so. (*PW* 1, 116)

Lewis Mumford seizes on this passage as an illustration of his case against baroque city planning. According to Mumford, the passage describes the triumph of mechanical principles over organic ones, of the "baroque despot's" will over the individuation of the Middle Ages, which had been rationalized but not destroyed by Renaissance city planning. The hallmark of this new, monolithic city planning was the avenue, with its impersonal vistas and wide traffic lanes that daunted pedestrians but facilitated the movement of the large national armies that had arisen in Europe.[23]

Mumford's observations have direct relevance for Descartes, but Descartes was by no means the eager spokesman for baroque uniformity that Mumford portrays. Descartes not only understood the threat that authoritarian uniformity represented to him and his work; he also felt keenly how difficult it is to authorize any uniform plan, whether architectural, political, or methodological. Moreover, as Mumford admits (without mentioning Descartes), Amsterdam, Descartes's adopted home, does not fit the baroque mold; Mumford dubs it "capitalism's one outstanding urban achievement, rivaled only by elegant Bath" (439). Leonardo Benevolo points to the fact that the political structure of Holland's city-states emerged from the Middle Ages relatively intact and notes both the individualized architecture of Amsterdam's houses and its closed visual spaces, limited by the curvilinear nature of the canals and the rows of elms planted along them according to the 1607 plan for the city's expansion. In fact, and it is a fact relevant to Descartes's urban metaphors, Amsterdam was seventeenth-century Europe's most rationally and efficiently designed city, but its design included a closely confined yet nonetheless expressive individualism, as conveyed in the facades of the houses, the only external detail not specifically controlled by city ordinance.[24]

Amsterdam must have seemed a figurative bonanza to Descartes, a place where he could at once represent himself as the aristocratic stranger standing aloof and a participant in a social structure whose ostentatious republicanism and public commerce could not have differed more from the universities and salons of Paris. The Amsterdam compromise between authoritarian plan and individual expression thus epitomizes nicely his own prevarication. Once he has put forward his analogy, asserting that in building a philosophical system as in building a city razing is the necessary precondition for raising, he immediately retreats into his apolitical pastoral stance and dissociates himself from any implications the analogy might have beyond describing his internal pursuit of method. "This example convinced me that it would be unreasonable for an individual to plan to reform a state by changing it from the foundations up and overturning it in order to set it up again" (*PW* 1, 117). Moreover, by shifting even his idealized role immediately from great architect to great city planner, he manages to have his cake and eat it too. While avoiding an exemplarity that implies absolutism, he suggests that the example of his method might stand over the product of other individuals in a loose, supervisory manner, just as the central planning of Amsterdam permits individuated architectural expression within defined limits. In the remainder of this chapter, I will examine how the "suburban compromise" that Descartes finds in Amsterdam becomes the basis for what might be called his social epistemology, his exploration of the possibilities for institutionalizing scientific endeavors.

This exploration combines concerns that appear in autobiographical, methodological, topographical, and in particular rhetorical forms throughout the *Discourse* and Descartes's works as a whole. Nowhere, however, does he pursue the exploration so single-mindedly as in Part VI of the *Discourse*. Part VI is the most prefatory section of the work, an extended apology for coming forward in print that outlines the conflicting motivations for privacy and publication. Descartes opens by alluding to the case of Galileo, then states his dilemma:

This [the condemnation of Galileo] made me fear that there might be some mistake in one of my own theories, in spite of the great care I had always taken never to adopt any new opinion for which I had no certain demonstration, and never to write anything that might work to anyone's disadvantage. That was enough to make me change my previous decision to publish my views. For although I had had very strong reasons for this decision, my inclination, which has always made me dislike the business of writing books, prompted me to find excuses enough for deciding otherwise. The reasons, on one side and the other, are such that not only do I have some interest in stating them here, but also the public may be interested to know what they are.   (*PW* 1, 142)

Once again Descartes is entering into the metadiscourse of the preface—this time not through epitome or even narrative apologue but through apology, the master discourse of the traditional preface. If Descartes has doubts about the decorum of relating his physical theories, he has none about describing his dilemmas as an author.

When forced to confess why he then bothered to publish this private discourse, Descartes appeals to *ususfructus*, or usefulness, a concept conventional to the exordium. Curtius labels this topos as "the possession of knowledge makes it a duty to impart it."[25] This topos stands very much in the public-spirited tradition not only of prefatory rhetoric but of the Baconian georgic of technology. Descartes sees his usefulness as author in terms of the "bodily": the very body he had sundered from the mind and banished in his method now returns, strengthened by the sundering itself. For, as Timothy Reiss has shown, Descartes had taken part in the creation of an entirely new "discourse" for understanding the world in terms of the manipulation of matter rather than as a system of correspondences.[26] Descartes does not yet have the word, but it is the creation of technology that gives him a new world comparable to the new world of *Le Monde* (and with it a new version of the "public") to move back into and take possession of:

For they [his "speculations"] opened my eyes to the possibility of gaining knowledge which would be very useful in life, and of discovering a practical philosophy which might replace the speculative philosophy taught in the schools. Through this philosophy we could know the power and action of fire, water, air, the stars, the heavens and all the other bodies in our environment, as distinctly as we know the various crafts of our artisans; and we could use this knowledge—as the artisans use theirs—for all the purposes for which it is appropriate, and thus make ourselves, as it were, the lords and masters of nature.   (*PW* 1, 142–43)

It is difficult to imagine a clearer statement of the ideology permeating the New Science. The world Descartes returns to is not the object of speculation but manipulation, the world of the artisan.

If, however, this "bodily" world is as free from scholastic overlay as the new world of *Le Monde*, it is equally idealized. That is, this constructed world is still not a public world in any real sense, lacking the institutional structure to make public the fruits of Descartes's lucubrations. In the final part of the *Discourse on Method*, then, Descartes engages in an attempt to work out a compromise between public and private, composing in effect an oblique meditation on the possibilities for institutionalizing his method. Hovering over this meditation is the fate of Galileo and the implications of his condemnation for the publication of scientific speculations. Although *Le Monde*, a scientific summa of sorts, was couched as a fable of "imaginary spaces" (*PW* 1, 132), Descartes felt he could not risk publication. Why, one might ask, did he feel unprotected by the fiction of *Le Monde* yet go on to risk publication of the *Discourse* and the accompanying treatises on optics, meteorology, and geometry? The answer, I believe, is to a large extent a hermeneutic one; that is, Descartes had no doubt about the legibility of *Le Monde*'s fable but could nonetheless put his faith in the indeterminacy of the generic fiction of a "discourse." Not only does the *Discourse* bear a prefatory relation to the texts that follow, but both sets of texts are presented as conative, exploratory documents, essays spoken in a private voice rather than imprinted with the public designs of the written treatise. It is this fiction that Descartes hides behind, but it is also this fiction that exposes the difficulties he will have in grounding a public science on an almost Montaignesque personal discourse.

Part VI, in other words, must return to the question of exemplarity: why should he publish a purportedly private discourse unless he sees himself as a model for the pursuit of scientific research? Acknowledging once again that "we might find as many reformers as heads," Descartes nonetheless appeals to "the law which obliges us to do all in our power to secure the general welfare of mankind" (*PW* 1, 142). In a momentary flush of goodwill toward his fellow man, he seems to forget the problematic nature of self-publication and to suggest the possibility for cooperative research. He reasoned, as he explains to the reader, that the huge scope of the endeavor could be overcome if he published his findings to incite others to contribute their observations and talents. "Thus, by building upon the work of our predecessors and combining [*joignant*] the lives and labours of many, we might make much greater progress working together than anyone could make on his own" (*PW* 1, 143; *A & T* 6, 63).

But if this vision seems to partake of a kind of Baconian institutionalization of science, it stalls at key moments. Descartes never admits a truly collaborative project, only a collective one passed from hand to hand after each experimenter has made his contribution. The metaphor of "combining," chosen by the translator of this passage, is a Baconian concept fundamentally foreign to Descartes. His metaphor of joining suggests not a system in which one's work circulates and mixes with others as a commodity might in the marketplace but one in which information descends to a new researcher as a legacy, not unlike an aristocrat's estate. This genealogical model for experimental research, with its comfortingly abstract and hierarchically constituted ligatures binding an experimenter to his indebted progeny, is as far as Descartes is able to proceed into a publicly articulated system of knowledge.

Posthumous publication would seem the mode of transmission most fully fitted to this lonely collective of discrete and solitary acts of scientific inquiry. But if Descartes prefers not to open his researches to the public eye, he also realizes that his labors are of a magnitude that requires aid while he is still alive to supervise that aid. Even the best-intentioned he had enlisted were hampered by the privacy of the method; "highly intelligent persons" (*PW* 1, 146) to whom he outlined his opinions recounted them to him in such a way that they were hardly recognizable as his own. The only glimmer of hope lies in his limited faith in the "artisan," a faith that implies a mechanization of progress wherein the skilled technician can hammer out the details of a prearranged master plan, a plan not unlike the hierarchic, centralized uniformity of Mumford's baroque city: "As regards observations which may help in this work, one man could not possibly make them all. But also he could not usefully employ other hands than his own, except those artisans . . . who would be led by the hope of gain (a most effective motive) to do precisely what he ordered them to do" (*PW* 1, 148).

Descartes's artisans recall his bustling burghers: anonymous but necessary participants in an otherwise solitary undertaking. Even when he grants his "co-workers" something more than artisinal status, there is no doubt who holds the master plans. Explaining that posthumous publication will not suffice to further his work, he argues: "This would oblige all who desire the general well-being of mankind . . . both to communicate to me the observations they have already made and to assist me in seeking those which remain to be made" (*PW* 1, 144). Publication is therefore a necessary evil designed to "oblige" others to share their research and to reduce them to the status of assistants.

In the end, even this heavily compromised form of collaboration seems too unsystematic, too messily disparate, for Descartes. "So if there were someone in the world," he coyly suggests, "whom we knew for sure to be capable of making discoveries of the greatest possible importance and public utility . . . I do not see how they [other men] could do anything for him except to contribute towards the expenses of the observations that he would need and, further, prevent unwelcome visitors from wasting his free time" (*PW* 1, 148). Thus, after an elaborate maneuver around the question of collective research and the institutionalization of science, Descartes brings the *Discourse* to an end by suggesting that his fellow workers might best serve as fund-raisers and security guards. While private speculations contribute to the public weal, the public, with its "common sense," can do no better than appreciate which private discourse deserves its (primarily financial) support. The ironic result of the failure of Descartes's narrator to serve as an intermediary between private accomplishment and public dissemination of that accomplishment is that Descartes passes beyond establishing himself as a merely paradigmatic figure in the search for knowledge to exhibiting a truly proprietary interest in the discourse of the new science: "In short, if there was ever a task which could not be accomplished so well by someone other than the person who began it, it is the one on which I am working" (*PW* 1, 148). The *Discourse on Method* thus becomes the prototypical grant proposal.[27] And like Luther's amalgam of inspiration and historical compulsion, Descartes's inside position in his project closes down the possibility of meaningful imitation.

The spatialized version of these irresolvable public and private discourses, Descartes's Amsterdam compromise, reveals the limited sense in which he can allow himself to accept the new discourse of common sense or to synthesize it with older notions of an authority that stands outside public utility. The licensing of individualized facades in a rigid master plan embodies, within the city limits, the kind of compromise we would now call suburban, the subdivision of the public realm into small private plots. Descartes's final rhetorical stance involves just such a retreat to a kind of public privacy: "I have never tried to conceal my actions as if they were crimes. . . . For if I had done this I thought I would do myself an injustice, and moreover that would have given me a certain sort of disquiet, which again would have been opposed to the perfect peace of mind I am seeking" (*PW* 1, 149). He describes here a delicately poised *otium*, one that depends on going public only to the extent required to defuse curiosity and idle gossip about the product of his "perfect peace of mind." Once again, since Descartes is quick to add that he seeks leisure for the sake of the public good that it will produce, this leisure must be understood in the context of a scientific georgic. Yet public service that requires public exposure is clearly at odds with an older tradition of aristocratic privacy that he is unwilling to abandon. His solution is to offer only a partial version of his researches, a partial version of his self.

Descartes leaves the reader with this paradoxical combination of public and private. He has taken up residence in the city, but he retains his solitude. He cannot speak clearly and univocally the public discourse of universal scientific method that he was instrumental in shaping: there is an "I" that remains distinct from the "we" of common sense. But he has already pointed the way to a new rhetoric in which the author is figured as a public judge, a spokesman for a shared discourse, rather than a private advocate arguing for the relevance and legitimacy of his words against an authoritative tradition. Bacon, as spokesman for the new forces of "method," asserts, "I cannot be fairly asked to abide by the decision of a tribunal which is itself on its trial."[28] Descartes, arguing against the value of academic disputation, uses the same figure: "Those who have long been good advocates do not necessarily go on to make better judges" (*PW* 1, 146). But it is in his suburban compromise rather than his understanding of forensic rhetoric that Descartes makes his contribution to the figurative storehouse of the public sphere. Through his narrative of urbanization, Descartes gives Bacon's new venue a local habitation in the georgics of public technology, although he seems unwilling to settle there himself. It is to Bacon that we must turn in order to find a plan for settling this new public space.

5

An Induction into Nature's Inner Courts

EMPIRE AND INSTITUTION IN
BACON'S PREFATORY METHOD

It has often been noted that Francis Bacon's contribution to the history of science lies not so much in his experimental work as in his methodological speculations.[1] One might go further and argue that Bacon's most momentous accomplishment was his relentless and ultimately successful pursuit of a framework and a language within which the New Science could be institutionalized. He understood that if the new discoveries were to be consolidated and methodized, they required an institutional backing that could compete with Aristotelianism's well-ensconced place in the universities. Given Bacon's lifelong career as a seeker and holder of public office, it is not surprising that he looks to the state as the best source of such an institutional backing. This pursuit of state support gives Bacon's rhetoric a political element absent in earlier scientific writers who sought patronage from powerful figures but lacked Bacon's (to risk a contradiction in terms) bureaucratic vision.[2] It is this vision that makes Bacon rather than Descartes or Galileo the starting point of the rhetoric modern science employs to speak about its public role. Although Bacon voices many of the same conflicts that stand behind much of Descartes's metascientific discourse—between leisure and labor, between aristocratic and popular constructions of the public sphere—he feels comfortable in building his Great Instauration on foundations provided by the state. Even though his attempt to produce a state-supported scientific apparatus was unsuccessful during his lifetime, Bacon was able to submerge questions of vocation more successfully in the vocabulary of the public weal than could Descartes a generation later.

In this chapter, I will pursue Bacon's rhetoric of science or, more accurately, his rhetoric of the scientist—his language of authority and authorship. I begin by examining his alignment of scientific endeavor with other public activities. This alignment provides Bacon with the means to figure his authority and relation to public discourse. In particular, Bacon models the structure of his particular representation of science on propaganda (much of which he wrote himself) that articulates a particularly English form of imperialism, an imperialism that valued not the quick wealth of gold sought by the Spaniards but the solid investment of good agricultural colonies. As we shall see, Bacon translates this model for imperialism into not just a methodology that valorizes "pure" science over applied technology but a model for the scientist himself, who knows when and how to turn science to "use" for the public good rather than personal gain. Bacon's role is that of "a guide to point out the road; an office of small authority" (*Works* 4, 41),[3] a role that defers any glory or gain to the next generation. This self-denial, however, proves a powerful rhetorical tool, a means for converting weakness to strength by identifying Bacon's voice with public good rather than personal aggrandizement.

Bacon's rhetorical method, therefore, in its emphasis on the conative and its portrayal of the self-denying public man, is highly prefatory. Like Descartes, Bacon hints that he saw his works as a series of interlocking prefaces, preparatory gestures that took him closer to articulating a central work that was never completed— and perhaps never could be. The importance he places on the prefatory can be judged from a letter to Sir Tobie Matthew accompanying part of the *Instauratio*, dated October 10, 1609, in which he speaks of "that preface which you so much commend." Sir Tobie's commendation, he goes on to say, leads him to believe that his friend will not be displeased with "this other speech of preparation" (11, 137). In the first instance, Bacon seems to be referring to a "literal" preface to the *Instauratio*, perhaps "The Plan of the Work." The "speech of preparation," however, is very likely the *Redargatio Philosophiarum*, yet another of his methodological dry runs for his experimental work. In both instances, Bacon feels it worthwhile to propagate works of "preparation," perhaps realizing that he will never progress beyond such works. Regarding the *Advancement of Learning*, Bacon says in an earlier letter to Sir Tobie, probably written in November 1605: "I have now at last taught that child to go, at the swadling whereof you were. My work touching the *Proficiency* and *Advancement* of *Learning*, I have put into two books; whereof the former, which you saw, I count but as a Page to the latter" (10, 256). Even the "preface" of the *Advancement*, therefore, falls into two halves, the first serving as "a Page" to the second. Without insisting that by "Page" Bacon means "title page," I would emphasize the recursive conception Bacon shows toward his work in which each piece of writing is reduced to a kind of induction to the one that follows.

I use the word *induction* to highlight the homology between the rhetorical and the methodological in Bacon's thinking. The prefatory work of the *Advancement*—and there is no clearer example of the configuration of the methodological and the prefatory—is "to clear the way, and as it were to make silence to have the true testimonies concerning the dignity of learning to be better heard without the interruption of tacit objections" (3, 264). Bacon's odd articulation of his task—to make the tacit silent—is in fact a good statement of the prefatory project: to anticipate and answer criticism before it can even be spoken. Yet for Bacon, who has no desire to enter into the empty exercises of academic dispute with the Aristotelians, this proleptic silencing has a particular force. Baconian induction, in its rhetorical as well as its methodological sense, involves "clearance" of past voices to an extent perhaps unprecedented. His primary goal, it might be argued, was to redress the lack that he laments in *Novum Organum*: "No one has yet been found so firm of mind and purpose as resolutely to compel himself to sweep away all theories and common notions" (4, 93).

This imperative was so urgent to Bacon that he never effectively advanced from clearing the field to actually cultivating it. The ambition of Bacon's prefatory rhetoric is not to find authority for his authorial voice, to move in from the margins to public "text," but to create a space for public consensus within that authorial voice. Bacon's prefatory method, then—despite his self-presentation as mere harbinger who lays no claims to any real scientific productivity—is not primarily modesty, which traditionally serves to clear room for private discourse, room for the author to make his case. Rather, he maintains that the space he clears rhetorically and scientifically will be both fertile field and open agora, a place where public profit and public information meet, undisturbed by private ambition or personal profiteering. Modesty has no function when the self has no case to make.

The often-reproduced frontispiece to the *Instauratio Magna* (1620) emblematizes its status as entrance to Bacon's book and his method, and in its self-conscious liminality is a good starting place for an investigation of Bacon's prefatory rhetoric. The engraving depicts a ship, followed by another in the far distance, passing through the Pillars of Hercules. Two malevolent sea creatures lurking on either side of the ship like Scylla and Charybdis indicate the difficulty of this passage. The Latin motto, however, reflects an optimism that the rewards of the journey will justify the peril: "Multi pertransibunt & augebitur scientia" (Many will pass through, and knowledge will be increased).

One need not rely upon an iconographic reading to make sense of this frontispiece since Bacon provides an interpretation of the image in the preface to the *Instauratio*. Men have misunderstood the relation between *store* (*opes*) and *strength* (*vires*),[4] thereby overvaluing tradition and undervaluing their ability to obtain knowledge:

These are as the pillars of fate set in the path of knowledge; for men have neither desire nor hope to encourage them to penetrate further. And since opinion of store [*copiae*] is one of the chief causes of want, and satisfaction with the present induces neglect of provision for the future, it becomes a thing not only useful, but absolutely necessary, that the excess of honour and admiration with which our existing stock of inventions is regarded be in the very entrance and threshold of the work, and that frankly and without circumlocution, stripped off, and men be duly warned not to exaggerate or make too much of them.   (4, 13)

Bacon, anticipating twentieth-century anthropology, figures his preface as *limen* and connects this threshold to a process of deculturation, a "stripping" that will produce a neophyte as tabula rasa, ready to exercise his natural powers of induction.

Thus he begins his instauration of a new science with another version of the trope we have seen play such an important role in

Protestant writers, the conversion of weakness into strength. Power seems to be taken on at the very moment of stripping—to remove the dependence on "store" is to expose the naked strength of the human mind. Yet what is interesting (and idiosyncratically Baconian) about Bacon's version of this topos is that it occludes entirely any sense that this narrative of weakness converted to strength might apply to the author. Characteristically, he does not portray this process as something he himself is undergoing but as one over which he is presiding. The passive constructions—"be . . . stripped off," "be duly warned"—distance Bacon from his own threshold and create the sense that he is merely the spokesman for a process that he will undergo along with the reader and society as a whole. In fact, although he does not specifically imply this here, one is to imagine that he has already experienced this process, that he is the captain of a ship that has already passed between the monstrous pitfalls of methodological error.

This conversion of authorial journeying into an emblem for the problematic of all scientific discourse operates through the analogy between Bacon's method and imperial politics. The connection of empirical "journey" with imperial voyage, if not clear from this emblem, is even more explicit in the frontispiece to the posthumously published *Sylva Sylvarum* in which it is now a globe marked *Mundus Intellectualis*, that sits between the Pillars of Hercules.[5] Thus the iconography of the *Instauratio* strongly suggests the device of Charles V—two columns representing the Pillars of Hercules surmounted by the motto *Plus ultra*. The assumption behind the open imperialism of the "more beyond" is that Christendom was already unified as the Holy Roman Empire and that the New World provided the only frontier available. Imperialism, in this conception, is the product of empire alone, and empire the property solely of the emperor.

Yet as Frances Yates has shown, the device of Charles V entered into and permeated royal iconography of sixteenth-century France and England.[6] Although Henry VIII seemed to entertain notions of empire consonant with older definitions of a universal *imperium*, circumstances also led him to appeal to other definitions of the word *empire*. The Act in Restraint of Appeals (1533), a prefatory gesture toward the Act of Supremacy (1534), states:

Where by divers sundry old authentic histories and chronicles it is mani-

festly declared and expressed that this realm of England is an empire . . .
governed by one supreme head and king having the dignity and royal estate of the imperial crown of the same, unto who a body politic, compact
of all sorts and degrees of people divided in terms and by names of spirituality and temporalty, be bounden and owe next to God a natural and
humble obedience.[7]

Behind this pronouncement stands the Donation of Constantine,
which (Valla's debunking notwithstanding) provides Henry with
an implicit definition of *imperium* as the yoking of temporal and
spiritual power, even if this power does not extend to all Christendom. It is this attenuated version of empire that develops into
the basis for Elizabethan imperialism.

This peculiar figuration of Elizabethan—and Jacobean—imperialism stands behind Bacon's portrayal of his task as scientific
explorer. Jeffrey Knapp has documented the tendency of late-
sixteenth-century Englishmen and Englishwomen, including Elizabeth, to stress the smallness, weakness, and isolation of their
country, especially in comparison to the imperial reach and wealth
of Spain. Knapp argues that these qualities, emblematized by the
"weak," "solitary" virgin monarch, are spiritualized and ultimately converted to their opposite by Elizabeth's successes as ruler
and symbolic propagandist: "What would otherwise have appeared dispiriting tokens of England's weakness—its littleness, its
circumscription by enemies, its female monarch—could signify instead England's abjuration of material or worldly means to power and its extraordinary reliance on God" (4). In their resulting obsession with "trifles," nugatory trinkets that suggest the spiritual
through the very paltriness of their materiality,[8] the English came
to expect a temporal power while high-mindedly refusing to pursue gold like the Spaniards. Like Solomon's choice of wisdom,
England's spirituality held out the promise of the thing not asked
for, and as Knapp shows, the defeat of the Armada served as more
than a material sign of the nation's grace; it promised imperial successes that would outstrip, not merely transcend, those of the
Spanish Empire.

As one piece of evidence, Knapp cites the "Device Made by the
Earl of Essex for the Entertainment of Her Majesty" (1592?) (14),
which, if composed in part by Bacon as it almost certainly was, reveals that the future Lord Chancellor had a hand in articulating

this Elizabethan myth. Among other things, Bacon carefully articulates the notion of limited imperium begun by Henry VIII and in
fact links the idea of an island empire to Elizabeth's inheritance:
"She hath made the possessions which she received the limits of
her dominions, and the world the limits of her name" (8, 128). Bacon's pointed rejection of the plus ultra, although it perhaps lies
athwart the internationalist ambitions of his patron Essex, fits well
with Elizabeth's circumscribed efforts at imperialism. Insofar as
she has established an imperium, it is the spiritual one of her
"name."

Yet Bacon also served as spokesman and speechwriter for the
Jacobean form of this topos, the form articulated by the Bacon of
the later scientific works rather than the Bacon of courtly enter-
tainments, and it is that form that interests me here. An aesthetic
and ideology of trifling would have had little appeal to Bacon,
who remained ambivalent toward poetic games even as he prac-
ticed them[9] and scrupulously bracketed spiritual concerns in order
to continue his pursuit of natural knowledge.[10] Even in the speeches from Essex's device, he is already promoting his new science, arguing, in a phrase that he would use repeatedly in his methodological works, that "we should command her [nature] in action"
(8, 126). If his New Atlantis bears a resemblance to Faerie Lond,
his imperial vision and his version of the powerful weakness topos
depart from Spenser's Elizabethan trifling in the directness of their
appeal. In a few short years after the death of Elizabeth, the English had finally established a permanent (if tenuous) plantation in
the New World at Jamestown, and the very accession of James
brought the promise of a kind of imperial expansion closer to
home. Speaking to Parliament in February 1607, Bacon presented
the following opinion as part of his argument in favor of joining
the crowns of England and Scotland:

For certainly the kingdoms here on earth have a resemblance with the
kingdom of Heaven; which our Saviour compareth, not to any great ker-
nel or nut, but to a very small grain, yet such an one as is apt to grow and
spread; and such do I take to be the constitution of this kingdom; if indeed we shall refer our counsels to greatness and power, and not quench
them too much with the consideration of utility and wealth. For, Mr.
Speaker, was it not, think you, a true answer that Solon of Greece made
to the rich King Croesus of Lydia, when he showed unto him a great
quantity of gold that he had gathered together, in ostentation of his great-

ness and might? But Solon said to him, contrary to his expectation, "Why, Sir, if another come that hath better iron than you, he will be lord of all your gold." (7, 39–40)

The speech depends heavily on the myth of English smallness and poorness; yet there is nothing nugatory about Bacon's imprecations against the power of gold: his dichotomy does not oppose wealth to toys but to inherent human strength, the "iron" in the muscle of the English yeoman soldier.

Bacon makes this Machiavellian argument more explicitly in an essay based on this speech, "Of the True Greatness of Kingdoms and Estates": "The principal point of greatness in any state is to have a race of military men. Neither is money the sinews of war (as is trivially said), where the sinews of men's arms, in base and effeminate people, are failing" (6, 446). The strength of England lies in the yeoman soldiery that prevailed at Agincourt and its solid agricultural practices, not in its accumulation of gold. In "Of Plantations," Bacon makes the contrast to the gold-hungry Spanish even clearer: "But moil not too much under ground; for the hope of mines is very uncertain, and useth to make the planters lazy in other things" (6, 458). And more essentially, he connects the success of a colony to its ability to defer profit taking (which ability depends on the limited participation of merchants in the venture): "For the principal thing that hath been the destruction of most plantations, hath been the base and hasty drawing of profit in the first years" (6, 457).

Bacon introduces here one of his central concerns, one that would become a virtual *idée fixe* among his seventeenth-century followers writing on scientific and technological subjects: the essential but potentially corrosive contributions of mercantilism to scientific enquiry. As Richard Helgerson notes, already under Elizabeth "the pursuit of trade rather than conquest becomes a sign of England's virtuous difference [from Spain]."[11] The description of the "Merchants of Light" in the *New Atlantis* reveals Bacon's appreciation for the inquisitive power that propels English entrepreneurs, but one also hears a cautionary note concerning their acquisitive nature in his proviso that their idealized counterparts "maintain a trade, not for gold, silver, or jewels; nor for silks; nor for spices; nor any other commodity of matter; but only for God's first creature, which was *Light*" (3, 146–47). Although Bacon's ultimate desire was a discourse of public utility to govern science, this discourse could not be confused with a "premature and unseasonable eagerness" to pursue "experiments of Fruit, not experiments of Light" (4, 17). Like the English who forbear from pursuing the quick wealth of gold in favor of the solid if unspectacular profits of plantation, Bacon scorns any attempt to garner too soon any practical "works" from his method.[12] He thus considers technological profit taking, which hamstrings science by not returning capital to scientific investment, a form of the Old Adam corrupting man's better intentions and inventions.

This insistence on a science that would not settle too soon into the profitable realm we would now call technology thus bears an obvious relation to Bacon's strictures against the Spanish model of accumulated wealth and his praise of an English model of unadorned strength. To quote once again from "Of Plantations": "I like a plantation in a pure soil; that is, where people are not displanted to the end to plant in others" (6, 457). It would be a mistake, I think, to attribute Bacon's preference for "purity" of soil to consideration for the indigenes. The New World, with its complete lack of any acculturated "store" (at least any that Bacon could recognize), provides a fertile conceptual alternative to the endless intellectual and political reshuffling of the old empire of Christendom. Speaking of the detrimental effect of custom on research, Bacon writes of the dichotomy between approaches to knowledge, approaches he elsewhere labels "cultivation" and "invention" (4, 42): "For it is hardly possible at once to admire an author and to go beyond him. . . . Men of this kind, therefore, amend some things, but advance little; and improve the condition of knowledge, but do not extend its range" (4, 16).

Like so much of Bacon's scientific language, his distinction between *improvement* and *extension* resonates with cultural and political overtones. The significance of these overtones becomes clearer a moment later when he criticizes those who overturn custom but do so "not to extend philosophy and the arts in substance and value, but only to change doctrines and transfer the kingdom of opinions to themselves" (4, 16–17). One begins to discern here what an imaginative and conceptual resource the North American territories became for both political and intellectual discourse. Like his monarchs, who refused to define their kingdom in relation to Continental events, Bacon could turn his back on Aristotelian disputation as at best the "transfer of kingdom" from one disputant to another. When he claims that "there are found in the intellectual as in the terrestrial globe waste regions as well as cultivated ones" (4, 23), there can be little doubt that it is precisely those waste regions that enable Bacon to claim his own intellectual imperium independent of cultivated kingdoms.

Bacon's transformation of the scientific imperium required a new rhetoric, one that could register the scientific scruples and the self-denying (yet self-authorizing) prophetic stance we have already seen. It is possible to view these rhetorical features as neat translations of an array of prefatory commonplaces absolving the author from responsibility for his text. Charles Whitney connects this Baconian "humility" with Montaigne's "metaleptic" stance toward authority. For Whitney, metalepsis constitutes an "adjacent" as opposed to "dynastic" relation toward one's predecessors.[13] Adjacency, while not directly challenging traditional authority, effectively devalues it by allowing the concept of "store" a power at best parallel to individual strength. Thus modesty takes on a paradoxical ability to empower: "For Bacon, the office of small authority clearly is the highest office, since the whole idea of authority is devalued: such is the function of Bacon's claim to humility."[14] When Bacon does produce scientific results, he does so only provisionally, taking care that the reader see such speculations as "wayside inns," and he adds, "Nevertheless I wish it to be understood in the meantime that they are conclusions by which ... I do not at all mean to bind myself" (4, 32).

Bacon employs a variety of metaphoric strategies for portraying the role he plays as the prophet of this new empire of the mind, strategies that allow for personal agency without allowing for personality. His project is the foundation, the machine: "I have provided the machine, but the stuff must be gathered from the facts of nature" (4, 12).[15] He is "a bell-ringer," happy merely "to awake better spirits" (10, 254). He is a planter who realizes he may never see the harvest: "For though it be true that I am principally in pursuit of works and the active deportment of the sciences, yet I wait for harvest-time, and do not attempt to mow the moss or to reap the green corn" (4, 29). Bacon sees himself as a kind of scientific Moses, forced into deferring technological gratification, never able to pass into the promised land of the New Science.[16]

This ethos of deferred gratification maintains only distant filiations with traditional modesty. When at the end of the preface to the *Instauration* Bacon writes, "I cannot be fairly asked to abide by the decision of a tribunal which is itself on its trial" (4, 21), one senses no humility in the face of the authority of tradition. His role as harbinger "humiliates" him only in relation to the new discourse he is inaugurating. In fact, rather than "modesty," it is perhaps more accurate to see Bacon's new form of humility as a prototype of scientific objectivity, the submergence of self in method. And it is in the method of induction that the key to Bacon's rhetorical ethos of humility lies.

Baconian induction both problematizes and reinforces the connection between method and preface.[17] On the one hand, it provides a ground for questioning whether there is any proper place for method prior to practicing science. If method and practice are identical, then the prefatory (and the extrinsically methodic) are mere appendages, the unnecessary supplements of Aristotle's slave. On the other hand, induction could be taken to imply that all science is prefatory, the continuous entrance to the next experiment. The rhetorical element of this endless preface becomes clear when Bacon speaks of his method of relating and teaching discovery, the "aphoristic" or the method of "probation." As opposed to the "magistral" method, the sustained, informing, and forming discourse of the lecturer that predisposes the student to follow a path already cleared, Bacon's method delivers knowledge in brief, unelaborated aphorisms that the student must struggle to connect. In the *Advancement*, he describes the reason behind the efficacy of his method: "But knowledge that is delivered as a thread to be spun on, ought to be delivered and intimated, if it were possible, *in the same method wherein it was invented*" (3, 404).[18] The aphoristic method, then, necessitates the constant reconversion of product to process, not merely to facilitate the next experiment but to make itself persuasive and intelligible.

In this reconversion we can glimpse the ethos of the Baconian scientist, at once humble and exalted, sallying out to conquer both the natural world and the imagination of the student but at the same time sublimely self-effacing: "But in this same anticipated and prevented knowledge, no man knoweth how he came to the knowledge which he hath obtained. But yet nevertheless, *secun-*

dum majus et minus, a man may revisit and descend unto the foundations of his knowledge and consent; and so transplant it into another as it grew in his own mind" (3, 404).[19] This coloniz-ing "transplantation" always requires an imaginative humbling, a recreation of one's ignorant first steps that enables one to imagine the mind of the student but also to rediscover the foundations of one's knowledge. This linking of rhetorical and epistemological humbling recalls the master-slave dialectic that Bacon always maintains man holds with nature: "Nature to be commanded must be obeyed" (4, 47).

Humility in the face of what one wishes to dominate might be taken as a description of all the rhetoric I describe in this book, but in Bacon the volume is turned up in the service of his one goal: "human power" (4, 47). In this new imperialism, humanity, hav-ing learned the lesson of strength through weakness, has taken the place of the English, and nature, through a metaphorical transfor-mation so intensive that it hardly seems metaphorical, takes the place of the New World. I will return at the end of this chapter to Bacon's figuration of nature and the relation of that figuration to ideas of public and private, but for the moment I will focus on the more purely rhetorical element of Bacon's new imperialism. In the transformation of a literal imperialism to a scientific one, Bacon's voice must take on the paradoxical characteristics of modesty and arrogance, parsimoniousness and acquisitiveness. But the overrid-ing quality of his rhetorical ethos is the attempt to render itself ful-ly public, thus engaging in a new kind of authorial self-effacement.

The prefaces to the three editions of Bacon's *Essays* trace the process of "going public" with some accuracy. Appropriate to a genre Montaigne claims to have invented for "the private conve-nience" of "relatives and friends,"[20] Bacon dedicates the first edi-tion (1597) to his brother Anthony, and he opens his letter with a conventional excuse for showing oneself in print, the piracy topos: "I doe nowe like some that haue an Orcharde il neighbored, that gather their fruit before it is ripe, to preuent stealing" (6, 523). This topos, however, with its implication that private fruits need to be protected from the public appetite, proves inadequate to de-scribe Bacon's attitude toward publication. These essays, after all, composed throughout the 1590s when Bacon was struggling to find a secure position at court, are vastly different from Montaigne's retired musings. As F. J. Levy has shown, the 1597 *Essays* are political in intent as well as content, the display of a would-be counselor.

The first edition of the *Essays* thus stands at the confluence of two definitions of *public*. Intended to demonstrate that he possesses the wisdom to be a public man, no matter how privately this counsel would be imparted, the book needs the larger public of a reading audience to demonstrate that wisdom. Not surprisingly, then, Bacon shows less regret over the supposed piracy than is customary:

> And as I did euer hold, there mought be as great a vanitie in retiring and withdrawing mens conceites (except they bee of some nature) from the world, as in obtruding them: So in these particulars I haue played my selfe the Inquisitor, and find nothing to my vnderstanding in them contrarie or infectious to the state of Religion, or manners, but rather (as I suppose) medicinable.   (6, 523)

Bacon readily accepts the role of public censor he finds in the decision to publish and just as readily grants his work his imprimatur. His green fruit soon metamorphoses into the less modest and less private metaphor of currency: "Only I disliked now to put them out because they will be like the late new halfe-pence, which though the Siluer were good, yet the peeces were small" (6, 523). If the *Essays* were first intended as a courtly performance, by the time Bacon wrote the preface he was clearly ready to see their bullion dispersed in a more fully public circulation.

In the brief preface to the 1612 edition, which is dedicated to his brother-in-law, Sir John Constable, Bacon maintains the metaphor of addition to a public discourse while still addressing his work to a private relation: "Looking amongst my papers this vacation, I found others of the same Nature [as that of the 1597 *Essays*]: which if I my selfe shall not [*sic*] suffer to be lost, it seemeth the World will not; by the often printing of the former" (6, 539). The success of the first edition has transformed Bacon into a public man whose innermost searchings have significance in the "World"; at the same time, he had become a public man in the narrower political sense by holding a series of important offices under James I. But the importance of the literary sense of publication can be inferred from the preface to the final edition of 1625, published the year before his death. Here, despite a fall from power that no doubt compromised any pretense to a public voice, Bacon can nonetheless articulate the alignment of public and private in his writings with even more clarity than in the 1612 edition. He dedicates his work to none other than Buckingham, and both the rhetoric of the preface and his generic conception of the essay seem to have changed concomitantly, becoming less "brotherly" and more confidently public-spirited. He now states directly the link between private expostulation and public discourse that distinguishes the essays of the privy councilor (though banished from court) from those of the voluntarily retired mayor of Bordeaux: "I do now publish my Essays; which, of all my other works, have been most current; for that, as it seems, they come home to men's business and bosoms" (6, 373). It seems that the content of the essay can never become fully public; the genre, even in Bacon's highly politicized form, still appeals as much to the "bosom" as to "business." Yet Bacon sees that the private value of his counsels still creates a public "currency," so that the *Essays*, looking forward to the *Leviathan* (which I will discuss in the next chapter), create a miniature polity out of their readership.

In the *Advancement of Learning*, Bacon carries the counselor's adjudication of public and private into the realm of scientific inquiry, and it is here that one feels Bacon's urgent need to convert his new method into bureaucratic structure. This urgency is nowhere more apparent than in Bacon's dedication of the book to King James, but he is not unaware of the rhetorical problems this dedication involves. In the middle of the first book he pauses to condemn "the dedications of books and writings, as to patrons," since "books . . . ought to have no patrons but truth and reason." As if sensing the irony, Bacon provides himself with an escape hatch; ancient practice, he says, was to dedicate books "to private and equal friends . . . or if to kings and great persons, it was to some such as the argument of the book was fit and proper for" (3, 281). This deft transformation of self-exposure into further praise for James finds analogues in other structural elements of the *Advancement*. Rather than attaching an epistle dedicatory to James, Bacon forgoes front matter altogether and embeds his address to James in the opening pages. This adjustment of traditional dedicatory form does more than downplay Bacon's flattery; it adds to the sense that James is somehow integral to the book, that he is "some such as the argument . . . was fit and proper for."

Bacon's actual address to the king is an epideictic masterpiece, a deeply studied piece of flattery cleverly manipulating prefatory commonplaces to win James's approval for both the book and Bacon's scientific projections. He opens with a piece of praise that translates the dichotomy of *otium* and *negotium* into epideictic phraseology:

There were under the Law (excellent King) both daily sacrifices and freewill offerings; the one proceeding upon ordinary observance, the other upon a devout cheerfulness. In like manner there belongeth to kings from their servants both tribute of duty and presents of affection. In the former of these I hope I shall not live to be wanting, according to my most humble duty. . . . For the later, I thought it more respective to make choice of some oblation which might rather refer to the propriety and excellency of your individual person, than to the business of your crown and state.   (3, 261)

Here Bacon displaces the conventional split of the preface—between privately pursued knowledge, the fruit of leisure, and publicly constituted duty—onto the king, by juxtaposing it with the similar dichotomy of the king's two persons. And although he creates an elegant compliment through the appeal to the private person of the king, he must quickly retreat from the approach to the "individual" and look on the king "but with the observant eye of duty and admiration" (3, 261). By displacing his private status onto the king and then allowing the king's public face to subsume the private, Bacon carefully creates a fully public status for his own lucubrations. He thus implies that his writings, like the king's voice, are "flowing as from a fountain, and yet streaming and branching itself into nature's order, full of facility and felicity, imitating none, and inimitable by any" (3, 262).

By the time he has finished his quite extensive piece of epideixis, Bacon has converted the private from the modest refuge of the orator to the stamp of individuality set upon public works: "This propriety inherent and individual attribute in your Majesty deserveth to be expressed not only in the fame and admiration of the present time, nor in the history or tradition of the ages succeeding; but also in some solid work, fixed memorial, and immortal monument, bearing a character or signature both of the power of a king and the difference and perfection of such a king" (3, 263). This description of individual "signature" has a dual importance; first, aligning James with Bacon's project of instauration, acquiring for it a proleptic imprimatur of sorts, and second, alluding to the relation between the "propriety" (i.e., the proprietary) and the traditional in Bacon's rhetoric and method. The Great Instauration is "monumental" in that it stands as a public fixture and institution—but monuments also bear the "character" of their creator. Thus while Bacon may wish to defer person and personality indefinitely through the agency of public method, he is not averse to monumentalizing his own heroic deferral and recognizing "the difference and perfection of such a scientist."

With the *Instauratio Magna* itself we come to the center of Bacon's work, the book he regarded as the culmination of his labors, even though he never completed it. In purely scientific terms, the *Instauratio* remains an "induction"; it continues the project of laying out the division of the sciences and articulating the proper method of experimentation. The most finished part of the work is the *Novum Organum*, a series of aphorisms outlining once again the "idols" that need to be overcome to begin providing a foundation of true knowledge. Fittingly enough, the grandest of Bacon's inductions is fitted with an elaborate prefatory apparatus, consisting of a "Prooemium," an epistle dedicatory (once again to James I), a preface, and "The Plan of the Work."

The "Prooemium" is the most emblematic of all Bacon's prefatory writings. Even though a proem is traditionally given over to stating the plot or contents of a work rather than making rhetorical overtures, a reader coming to the *Instauratio* for the first time cannot help being surprised by the impersonal nature of the opening heading: "Francis of Verulam reasoned thus with himself, and judged it to be for the interest of the present and future generations that they should be made acquainted with his thoughts" (4, 7). The prooemium continues in the third person, maintaining the fiction that the reader simply overhears Bacon's musings on his place in the history of science. The effect of this prefatory eavesdropping is to efface and to institutionalize Bacon as author. If he seemingly hurried into print, it was not because he was ambitious but because of his concern for the public weal. As in the *Advancement*, it is the memorial that provides the interface between the personal and the institutional: "The cause of which haste was not ambition for himself, but solicitude for the work; that in case of his death there might remain some outline and project of that which he had conceived, and some evidence likewise of his honest mind and inclination towards the benefit of the human race" (4, 8). Self and work, private achievement and public benefit, meet in the monument of the *Great Instauration* and in the monumental third person of the proem, a syntactical device that only makes more explicit the central ploy of Bacon's rhetorical self-presentation. In the epistle dedicatory to James, for instance, Bacon speaks of his work as "a child of time rather than of wit" and attributes his discoveries to "the felicity of your Majesty's times" (4, 11). Self is swallowed up, but not by anything resembling conventional modesty; the work is too important to be introduced modestly. Instead, personal accomplishment becomes part of a historical process in which Bacon's role is that of the "machine" (4, 12).

Part of Bacon's critique of traditional philosophy in the preface to the *Instauration* focuses on the very role that modesty plays in expositions of this philosophy. Philosophers "think they have done some great thing if they do but add and introduce into the existing sum of science something of their own; prudently considering with themselves that by making the addition they can assert their liberty, while they retain the credit of modesty by assenting to the rest" (4, 16). Thus modesty contributes to the tendency of men to continue in "mediocrities and middle ways" (4, 16) without ever reconsidering the foundations of knowledge. Moreover, this modesty is palpably false; when these philosophers describe the vast areas of knowledge they have been unable to penetrate, "they fall to complaints of the subtlety of nature, the hiding places of truth, the obscurity of things, the entanglement of causes, the weakness of the human mind; wherein nevertheless they show themselves never the more modest, seeing that they will rather lay the blame upon the common condition of men and nature than upon themselves" (4, 16). True modesty, modesty that signifies more than a rhetorical gambit to deceive the reader, must lie in "the true and legitimate humiliation of the human spirit" (4, 19) before its object, nature.

I have already spoken of the dialectic of commanding and obeying in Bacon's notion of the humiliation of the spirit. Such humiliation may not seem in keeping with Bacon's avowed object "to command nature in action," "nature under constraint and vexed" (4, 24; 4, 29). Yet to command nature, men must quash their individual proprietary drives toward acquisition and glory, must become, in effect, truly modest. Here lies what I called at the beginning of this chapter Bacon's bureaucratic vision. For science to advance, scientists must see their work in terms of *office*, both in the sense of public duty and in the more modern sense of institutional place. In the preface to the *Novum Organum*, Bacon alludes to this "office" and its implications for his relation to the ancients:

As it is however,—my object being to open a new way for the understanding, a way by them untried and unknown,—the case is altered; party zeal and emulation are at an end; and I appear merely as a guide to point out the road; an office of small authority, and depending more upon a kind of luck than upon any ability or excellency. And thus much relates to the persons only. (4, 41)

One can see here the extent to which Milton's claims of *officium* depend on Bacon's revisions of civic humanism, which allowed the retrenchment of the ideal of public service, but at the expense of authorial "personality." If Bacon's insistence on his "small authority" and his "kind of luck" sounds like a return to the false modesty of traditional prefatory rhetoric, the fact should not blind us to the thrust of the passage, which is first to oppose "office" to "party zeal and emulation" and then, more important, to marginalize the whole discussion as concerning only "persons" (whom he contrasts to "matter"). Questions of "person" are after all merely prefatory necessities to be dealt with before proceeding to the "matter" of science. And if one senses in the denouncement of party the anticourtly sentiments of a confirmed courtier and politician, one nonetheless finds him unable to describe the inner sanctum of the new learning as anything other than the royal presence: "I invite all such [who follow the new method] to join themselves, as true sons of knowledge, with me, that passing by the outer courts of nature, which numbers have trodden, we may find a way at length into her inner chambers" (4, 42).

I have insufficient space to unwind the various metaphorical threads that knot themselves into this passage. It cannot pass without comment, however, that the "object" of scientific enquiry, nature, is equated not merely with the royal presence but with a *female* royal presence. This presence in Elizabethan England has been the subject of a great deal of recent commentary, but I would like to focus on the relation of this figure to my discussion of Bacon's ideology of science. I have commented on Bacon's first recorded reference to commanding nature in action, in a speech to Elizabeth contained within Essex's "Device." Without insisting on any local psychosexual reading of Bacon's relation to Elizabeth (although one could point to his description of her in the *Advancement* as "solitary and of herself" [3, 307]), one can see how relentlessly nature is figured as an obscure object of desire, the attainment of which signifies "human power."[21] Perhaps not surprisingly, that object often takes on dark overtones in Bacon's rhetoric: "The universe to the eye of the human understanding is framed like a labyrinth; presenting as it does on every side so many ambiguities of way, such deceitful resemblances of objects and signs, natures so irregular in their lines, and so knotted and entangled" (4, 18).

Not only is nature herself a "knotted" and labyrinthine entity; scholastic attempts to master her through discourse rather than more manly experimentation can at best only echo her deceits:

That wisdom which we have derived principally from the Greeks is but like the boyhood of knowledge, and has the characteristic property of boys: it can talk, but it cannot generate; for it is fruitful of controversies but barren of works. So that the state of learning as it now is appears to be represented to the life in the old fable of Scylla, who had the head and face of a virgin, but her womb was hung round with barking monsters, from which she could not be delivered.   (4, 14)

I will resist the temptation to find an allegory of Elizabeth's court in the barking dogs that surround the virgin's womb. What I would like to call attention to is the yoking of boyish impotence with Scylla's unfortunate progeny. Although the two might seem parallel examples of ungenerative discourse, the passage strongly suggests a different linkage where immature attempts to father what Bacon elsewhere calls "the patrimony of knowledge" (3, 294) lead to premature, half-formed monsters that recall the perils of over-hasty profit taking. In such a schema, Scylla resembles not scholasticism itself but nature, which has been *represented* through discourse but not mastered through empirical method.

In general, Bacon seems suspicious of fertility when it is figured as feminine. Nature's bounty is profligate and even dangerous without the shaping fecundity of science. He alludes to both the terrifying "nothing" of nature that lies behind her bounty and the necessity of harnessing that bounty with male potency in an important passage from the *Advancement*:

But as both heaven and earth do conspire and contribute to the use and benefit of man, so the end ought to be . . . to separate and reject vain speculations and whatsoever is empty and void, and to preserve and augment whatsoever is solid and fruitful; that knowledge may not be as a curtesan, for pleasure and vanity only, or as a bond-woman, to acquire and gain to her master's use; but as a spouse, for generation, fruit, and comfort.   (3, 294–95)

Marriage—one of Bacon's favorite metaphors for the joining of the mind to the facts of nature, for the undoing of the "ill-starred divorce" between "the empirical and the rational faculty" (4, 19)—serves him here as a means of distinguishing methodical masculine science both from the boyish scholasticism that does nothing to tame the "void" of nature and from the premature profit taking that treats nature like a "bond-woman." The ostensible mutuality of marriage thus describes the perfect Baconian approach to the world of nature, although there can be little doubt about the ultimate outcome of the dialectical marriage in his aphorism "Nature to be commanded must be obeyed" (4, 47).

If I may seem to have drifted a long way from my discussion of Bacon's creation of a public voice, a look at one final Baconian marriage may serve to demonstrate the relevance of his figuration of nature. In *New Atlantis*, Bacon describes a ceremony of Bensalem known as the "Feast of the Family." In this ceremony, the Bensalemites celebrate fecundity of "the Father of the Family, whom they call the *Tirsan*" at such a time as "any man . . . shall live to see thirty persons descended of his body alive together" (3, 147). I quote only one detail from the rite:

The Tirsan cometh forth with all his generation or lineage, the males before him, and the females following him; and if there be a mother from whose body the whole lineage is descended, there is a traverse placed in a loft above on the right hand of the chair, with a privy door, and a carved window of glass, leaded with gold and blue; where she sitteth, but is not seen.   (3, 148–49)

Although the initially arresting phrase "if there be a mother" is softened by the further revelation that maternity is not considered a contingent part of childbearing, there can be no doubt that the ceremony is designed to occlude female generation. This occlusion is perhaps shocking only in the ostentatious way it is carried out—this is after all a feast celebrating the father's fertility. But what is interesting about this passage is exactly how the hiding of the mother is *foregrounded*. The leaded window seems to be intended as a perspective of honor. I would suggest that the simultaneous lifting up and sequestering of the mother is an operation that parallels the mythopoesis of nature's "inner chambers." The "privy door" of the Tirsan's wife does suggest a domestic confinement, but at the same time, "privy" recalls the inner apartments of the royal palace.[22]

In Bacon's system of representing his endeavor, the privateness of the mother seems to perform at least two functions. First, it keeps the ultimate object of enquiry, the "inner court" of Nature, shrouded from the scrutiny of the unworthy. If Bacon's New Science was one of public utility, this did not mean it was one of public access.[23] Second, the private and mysterious nature of Nature, although creating a desire to master these hidden recesses, nonetheless serves to foreground the "strength" of the scientist who scorns the ready fruits of uncultivated nature. Translating these terms back into the ones I have been using, we can see that only by putting aside private desire can the seeker obtain the desired object. And this object, figured as the queen's privy chamber, exemplifies the same doubleness: it is at once the most obscure, inaccessible, and threatening of places and the seat of all the public good.

I ended my discussion of Descartes by concluding that he was unable to reconcile the split between public and private, labor and leisure, that plagued his conception of scientific vocation. He mapped his endeavors with spatial and social coordinates that allowed him no way to triangulate his sense of his aristocratic social "place" and his sense that the public sphere had become both overwhelmingly bourgeois and unrelentingly "public" in the modern sense: open to the eye and to interference. Yet his need to justify his labor—and indeed to justify the very act of laboring—made it impossible for him to figure his activities as the retired musings of an intellectual aristocrat. The result was his restless ideological commuting between sets of values and his inability to accept his own solution of an artisanal technology that would render science fully public and fully faceless.

Bacon remains unhampered by Descartes's ambivalences for reasons both reactionary and revolutionary. Reactionary because, as we have just seen, he still equates the public sphere with the innermost recesses of power. The "private" person of the monarch does more than *represent* the public—it would take Bacon's young acquaintance Hobbes to suggest this possibility—it *is* the public. Yet it is also revolutionary because he can nonetheless imagine that public power as separate from the state. In the utopian *New Atlantis*, written after a public disgrace from which James had refused to rescue him and therefore after any realistic chance of effecting his instauration through the king's person, we see how such a definition of the public can begin to take on a new, progressive force. The Fathers of Salomon's House, the ultimate benefactors of the public realm, are also the greatest guardians of secrecy, so much so that they do not even answer to the state: "We have consultations, which of the inventions and experiences which we have discovered shall be published, and which not; and take all an oath of secrecy for the concealing of those which we think fit to keep secret, though some of those we do reveal sometimes to the state, and some not" (3, 165).

Bacon has created a new sense of institutionalized learning that is based on and connected to the power of state but not completely answerable to it. He has, in short, created the idea of scientific community, designed to serve the larger public yet taking its institutional definition from its more circumscribed public, its "consultations," and finding its raison d'être in its confident belief that a correspondence can be attained between scientific inquiry and the objects of nature, a correspondence that grants this new public an "objectivity." Thus this community, although still only imagined, is sufficiently powerful to subsume Bacon's rhetorical "person." The resulting voice, the voice of "Francis Bacon reasoning with himself," presages the revolution in prefatory rhetoric that would take place during the seventeenth century, a revolution that would make traditional rhetorical forms seem forever outmoded.

6

From Instauration to Restoration

HOBBES, SPRAT, DRYDEN, AND THE
POLITICS OF COMMON SENSE

Sir Charles Cavendish records (in an unfortunately terse fashion) the only known meeting between Descartes and Hobbes, a brief encounter in 1648:

Mr de Cartes & Mr Hobbes have met & as they agree in some opinions so they extreamlie differ in others, as in the nature of hardness. Mr Hobbes conceiving the cause of it to be extream quicke motion of the atomes or minute partes of a bodie which hinders an other bodie from entring & Mr de Cartes conceives it a close joining of the partes at rest, which appears to me more reasonable.[1]

In fact, extreme differences governed nearly every intellectual encounter between the two philosophers, from their views on atomic theory to Hobbes's claim to have preceded Descartes in discovering the secondary characteristics of matter—a claim that Descartes called "puerile and laughable" in a letter to Mersenne.[2] Nor were these disagreements carried out in the spirit of the disinterested pursuit of knowledge, as Descartes's comment to Mersenne shows. Seven years before their only meeting, Hobbes, in the third set of "Objections" to the *Meditations*, tosses in several criticisms of Descartes that could only be considered gratuitous, including his lament that he is "sorry that the author, who is so outstanding in the field of original speculations, should be publishing this ancient material," namely, the observation that it is difficult to distinguish dreams from waking experiences.[3] Descartes, however, is even less gentle with Hobbes. Though Hobbes's criticisms are in no way the least interesting of the seven sets of responses Mersenne solicited, Descartes reserves his most dismissive comments for the Englishman's objections.

Without attempting to catalog and analyze all the possible causes for an antipathy that clearly transcended their scientific disagreements but could not have been based solely on personal contact, I would like to concentrate for a moment on one dispute that has resonances for the historical narrative I am tracing. In his "Objection XIII" to the *Meditations*, Hobbes challenges Descartes's dependence on "clear and distinct" ideas: "The phrase 'a great light in the intellect' is metaphorical, and so has no force in the argument. Moreover, anyone who is free from doubt claims he has such 'great light' and has no less strong a propensity of the will to affirm what he has no doubt about than someone who possesses real knowledge" (*PW* 2, 134). What Hobbes objects to is in effect the lack of a Cartesian anthropology to accompany his philosophy. Descartes makes universal assumptions about human cognition on the basis of his own "illumination" without asking whether his private experience can be thus extrapolated. As we have seen, Descartes does worry the problem of exemplarity in the *Discourse on Method*, but always at the level of his institutional *histoire*, never allowing it into his account of the cogito. For Hobbes, until a sufficient theoretical basis has been formulated to establish what is human, no system founding public knowledge on private experience can claim legitimacy.

It is no surprise, then, that the *Leviathan* is first and foremost an extended meditation on the possibilities of mending the breach between private speech and public discourse. The social contract enacts at the level of the polity what Hobbes first articulates as ontological and epistemological principle. The Golden Rule, which Hobbes raises from platitude to the basis for a systematic understanding of social construction, is preceded in his analysis by the explication of another ancient saw that provides his political science with an anthropological grounding. In his introduction he writes,

But there is another saying not of late understood, by which they might learn truly to read one another, if they would take the pains; and that is, *Nosce teipsum, Read thy self*: which was not meant, as it is now used, to countenance, either the barbarous state of men in power, towards their inferiors; or to encourage men of low degree, to a sawcie behaviour towards their betters; But to teach us, that for the similitude of the thoughts, and Passions of one man, to the thoughts, and Passions of another, whosoever looketh into himself, and considereth what he doth, when he does *think, opine, reason, hope, feare*, &c, and upon what grounds; he shall thereby read and know, what are the thoughts, and Passions of all other men, upon the like occasions.[4]

Here Hobbes makes explicit what Descartes only assumed—namely, that there is such a thing as human nature to which one can appeal in constructing philosophical or political systems. But Hobbes's retooling of self-analysis to serve as a method for reading what is "human" logically extends Descartes's exemplarity of self by admitting, however tentatively, the political implications of this extension. Although Hobbes's common "ground" does not lead him to champion democratic principles, there is nothing in his anthropology that keeps him from doing so,[5] an anthropology that implies at every turn a polity of shared interests and mutual legibility.[6] Descartes's hesitant exemplarity assumes that his experience, if not precisely imitable, can nonetheless trickle down to the public. Hobbes sees this "reading" of character as continuous and reflexive; the reader and the read are not readily distinguishable.

The famous frontispiece to the *Leviathan* is a representation of this new political legibility. In its outline, the engraving describes the hierarchical body politic that had governed medieval and Renaissance models of the state, but its anatomy includes a homogeneity of tissue between organs that had not been present in earlier political analyses. "Nature hath made men so equall," writes Hobbes, that "the difference between man, and man, is not so considerable, as that one man can thereupon claim to himselfe any benefit, to which another may not pretend, as well as he" (183). Menenius's fable of the articulated body, which I have had several occasions to recall earlier, has given way to a body of equal members of indeterminate function, organized only by the head of sovereignty that creates the "artificial man" of the state.[7] Man may array himself in an articulated political structure, but he does so for political reasons.

As Descartes was forced to recognize, no member of the body politic has an *essentially* public function independent of his or her content. Man's natural inclinations are toward private gain or gratification; what is "public" must now be a matter of constant negotiation. Asking himself why creatures like ants and bees can, unlike man, live socially without "coercive Power," Hobbes speculates, "Amongst these creatures, the Common good differeth not from the Private; and being by nature enclined to their private, they procure thereby the common benefit. But man, whose Joy consisteth in comparing himselfe with other men, can relish nothing but what is eminent" (226). Hobbes can imagine the perfect fusion of public and private goods only in a subhuman condition or in a political state where every man's "relish" in superiority is surrendered out of fear of anarchy (or in the case of tyranny, simply out of fear of the man with the most power). Even if, however, such a fusion of the public and private can exist for Hobbes only as an artificial imposition on man's natural desire, the terms on which he understands both the merger and the natural resistance to it are unremittingly psychological rather than theological. Thus even the force that would seemingly block a mutually intelligible public language, man's desire for "eminence," is itself mutually intelligible, based on no innate distinction between kinds or classes of men.

Implicit in this new picture of political organization is a new conception of authorship and authority. Perhaps the most significantly placed chapter of *Leviathan* is Hobbes's discourse on authority, "Of Persons, Authors, and things Personated," which serves as a bridge between the first part of the book, "Of Man," and the second, "Of Common-wealth." Here Hobbes works out a theory of political representation based on the "Covenant" between an "Actor" and an "Author" whom the "Actor" "personates." Thus questions of authority and representation provide the vital link between man and the "artificial man" of the commonwealth. As part of his definition of *personation*, Hobbes turns to classical rhetorical theory: "To *Personate*, is to *Act*, or *Represent* himselfe, or an other; and he that acteth another, is said to beare his Person, or act in his name; (in which sence *Cicero* useth it where he saies, *Unus sustineo tres Personas; Mei, Adversarii, & Judicis*, I beare three Persons; my own, my Adversaries, and the Judges)" (*Leviathan*, 217–18). Hobbes's allusion to Cicero's dialogue *De oratore* (2.24.102) involves a complex series of associations. Conveniently, the passage alludes to three of the four sources of goodwill classical theorists said an orator should attempt to exploit in a forensic exordium (the fourth being the cause itself). More important, it makes explicit the connection operative throughout this chapter between self-presentation and political representation.[8] The rhetorical exercise in "acting" out the different personae involved in a case becomes for Hobbes an analogy for the way a political agent can "beare" the authority of those who actually "own" an action.

Yet the ironic possibilities of his position are familiar to anyone living in a modern democracy: more often than not, power lies not in the hands of the "Author" but of the "Actor" or "Artificiall person." Hobbes describes the origin of the commonwealth:

A *Common-wealth* is said to be *Instituted*, when a *Multitude* of men do Agree, and *Covenant, every one, with every one*, that to whatsoever *Man*, or *Assembly of Men*, shall be given by the major part, the *Right* to *Present* the Person of them all, (that is to say, to be their *Representative;*) every one, as well he that *Voted for it*, as he that *Voted against it*, shall *Authorize* all the Actions and Judgements, of that Man, or Assembly of men, in the same manner, as if they were his own.   (228–29)

The well-known frontispiece to the *Leviathan* emblematizes this ironic reversibility of representation. The king's body both incorporates and is incorporated by the English people, suggesting that if the people now partake of power metaphorically rather than synecdochically, not as part to whole but as a microcosmic mirroring of the macrocosm, in practical terms sovereignty is still synonymous with power. Political representation, as Hobbes views it, is not passive reflection but the active appropriation of another's authority.

I would like, however, to concentrate on another question Hobbes raises implicitly through his concept of representation, namely, whether the writer is an "Author" or an "Actor." Does the writer originate or represent—impersonate—the common sense of the audience? It is worth returning for a moment to *De oratore*. Throughout the dialogue, Cicero's speaker, Anthony, argues against the doctrine of Crassus that the orator must be learned in law and the arts. Instead, Anthony states, the orator should be a man of common sense and experience, able to understand fully the situation of his client and to intuit the attitudes of judge and jury. Thus Anthony's orator is an appropriate model for Hobbesian "personation" and the theory of human legibility. Yet his stance does not address directly the question we asked of political representation: is author or actor the locus of cultural authority? The connection between political and writerly authority becomes explicit in another detail of the *Leviathan*'s frontispiece: the face of the "king" whose body represents and is represented by the people is actually a portrait of Hobbes himself.[9] Thus, if one turns Hobbes's theory of representation onto the question of the authority of the writer, an irony analogous to that contained in political representation emerges: the writer becomes both "Actor" and "Author."

C. B. Macpherson, in his classic study of seventeenth-century possessive individualism, locates the origin of this double-sidedness of representation in the marketplace:

The paradox of Hobbes's individualism, which starts with equal rational individuals and demonstrates that they must submit themselves wholly to a power outside themselves, is a paradox not of his construction but of the market society. The market makes men free; it requires for its effective operation that all men be free and rational; yet the independent rational decisions of each man produce at every moment a configuration of forces which confronts each man compulsively. All men's choices determine, and each man's choice is determined by, the market. Hobbes caught both the freedom and the compulsion of possessive market society.[10]

Macpherson's formulation is important to my picture of Hobbes's rhetoric of representation since it suggests the difficulty of making a distinction between author and actor in market culture. Hobbes can define property itself only in a sublimely circular fashion as that "which by mutuall Contract men acquire, in recompence of the universall Right they abandon. . . . And therefore where there is no *Own*, that is, no Propriety, there is no Injustice; and where there is no coërceive Power erected, that is, where there is no Common-wealth, there is no Propriety; all men having Right to all things: Therefore where there is no Common-wealth, there nothing is Unjust" (202). These mutually embedded definitions—of property, justice, power, commonwealth—like Macpherson's paradox of individual freedom, lie in a matrix of reflexive representation created by the market. Put otherwise, the fiction of the market creates the concept of representation, but it also collapses the question of agency implied by the concept: the writer is both a function and the determining origin of the audience.[11]

It is in this context that I turn to Hobbes's introduction to the *Leviathan*, in which we can see how the paradoxes of representation shape his prefatory rhetoric. We have already seen how the introduction resorts to a novel translation of an ancient dictum—"*Nosce teipsum, Read thy self*"—to establish a mutual legibility between audience and author. Hobbes complicates, if not compromises, this legibility by admitting that one must always temper any conclusions about human nature drawn from introspection with observations of particular men's actions. Gary Shapiro suggests that this prevarication shows that Hobbes "has one foot in the literary and analogical world of the Renaissance and the other in the emerging mechanism and nomimalism of the seventeenth century."[12] Put otherwise, Hobbes exemplifies, in the words of Timothy Reiss, that moment when "the fluid and ambiguous concept of meaning characteristic of the Renaissance gives way to a fixed concept and practice of signification—[when] representation, however complex, becomes fundamentally monolithic." Hobbes's monolith, the leviathan of the state itself, continues to operate along the "readerly" lines of analogy even as it attempts to totalize in the image of the writer himself. As Reiss goes on to observe, "Responsibility and intention pass from reader to writer, before such responsibility and intention are both occulted, subsumed in the objectivity of a universal reason whose eventual model will be the scientific order of mathematical experimentalism."[13]

As "responsibility" changes hands from reader to writer, the ironic result is that the rhetorical persona of the author, to garner authority to itself, must be more and more restricted until it is, as Reiss points out, fully occulted in the cult of objectivity. The humanist flexibility of Erasmus and Montaigne is a flexibility based on their infinite readability; Hobbes takes his authority by systematizing and essentializing the "nature" of his reader and mirroring that nature in his own persona. The prudential tradition of humanist rhetoric, however, still prevents Hobbes from settling into an easy reliance upon a universalized conception of language or human nature. He concludes his preface:

But let one man read another by his actions never so perfectly, it serves him onely with his acquaintance, which are but few. He that is to govern a whole Nation, must read in himself, not this, or that particular man; but Man-kind: which though it be hard to do, harder than to learn any Lan-

guage, or Science; yet, when I shall have set down my own reading orderly, and perspicuously, the pains left another, will be onely to consider, if
he also find not the same in himself. For this kind of Doctrine, admitteth
no other Demonstration.   (83)

As compensation for this remittance of authority to the audience,
however, the writer receives the authority to articulate for the audience a "representative discourse," a discourse limited by common sense, or in Hobbesian terminology, natural law. The reader
is given a yes-or-no vote on the authorial candidacy, like that of
the constituents of a representative democracy, but if Hobbes's
"own reading" has been acute, common sense should grant him
authorial sovereignty.[14]

As I have suggested, Hobbes's assumption of human legibility
has significant echoes in the shifts that were taking place in the
alignment of author, text, and audience. The primary "textual"
implication of Hobbes's theory is a configuration in which the author tends to be assimilated not to his material, not to the master
text, but to his audience, with whom he shares a common bond.
The preface serves both to stake the author's claim to eminence
and to smooth this disruption of social discourse. Thus the problem of a shared commonsensical discourse defines the new direction of prefatory rhetoric: if the author's discourse is common
sense, is he doing anything more then reiterating what each man
possesses innately? Is common sense always *only* common sense?
In other words, does Descartes's ambivalence concerning the dissemination of his experience and his uneasy suburban compromise
continue to haunt the discourse of public utility?

For the real theorist of this discourse, a discourse I described in
Chapter 4 as "suburban georgic," we must wait for the work of
another philosopher who retired to Amsterdam, John Locke.[15]
Locke extends Hobbes's solution to Descartes's dilemma by point-
ing to the way the author can at once participate in public parlance and "own" his words. His solution appears in the famous
discussion of property in *The Second Treatise of Government*,
where he provides a public justification for private enclosure.[16] The
major thread of his complex argument, teased out, runs as follows:

God, who hath given the World to Men in common, hath also given them
reason to make use of it to the best advantage of Life. . . . No body has

originally a private Dominion. . . . Yet being given for the use of Men, there must of necessity be a means *to appropriate* them some way or other before they can be of any use. . . . Every Man has a *Property* in his own *Person*. This no Body has any Right to but himself. The *Labour* of his Body, and the *Work* of his Hands, we may say, are properly his. . . . *As much Land* as a Man Tills, Plants, Improves, Cultivates, and can use the Product of, so much is his *Property*.[17]

Locke thus provides a historical origin and a theoretical basis for the cooperative endeavor Bacon and Descartes were attempting to found. By locating the right to property in our ownership of our bodies and then in the labor that these bodies can produce, he not only legitimates the personal enclosing of the "common" world but also finds in this enclosure the source of "improvement" and "cultivation." Therefore, we have a right to property only insofar and as long as we make it productive and useful, thereby promoting the public welfare as well as our own.[18] The georgic ideal thus becomes at once the justification of private property and the basis for the common good since for Locke, appropriation is indistinguishable from use, and use the basis of public as well as private wealth.[19] By extension, I would add, common sense exists only as articulated by acts of private discourse.[20]

The rhetorical work of the preface in such a context is essentially less difficult than that of the Renaissance preface since the post-Renaissance preface no longer needs to bridge the theoretically unbridgeable gap between the "structure" of authorized texts and the marginal status of belated "commentaries." The author is not divided automatically from his audience, and the authority of the discourse lies in its compliance with the laws of common sense, a compliance the audience is assumed able to judge. This compliance, and therefore the writer's authority, can be judged from the text itself; the ethical proof of the preface is, at least theoretically, irrelevant. In such a context, the theoretical bond between author and audience inevitably compromises and slightly displaces traditional prefatory forms. The epistle dedicatory becomes more purely panegyric, a functional plea for patronage. The apology becomes more parodic, and the preface itself a piece of criticism, an act of public service carried out in a common space in which disagreements, however fundamental, are fully intelligible. I will conclude this chapter with an analysis of this new emphasis on the "critical" preface as it appears in Dryden's "Preface to the *Fables*"; first, however, I must elaborate on the picture of this public space in which the late-seventeenth-century preface articulates itself.

Descartes was not the only thinker with whom Hobbes engaged in intellectual fisticuffs. His altercations with the mathematician John Wallis reached vituperative levels unusual even for an age that did not scrupulously police the borders between invective and debate. Another of his disputes, with Robert Boyle and with the Royal Society as a whole, if somewhat less virulent, is of greater interest here. The controversy centered around Hobbes's challenge—shocking to our scientifically tuned sensibilities—to experimentalism as the basis for knowledge and more specifically to Boyle's air pump as an instrument of any philosophical value or scientific use. Steven Shapin and Simon Schaffer, in their book-length study of the dispute, *Leviathan and the Air-pump*, have shown that although the history of science has vindicated Boyle, this history, like the controversy itself, is part of a cultural and political contestation.[21] The stakes of the historical contest included the right to declare the winner of the debate between Hobbes and Boyle, but Shapin and Schaffer recontest the grounds on which that declaration was made. They argue that Hobbes's case against the Royal Society centers around his criticism of a restricted community of experts. In his *Dialogus physicus* (1661), his interlocutor, addressing the representative of those who "meet each week at Gresham College," asks incredulously, "Why do you speak of fifty men? Cannot anyone who wishes to come, since, as I suppose, they meet in a public place, and give his opinion on the experiments which are seen, as well as they?"[22] His insistence on a public witnessing is somewhat disingenuous since for Hobbes experiment can never be fully public. According to Hobbes, any knowledge that relies on physical "facts" can exist only in the localized sphere of the experiment rather than the public world of philosophical discourse.

Shapin and Schaffer locate Hobbes's objection and Boyle's defense in the cultural and political world of the Restoration, a world that necessarily entertained suspicions about the theories of fully integrated knowledge espoused not just by Hobbes but by

Puritan radicals such as Comenius, Samuel Hartlib, John Dury, and John Milton. Scientific objectivity thus shows itself as another side of the latitudinarian position that religious and political convictions are best sequestered from other intellectual pursuits. To quote from the conclusion of *Leviathan and the Air-pump*,

For Hobbes, the activity of the philosopher was not bounded: there was no cultural space where knowledge could be had where the philosopher should not go. The methods of the natural philosopher were, in crucial respects, identical to those of the civic philosopher, just as the purpose of each was the same: the achievement and protection of public peace. . . . For Boyle and his colleagues, the topography of culture looked different. Their cultural terrain was vividly marked out with boundary-stones and warning notices. Most importantly, the experimental study of nature was to be visibly withdrawn from "humane affairs." (337)

It is difficult not to respond sympathetically to the call for integrated and politicized intellectual life in Shapin and Schaffer's conclusion: "Hobbes was right" (344). Yet it is equally important to reiterate their starting point (even if we seem less likely to forget it): Hobbes lost.

One can detect the outline of this battle, as well as its outcome, in Thomas Sprat's *History of the Royal Society* (1667). The *History* documents a cultural compromise that was taking place not just between the ideas of Hobbes and Boyle but between two conflicting definitions of how knowledge was constituted. The Royal Society came into being as an uneasy truce between radical Puritan notions of public utility and older aristocratic ideas of a retired, leisured pursuit of learning.[23] Sprat's own prefatory modesty points to this institutional compromise; his protestations about his work merely reiterate his evaluation of the Royal Society: "What I am here to say, will be far from preventing the labours of others in adorning so worthy a Subject: and is *premis'd* upon no other account, then as the noblest Bui[l]dings are first wont to be represented in a few *Shadows*, or small *Models*."[24] Descartes's architectural model has been interestingly altered. Sprat makes no reference to privatized architecture. He is not merely putting his own house in order; he is laying out a Baconian instauration. His modesty lies in the provisional nature of his outline and in a deference toward those who will actually build the structure—and as we shall see, Sprat retains a healthy Baconian respect for the artisan.

Sprat begins his work with a history of learning from its origins in ancient Egypt. His fascinating account is unfortunately too long and nuanced to explicate in any detail here, but certain moments are worth singling out for what they reveal of the dialectical process of public and private that Sprat finds in history. The Egyptians, we learn, created science but corrupted it almost immediately by shrouding it "in the dark Shadows of *Hieroglyphicks*" in order "to beget a Reverence in the Peoples Hearts towards *themselves*" (*History*, 5). The Greeks, in general inferior to the Egyptians because of their tendency to poeticize knowledge, improved on the Egyptians by combating this tendency to privatize knowledge: "The *Greeks* being of a vigorous, and active humour, establish't their Philosophy, in the *Walks*, and *Porches*, and *Gardens*, and such publick places about their Cities" (6–7). Keeping the dialectic dialectical, however, Sprat finds that the Romans took the Greek penchant for public philosophizing to unfortunate lengths, using it only to "make their speech more plentiful; or else, that when they were at leisure from Civil affairs, they might have that as a companion, and comfort of their Retirements" (10). In other words, falling into the trap of finding philosophy's value only in the completely democratized form of rhetoric, they created a non-dialectical opposition by giving rhetoric a compensatory private side—the consoling moralizings of Stoicism—that had no public value.

However inaccurate Sprat's understanding of both rhetoric and Stoicism might be, his historical narrative has a compelling consistency. All the more compelling since the story of antiquity repeats itself in the modern world where humanists and reformers play the role of public liberators, freeing learning from the "solitary, and idle" (14) existence of the monks. Here as elsewhere in this history of learning Sprat depends upon the similar history embedded in Book 1 of the *Advancement of Learning*. Bacon, however, still sees the story of knowledge primarily in the traditional humanist terms of *res* and *verba* (even as he attacks the humanists), while Sprat has translated that story into one of public and private interests. Sprat's humanist liberators, for instance, once again fall into an excess, worshiping the ancients (the very tool they had used to battle Scholasticism), and undervaluing the strength of the individual to contribute to knowledge. At this point in his narrative, Sprat must pause since he has raised the very real danger that learning will never progress because of the eternal recurrence of this incomplete dialectic between public and private interests. His solution lies in the articulation of a political anthropology. Certain kinds of governments and institutions produce certain kinds of men and, he adds, certain genres of intellectual production. The cloister breeds Scholastic philosophy; commonwealths produce eloquence; and courts encourage poetry (19). Science, Sprat implies, must find its own ideal matrix to flourish in a world where intellectual life responds so readily to political structures.

And that ideal matrix, not surprisingly, is remarkably similar to the British empire that has spawned the Royal Society:

> Whoever shall soberly profess, to be willing to put their shoulders, under the burthen of so great an enterprise, as to represent to mankind, the whole Fabrick, the parts, the causes, the effects of Nature: ought to have their eyes in all parts, and to receive information from every quarter of the earth: they ought to have a constant universall intelligence: all discoveries should be brought to them: the Treasuries of all former times should be laid open before them: the assistance of the present should be allow'd them: so farr are the narrow conceptions of a few private Writers, in a dark Age, from being equall to so vast a design.   (20)

Sprat's rhetoric here is Baconian in its essence, but it possesses a new brio, courtesy of an expanding British mercantile order. Empire, with its continuous circulation of goods and ideas, is the perfect medium for scientific inquiry. And it matters not at all that a good deal of the mercantile success was achieved under the Commonwealth; empire, like science, transcends forms of government. All political differences between the members of the Royal Society can be subsumed under the mutual benefits of a freely available knowledge that has been sanitized of overt moral and political concerns. "The narrow conceptions of a few private Writers" stand little chance in a world of public information. Nor is this new scientific polity in danger of the intellectual stagnation that beset Rome since a mercantile empire, unlike a military one, does not reduce peoples and knowledge to a homogenized uniformity.

But if the Royal Society and its cultural matrix begin to resemble the liberal state for which Hobbes laid the foundation, one does well to remember that what I have called the world of public information was public in only a limited sense, a sense that Hobbes himself interrogated. To investigate this limitation on the concept of the "public," I need to rehearse Sprat's often-cited description of the social makeup and organization of the Royal Society. The Society, says Sprat, based its methodology on the Baconian idea of collective inquiry, proceeding step by step with no master planner standing magisterially over the proceedings: "If then there can be any cure devis'd for this; it must be no other, than to form an *Assembly* at one time, whose privileges shall be the same; whose gain shall be in common; whose *Members* were not brought up at the feet of each other" (70).

This democratization, however, still has an aristocratic cast to it since Sprat maintains that the Society, although "compounded of all sorts of men . . . all mutually assisting each other" (76) and including the "*Inquisitive Genius* of our Merchants" (88) who gather the "stuff" of scientific inquiry, nonetheless relies most fully on the involvement of the nobility and the gentry, "who, by the freedom of their education, the plenty of their estates, and the usual generosity of Noble Bloud, may be well suppo[s]'d to be most averse from such sordid considerations [i.e., profit]" (68). Sprat, mostly by implication, sets both of these classes against the cloistered virtuosity of the professional scholars of Oxbridge. His alternative to the traditional academy is a sort of suburban think tank constructed on the ideal readily available to him in Gresham College, the first home of the Royal Society.[25] The college, with its extensive walled gardens, was located in the center of the City, making it the ideal model for Sprat's notion of a community of scientists sheltered from the concerns of business and the affairs of state and at the same time open to all the "intellegence" and "discoveries" (20) that a thriving merchant (and imperial) city could bring.

The "suburban" nature of this model is perhaps even clearer in Cowley's *A Proposition for the Advancement of Experimental Philosophy* (1661). Cowley proposes that a "Philosophical Colledge," obviously constructed on the model of the Oxbridge colleges, "be scituated within one, two, or (at farthest) three miles of Lond[o]n, and, if it be possible to find that convenience, upon the side of the River."[26] The college's placement on the Thames, one might add, would almost certainly not be for the view but to facilitate communication with London and the rest of the world. This model of simultaneous isolation and communication seems to have passed down to the present in an almost unaltered form as the ideal for the university, a public space of free communication but a space protected from overt political pressures.

As a means of closure, I turn now to the first purely literary text I have discussed at any length, Dryden's "Preface to the *Fables*." I turn to literature so late partially because, as Michael McKeon has pointed out, "literature" in our sense does not actually begin to exist as a separate category until the time of Dryden. Even more significantly, McKeon argues that during the Restoration literature begins to fill some of the cultural functions of religion. As religion becomes more and more compartmentalized, it is literature (and "the aesthetic" in general) that serves as a secularized but nonetheless dominant cultural discourse. The "literary spirituality" (36) of the nineteenth century that McKeon finds rooted in the seventeenth "entails a humanizing of Spirit" (49) that parallels one of the stories I have been tracing, the progressive secularization of authority. It is not surprising, then, that a text like Dryden's provides the best example of a new system of authority, a system in which hierarchy has been not replaced, but displaced into a Hobbesian polity of readership. Authority is now a contractual matter between reader and author. What the author must demonstrate is not access to the ultimately divine text of tradition but the possession of "judgment," the criterion for a suitable representative of the reader's common sense.

This shift in political models for authority implies a concomitant shift in the forensic model that has governed prefatory rhetoric (however uncomfortably) in the texts I have been examining. In a passage quoted earlier, Bacon argues for a change of venue because the tribunal of tradition is insufficient to understand the New Science: "I cannot be fairly asked to abide by the decision of a tribunal which is itself on its trial" (4, 21). The question of judgment, it is important to note, has not been suspended but appropriated. In a similar fashion, when Descartes dismisses Scholastic disputes—"Those who have long been good advocates do not necessarily go on to make better judges" (*PW* 1, 146)—he is seizing the role traditionally reserved for the audience, that of judge.

This seizure necessitates a radical revision of prefatory rhetoric, a revision that Dryden takes several large strides toward articulating. His understanding of the combined roles of author and critic was undoubtedly influenced by the prefatory practice of the seventeenth-century French dramatists and poets, in particular Corneille, who formulated much of his influential theoretical work on drama in the prefatory matter of his plays. Especially worth noting is Corneille's habit of distinguishing between the *Préface* (alternately labeled *Avertissement* and *Au lecteur*) and the *Examen.*[27] Although not without "critical" content, Corneille's prefaces are in the familiar, even essayistic tradition of prefatory writing. The *examen*, however, is a more frankly retrospective piece, taking into account the reception of the play. The author thereby becomes critic of his own work, and Corneille takes rhetorical advantage of the voice of detachment, although he is so often forced to admire what he has written.

If, however, Dryden's "Preface to the *Fables*" (1700) is by no means the first critical preface,[28] it is one that fully enacts the author's rise to public power as a critic, dramatizing what Corneille presents schematically in his division of prefatory matter. The "Preface" addresses the problems of tradition and authority I have been tracing in Renaissance prefaces, but from a position that can no longer be described as the liminal one of the private author approaching the public venue of textuality. Rather, in a project that epitomizes the rhetorical vectors I have been describing, Dryden *begins* with the assumption that he is a "member incorporate" articulating cultural knowledge for the rest of the social corpus. In the *Fables*, Dryden writes literary history by compiling an anthology; he considers his roles as critic and editor readily comparable to his role as author, and in fact he takes considerable pains to show that the two roles are not easily differentiated. By conflating critic and author, Dryden makes himself both subject and object of literary history, and both origin and arbiter of common sense and taste.

Dryden begins the "Preface" with a suitably Cartesian simile: "'Tis with a Poet, as with a man who designs to build."[29] Unlike Descartes, however, Dryden appears ready to embrace the ad hoc process the simile implies: "He alters his mind as the work proceeds, and will have this or that convenience more, of which he had not thought when he began. So has it happened to me; I have built a house, where I intended but a lodge" (*Essays*, 246). The distinction seems to go beyond one of size; Dryden will live where he had initially planned only to vacation. The narrative that follows describes the poet taking up a brief task of translation that grows until it takes on book-length proportions. It also suggests that the task of translation became a complicated entrance into literary history as the tradition the poet chose to represent swept over him:[30]

Milton was the poetical son of Spenser, and Mr. Waller of Fairfax; for we have our lineal descents and clans as well as other families. Spenser more than once insinuates, that the soul of Chaucer was transfused into his body; and that he was begotten by him two hundred years after his decease. Milton has acknowledged to me, that Spenser was his original. (247)

Dryden does not yet directly insert himself into this genealogy (except through the oral tradition that he receives from Milton), but he does outline the family that he "houses" in his collection of translations.

Unlike Descartes, then, Dryden does not seem to balk at the eclectic structure of tradition. He does, however, make a bid to control it, to play the architect, through the very medium of the anthology. By compiling his collection, he not only admits that as a poet he has predecessors but also claims a right as critic to select and evaluate those predecessors:[31]

An author is not to write all he can, but only all he ought. Having observed this redundancy in Chaucer, (as it is an easy matter for a man of ordinary parts to find a fault in one of greater,) I have not tied myself to a literal translation; but have often omitted what I judged unnecessary, or not of dignity enough to appear in the company of better thoughts. I have presumed further, in some places, and added somewhat of my own where I thought my author was deficient, and had not given his thoughts their true lustre, for want of words in the beginning of our language. And to this I was the more emboldened, because (if I may be permitted to say it of myself) I found I had a soul congenial to his, and that I had been conversant in the same studies. Another poet, in another age, may take the same liberty with my writings; if at least they live long enough to deserve correction. (265)

"Congeniality," a kind of personal sympathy, therefore serves as the basis for the formation of poetic genealogies, and it is always the final, or most recent, poet in the line who has the right to construct the tradition. The etymological connection between *genius* and *gens* underlies Dryden's understanding of literary history here. If genius is a matter of family, however, the poet seems to reserve the right, a right exercised as a critic, to name his family history: the child is father to the tradition.[32]

This fluid conception of tradition lies behind Dryden's ambivalence in the Ancients-Moderns debate. He feels the power of the ancients to such an extent that he is overwhelmed with "congeniality" and compelled to produce his anthology. At the same time, however, he is enough of a believer in a kind of literary "proficience," to use Bacon's term, that he must put forward the following literary judgment for schematic reasons: "We must be children before we grow men. There was an Ennius, and in the process of time a Lucilius, and a Lucretius, before Virgil and Horace; even after Chaucer there was a Spenser, a Harrington, a Fairfax, before Waller and Denham were in being; and our numbers were in their nonage till these last appeared" (259). This appraisal of Waller and Denham was common enough (even the critical Dr. Johnson speaks of both poets' technical "advancement"), but what is interesting here is the structural necessity for the judgment, given Dryden's schema for literary history, and the ascendancy of the critic that makes this schema possible. Poetic maturity is being measured in purely technical terms. Chaucer's thought and characters are anything but crude, but his "numbers" have been immensely improved upon.[33]

Dryden's critic-translator is empowered by the peculiar nature of *transfusion*. The *Oxford English Dictionary* gives as synonyms for this sense of the word "transference; transmission; translation." Dryden most often seems to use the word as a strict equivalent for *translation*: "I grant that something must be lost in all transfusion, that is, in all translations; but the sense will remain, which would otherwise be lost, or at least be maimed" (267). Even here, however, *transfusion* drifts toward *transmission*. Words are translated, but words are historically vulnerable and therefore suspect to Dryden; real content, however, "sense," can and must be transmitted by the translator.[34] But more important than this extended sense of *transfusion* is its metaphoric force; genius flows through tradition, but as with most fluids, the direction of its flow can be reversed.[35] The ambiguous pronouns in a sentence already quoted—"Spenser more than once insinuates, that the soul of Chaucer was transfused into his body; and that he was begotten by him two hundred years after his decease"—are the first of many suggestions that tradition is a two-way street on which the flow of poetical debt is countered by that of critical appraisal. The poet may owe a debt to his predecessors, but tradition is no longer univocal, so that it may be selected, anthologized—in fact, created.

The implications of *transfusion* for prefatory rhetoric tend generally toward breaking the supplicatory stance of the Renaissance author. We have seen Luther, Milton, Bacon, and Descartes (in very different ways) chafing at the tradition of modesty they all inherited. None, however, was able to brush aside the trappings of modesty with the casual gesture that Dryden achieves with seeming effortlessness:

I will not trouble my reader with the shortness of time in which I writ it, or the several intervals of sickness. They who think too well of their own performances, are apt to boast in their prefaces how little time their works have cost them, and what other business of more importance interfered; but the reader will be as apt to ask the question, why they allowed not a longer time to make their works more perfect? and why they had so despicable an opinion of their judges as to thrust their indigested stuff upon them, as if they deserved no better?   (250)

Dryden exposes modesty as its opposite: the prideful pretense of *sprezzatura*. Like Milton, he finds nothing modest in the modesty topos. Unlike Milton, however, he need not mount a major assault on modesty because he can adopt a voice of self-assertion that comes not from an isolated prophet but from a priestly, institutionalized critic.[36]

As I have already suggested, the major form taken by the new prefatory rhetoric is a refiguration of the authorial voice from that of an advocate to that of a judge. This refiguration is by no means consistent in the "Preface." Dryden must still separate poet and critic, even though his anthology serves to blur that distinction: "For these reasons of time, and resemblance of genius, in Chaucer and Boccace, I resolved to join them in my present work; to which I have added some original papers of my own, which whether they

are equal or inferior to my other poems, an author is the most im-
proper judge; and therefore I leave them wholly to the mercy of
the reader" (249). The irony here, of course, is that Dryden does
not allow the obvious question of whether his poems are equal or
inferior to Chaucer's and Boccaccio's works, only the question of
the relative value of *his* works. To allow the former question
would be to question Dryden the critic and editor as well as Dryden the poet. And if the reader is allowed to make the final judgment, Dryden determines the evidence that is allowed in court:
"Perhaps I have assumed somewhat more to myself than they [the
learned] allow me, because I have adventured to sum up the evidence; but the readers are the jury, and their privilege remains entire, to decide according to the merits of the cause; or, if they
please, to bring it to another hearing before some other court"
(248). The forensic situation, then, is a complex one in which the
judge works closely with the jury, outlining the pertinent facts of
the case, summing up the evidence. He allows appeals, realizing
that his version of public justice may be flawed, but the assumption remains that judge and jury share a public discourse that is
capable of ascertaining truth.

The test of this discourse comes when Dryden himself comes
under attack, or chooses to represent himself under attack. Having justified or, more precisely, explained his choices for the anthology, he remarks, "As a corollary to this preface, in which I
have done justice to others, I owe somewhat to myself" (270), and
he goes on to deal with charges against him by Milbourne and
Blackmore. The only catch is that Dryden refuses to defend himself; he stays relentlessly in charge of the proceedings. Of Milbourne he says, "Let him be satisfied, that he shall not be able to
force himself upon me for an adversary. I contemn him too much
to enter into competition with him" (271). So with Blackmore;
Dryden does not pause even momentarily for self-defense before
launching into an attack on Sir Richard's works.

The most interesting case on the docket is that of Jeremy Collier and his charges of obscenity. Dryden's tactic here is to admit
everything in order to admit nothing:

I shall say the less of Mr. Collier [actually this is by far the longest reply],
because in many things he has taxed me justly; and I have pleaded guilty
to all thoughts and expressions of mine, which can be truly argued of ob-

scenity, profaneness, or immorality, and retract them. If he be my enemy, let him triumph; if he be my friend, as I have given him no personal occasion to be otherwise, he will be glad of my repentance.   (272)

Dryden here attempts to avoid specific charges through a general admission of guilt. When he turns to the concrete points in his opponent's case, he decides that Collier "has perverted my meaning." But even this briefest of apologetic moments swerves into prosecution as Dryden turns to an attack of the quotations Collier used to mount his attack: "Perhaps, it became not one of his function to rake into the rubbish of ancient and modern plays: a divine might have employed his pains to better purpose, than in the nastiness of Plautus and Aristophanes, whose examples, as they excuse not me, so it might be possibly supposed, that he read them not without some pleasure" (273). This is more than a snide comment on a clergyman's prurient pleasures; it is an assertion that Dryden is a better anthologizer and thus a better critic than Collier since he has constructed a more salutary genealogy for himself.

Dryden's parting words return us to the blunt ironies of his non-apologetic apology: "But, being a party, I am not to erect myself into a judge. As for the rest of those who have written against me, they are such scoundrels, that they deserve not the least notice to be taken of them" (273). It is difficult to imagine a more judgmental statement. And Dryden's final word, a quotation from the end of Horace's first book of satires, is not the peroration of an apologist, but the parting curse of a satirist at his rivals.[37]

> Demetri, teque, Tigelli,
> Discipulorum inter jubeo plorare cathedras.   (1.10.90–91)
>
> (But you, Demetrius, and you, Tigellius, I bid you go whine
> amidst the easy chairs of your pupils in petticoats.)

The quotation does more than allow Dryden a Horatian dismissal of his own Demetrius and Tigellius. It is the final link in the literary lineage he has been constructing for himself, a lineage that chooses Horace rather than Plautus or Aristophanes for its satirist.[38]

Dryden has put his own house in order, but unlike Descartes's house, Dryden's abode is unambiguously intended as an example of public architecture—a kind of literary Salomon's House—designed to represent its readership even as it instructs and constructs that readership. I will conclude with a brief look at the ironic deformations this public rhetoric entered into almost immediately upon its inception, suggesting that in parody (itself a kind of criticism) as well as criticism we can see a new conception of the preface, and with it a new conception of authority and authorship.

7

The End of the Beginning

THE DECLINE OF THE RENAISSANCE PREFACE

An Author ought to consider himself, not as a Gentleman who gives a private or eleemosynary Treat, but rather as one who keeps a public Ordinary, at which all Persons are welcome for their Money.   —Fielding, *Tom Jones*

This quotation comes from Fielding's "Bill of Fare,"[1] his introduction that was intended to guarantee that no reader could claim that he, as an "honest and well-meaning Host" (*Tom Jones*, 25), misrepresented or withheld the content of his public feast. Fielding's tone betrays the fact that he does not consider this new figuration of writing as public dining hall an entirely salubrious development: "Men who pay for what they eat, will insist on gratifying their Palates, however nice and whimsical these may prove; and if every Thing is not agreeable to their Taste, will challenge a Right to censure, to abuse, and to d——n their Dinner without Controul" (25). A public discourse that made no ready distinctions between readers and writers allowed for the nightmare of the eighteenth-century author: a world where every reader, by dint of "pay," was a critic and "without Controul." Fielding's "menu" is thus both an articulation of this new discourse and a moment of resistance to it. If, as the ideology of public language caught hold, the privacy of the prefatory space rendered the preface increasingly suspect, the writer could nonetheless resent the demands of this newly enfranchised audience. But since Fielding's avowed subject is "Human Nature" (26) itself, he feels obliged to indulge his readers in the advertisement of a bill of fare so that they may properly judge whether they wish to partake of his novel.

The suspicion of the "private Treat" that informs Fielding's introduction drives the prefatory rhetoric of the late seventeenth and eighteenth centuries. In a sense, the resurgence of fiction that insists on calling itself "history"[2] parallels the plethora of prefatory writings like Dryden's "Preface to the *Fables*" that present themselves as critical "essays." Just as preface writers adopted the role of judge to arrogate to themselves a disinterested public voice, to prove the public-spiritedness of their craft by playing the critic, so novelists looked to the guise of history as a means of not just removing the ludic stigma of fiction but also covering the private fantasies of fiction-making with the veil of "the public record." It is not difficult to explain the paradox that even as a developing sense of "individualism" rose in the seventeenth century, making possible among other things the "rise of the novel," the repository of rhetorical motive should become *more* rather than *less* suspect. If man was going to take over "God's plot," he had better have an extrapersonal motive. There seems to be an homology, then, between the novelist's simultaneous impulses to create an original plot and to present that plot as a "history" and the preface writer's heightened awareness of both his place as an individual in society and the responsibility to suppress that individuality for the good of society.

Defoe provides an early and clear example of the ideological uses of the historical pretense. In *Journal of the Plague Year* and *Captain Singleton*, for instance, he presents his work with no prefatory markers at all, leaving the reader to assume that the books are historical accounts. He also employs the fiction of a preface written by an editor who has merely collected and published the account that follows, as in *Moll Flanders*, *Robinson Crusoe*, and *Memoirs of a Cavalier*—the last was not uncovered as a fiction until the next century. It is telling how often the insistence on historical verity is invoked as a means of "making Publick" a "private Man's Adventures."[3] The assumption here and elsewhere in these early novels is that although a private man's fictions will always remain a private exercise, even when published, the "historical" account of a "private Man's Adventures" can indeed be "made Publick." Moreover, those very "Novels and Romances" that bear no relation to history vitiate the claims of veracity put forward for "a private History" like *Moll Flanders*.[4] In other words, it is history that stands as a guarantor of a public sphere made up of private stories and fiction that threatens this cumulative model of common discourse. Thus Richardson subtitles *Clarissa* (1748) "the History of a Young Lady: Comprehending the most Important Concerns of Private Life," and even though his preface abandons the overt fiction of an editorial speaker that he used in *Pamela* (1740), he insists that he has not written "a *light Novel,* or *transitory Romance.*"[5] Although his book describes an intimate subject, it addresses matters that concern "every private family" (xix). Thus the exemplary and the historical are revealed as functionally homologous.

As meaningful experience moved more and more into the private arena of the domestic, public discourse needed ever more firm proofs of the verifiable. Yet other options remained for handling the suspect excrescence of rhetorical motive found in the "private" voice of the preface. Rather than containing the private within the fiction of the veritable, it could be played out and expelled through parody, the rumblings of which we have already seen in Fielding's more ambivalent form of historical fiction. There is a Renaissance tradition of mocking the necessity of courting the reader, the tradition of Folly's good-natured embrace of the reader as a fellow fool, of Rabelais's alternating salutations to and imprecations of his reader. In differing forms, the tradition also appears in More's elaborately constructed *parerga* that supports the existence of Utopia, in Cervantes's decision (at the prompting of a "friend") to write his own dedicatory poems, in the fictional correspondence prefacing George Pettie's *Petite Pallace of Pettie his Pleasure,* in Nashe's induction of *The Unfortunate Traveller* to "the dapper Monsieur Pages of the Court," in the gigantism of Burton's "Democritus Junior" preface, and in Jonson's truculent induction to *Bartholomew Fair.* Yet this tradition, Lucianic in origin, remains limited if not isolated through the middle of the seventeenth century, becoming pervasive only with the exponential growth of satire in the Restoration.

The novel was not the primary locus for this second strategy to contain the problem of personal authority and the appeal to the reader. As in so many other matters, however, *Tristram Shandy* is the exception that proves the rule. Sterne uses a prefatory deformation different from those we have seen previously to express the same discomfort with a personal address to the reader. Sterne's form of prefatory parody is the employment of an ectopic preface. *Tristram Shandy* has both an ectopic preface and an ectopic epistle dedicatory (dedicated to no one in particular, so that the author can put it up for sale). This literal dislocation echoes the "dislocation" in which prefatory forms remain intact but are stripped of their traditional content and purpose.

In his dislocated preface, which does not appear until the middle of Volume 3, Sterne envisages a utopian world in which both writer and reader are perfectly endowed with wit and judgment, at which thought he goes into "raptures":

I faint away deliciously at the thoughts of it!—'tis more than nature can bear! . . . I'm dying,—I am gone.—Help! Help! Help!—But hold,—I grow something better again, for I am beginning to foresee, when this is over, that as we shall all of us continue to be great wits,—we should never agree amongst ourselves, one day to an end:—there would be so much satire and sarcasm.[6]

Rather than the critics and wits being assimilated to the purposes of the author, the author is drawn together with them into a vortex of "satire and sarcasm." The seam in the utopian fabric is the seam in the idea of common sense. Sterne realizes that even perfect judgment does not guarantee a commonly held discourse.

The rage for prefatory self-consciousness exhibits itself most clearly in parodic redactions of "public" forms such as the treatise. The touchstone for such treatments must be *A Tale of a Tub* (1704). Swift carried his exuberant parody of prefatory convention to such an extreme that in later editions prefatory matter makes up almost exactly half the work's bulk. Unlike the prefatory gigantism of *The Anatomy of Melancholy*, which is in fact perfectly proportional to the gigantic text that follows, Swift's rambling apparatus is intended to be monstrous. The prefatory matter consists of "An Apology for the, &c.," a dedication to Lord Sommers, "The Bookseller to the Reader," "The Epistle Dedicatory, to His Royal Highness Prince Posterity," "The Preface," and "The Introduction."[7]

The motive force behind this agglutinative collection may be glimpsed in the preface, where the author writes of "perusing some hundreds of Prefaces," which were given over mostly to "declaiming . . . against the Multitude of Writers whereof the whole

Multitude of Writers most reasonably complains" (45). The irony here threatens to fall into infinite regress: how can the conservative Swift check the cornucopian textuality of the newly authorized public without adding to the clamor? If satire seems the only solution for differentiating oneself, it is significant that the satire takes the form of extensive *parerga*.[8] For it is in the extratextual additions of the preface that the author steps forward to engage the reader. Swift's speaker, conjuring a picture of himself writing "in Bed, in a Garret," hungry and "under a long Course of Physick" (44), adds,

> Whatever Reader desires to have a thorow Comprehension of an Author's Thoughts, cannot take a better Method, than by putting himself into the Circumstances and Postures of Life, that the Writer was in, upon every important Passage as it flow'd from his Pen; For this will introduce a Parity and strict Correspondence of Idea's between the Reader and the Author. (44)

Swift shows himself not just as a reactionary yearning for an age of a more aristocratic, selective institution of authorship but as a man of his time decrying authorial inductions that distract the reader from public content to private persona. It is not just the Grub Street hack and the popular reader Swift assaults in his prefatory parody but the humanist author, with his personal, bodily authority.

Swift's brand of prefatory parody is carried much further—to the point of theorizing prefatory satire—in Thomas D'Urfey's *An Essay Towards the Theory of the Intelligible World. Intuitively Considered. Designed for Forty-nine Parts. Part III. Consisting of a Preface, a Postscript, and a little something between,*[9] a satirical anatomy in the Lucianic tradition (D'Urfey quotes *The Praise of Folly* very early in his treatise). Not surprisingly, D'Urfey's title misrepresents the extent of his *parerga* (it misrepresents everything else as well), but the work contains a chapter entitled "Of Prefaces" that itself becomes an ectopic preface. The chapter opens with the speaker's appraisal of the purpose of a preface and then moves on to address the question of motive:

> Learned reader,
> When you have settled your grand Affair with Mr. Stationer concerning the Purchase of this Golden Manual, you are desired to receive a modest

Address from the Author. Some thing must be said to a Person of your Character and Office, towards rendring him *attent and docile* . . . and some Civilities must needs pass between Author and Reader, towards introducing a better Acquaintance, before they proceed to their main Business. It must indeed be own'd, that many Readers of great Candor and Judgment, being endued with a mighty timerous Constitution, can never enter upon a Preface, Introduction, or *Apparatus* without the utmost Circumspection, and very great Uneasiness, lest in every Line some sly thing should be lurking to circumvent their Judgments.   (19–20)

There seems to be no adversative relationship between the second and third sentences here; "a modest Address," designed to socialize the reader into the text, always raises the suspicion of chicanery. D'Urfey gives his assurances, however, that he has no designs on the reader and encourages that reader to barrel headlong and unsuspecting through the work (the only danger is that we might miss many "Graces of Composition"). Amid these ironic self-congratulations, D'Urfey articulates the georgic principle: "However, there is nothing to trepan any inadvertent Reader, nor the least Design upon him, but what is purely and solely for his own Good" (21). He then links the theme of public good with the structural deformation of the preface: "Alas, I am so far from drawing up a subtle Harangue to bespeak your good Will, or prepossess you in Favour of an idle, unorthodox, or injudicious Book, that I am fully resolved to make this very Preface almost as valuable as the Book it self, and perhaps twice as long" (21). The "subtle Harangue," the insinuating intrusion of private motive into a publicly circulating text, is not discarded in D'Urfey's inverted world but diluted as the "valuable" content of the book is allowed to rush into its bounds and overwhelm its rhetorical savor. D'Urfey's irony serves the same homeopathic purpose as this overwhelming content that swells the preface: to appropriate the problematic rather than excise it, to emphasize rather than obscure it.

After "Due Examination," D'Urfey decides that the preface is "more Worthy" and "more Honourable" than the "Book" itself. Playing on the position of the preface in the book, he argues that "it was always allow'd the Precedence" and that "the Book has no other Office but that of filling up a Gap in the Middle, when it happens that a few useless Inter-leaves may be spar'd from the Introduction and the Index" (21–22). He concludes with a jab at ectopic content—not the sudden intrusion of prefatory topoi into the middle of the text we saw in Sterne but the deferral of significant matters (which D'Urfey associates with the prefatory) to the body of the text:

This shows us what a strange Absurdity our modern Innovators have run into, who bring in the Book before their Chief Preface, or which is all one, put off what was promised in the Title-page, till the Candid Reader begins to grow impatient; for who can bear to see things so preposterously disposed, that all the principal Matters which have an undoubted Right to be admitted in the Preface, should violently be kept out, and reserv'd to make up a pitiful Appendage, that is appointed to come servilely in the Rear of it: as if the Head should be forced to change place with the Belly, or the Brains thrust down to take their Seat in the lower Region. (22)

Prefaces are by nature "preposterous" since they are often what was last thought but at the first expressed, but D'Urfey purports to have discovered a new preposterousness in which matters destined for the preface are banished to the "pitiful Appendage" of the book. D'Urfey's textual version of Menenius's political fable suggests a parodic ideal of a volume that is all preface: a huge, bodiless head. As we have seen, this disembodied preface was a specter that haunted Bacon, Descartes, and others: a method that could never escape itself and produce content. D'Urfey's parody raises this fear to a more conscious level in an attempt to bring it under the control that satire provides. It is disputable, however, that he successfully banishes it. The political (and textual) vision that D'Urfey's parody assumes is one of integration; head and body, preface and text, writer and reader, exist in an intelligible, unified organism not unlike a slightly democratized version of Menenius's body politic. The body is being dehierarchized: *every* part, including the head, must act for the good of the whole. D'Urfey has imagined the Hobbesian text.

The prefatory rhetoric this vision calls forth bears only a parodic resemblance to the Renaissance rhetoric of authority through modesty. The preface has become a place of criticism (or of a parodied individualism), which implies an attempt to establish the author as a representative speaker of public discourse rather than a voice struggling to inscribe itself in an already completed text, to move in from the margins. Romanticism challenged the hegemony of common sense, but we have not seen, nor are we likely to see, the return of a rhetoric of self-authorization like that which prevailed in the Renaissance. Authorship may never be entirely self-justifying, but the role of the preface in providing justification has diminished immeasurably from its Renaissance heyday. Aristotle's slave may continue to cringe, but the complexity of his gesture has been lost as textual franchise has been extended. Today more than ever, as the bounded status of the book becomes more and more blurry in the face of continuous and open-ended forms of information flow, the prefatory threshold has become little more than an ornamental facade, a facade that shows in its pillars and tracery the vestiges of a once functional structure of rhetoric.

REFERENCE MATTER

Notes

For complete author names, titles, and publication data for works cited here in short form, see the Bibliography, pp. 181–93. For the abbreviations used here, see p. xiii.

PREFACE

1. Patterson, *Censorship and Interpretation*, 48.
2. I am referring of course to the famous entry in the index to *Histrio-Mastix* (1633), "women actors, notorious whores," which was taken to be a less than complimentary reference to Henrietta Maria's love of taking part in masques.

CHAPTER I

1. *Rhetoric*, 3.14.10, in *Basic Works*.
2. Aristotle's is the only recorded use in Liddell and Scott of *iatreúmata* as a technical term in rhetoric.
3. *Rhetoric*, 3.14.7. I include the Latin versions given by Cicero in *De inventione*, 1.16.22. The Latin terms for these "sources of goodwill," however, vary even in Cicero's theoretical writings.
4. George Kennedy argues that the Romans took from Greek rhetoricians those elements that could pose as anti-Greek, namely, the Stoic "emphasis on substance rather than style," an adaptation that fit the forum well and pandered to Roman nationalism (*Art of Rhetoric*, 4).
5. There are three major sources of Roman rhetorical theory on the preface: the tracts of Cicero (especially *De inventione, De oratore*, and *De partitione oratoria*), the anonymous *Rhetorica ad Herennium* (long believed to have been written by Cicero), and Quintilian's *Institutio oratoria*.
6. *De inventione*, 1.15.20. The *Rhetorica ad Herennium* (1.4.6) lists only four kinds of cases: *honestum, dubium, humile*, and *turpe*.
7. *Rhetorica ad Herennium*, 1.4.6.
8. The first century B.C. saw an outpouring of poetry—in particular,

that of Horace and the elegists—that took as its subject matter the "private" life of eros and retirement. Although the suddenness of this outpouring is a topic of very great interest, for my purposes the important point is that this poetry continued to enforce the distinction between public and private as rigorously as other forms of writing, taking its very existence from the "rejection" of public life but never denying the meaningfulness of the dichotomy.

9. The new alignment of public and private in the language of literary authorization can also be traced to the disappearance of a literary public documented by Auerbach ("The Western Public and Its Language," in *Literary Language*). That is, the notion of the public sphere had necessarily to be shrunk before it could be reconstituted as a series of private acts, and the reduction of the literary world to the cloister aided this process immeasurably.

10. Veyne, "The Roman Empire," in *History of Private Life*, vol. 1, *From Pagan Rome to Byzantium*, 231–32. Veyne sees the transition from pagan to Christian as that "from 'civic man' to 'inward man' " (1). He also argues, however, that a parallel transition was occurring within paganism, as a Stoic morality of the individual and the married couple began to supplant the "old morality" of the *urbs* (36–37). See also Foucault, *History of Sexuality*, vol. 3, *Care of the Self*, esp. pt. 2, "Cultivation of the Self," for the idea of an "internal" transformation within paganism toward a greater emphasis on the "self."

11. Janson, 126. Janson extends the work of Curtius on the topics of the preface back to late antiquity.

12. Ibid., 159.

13. Habermas, 7, 8.

14. Auerbach, "La Cour et la Ville," in *Scenes from Drama*; see also Sennett.

15. For the early history of this movement, see A. Ferguson, *Articulate Citizen*.

16. Reiss, *Discourse of Modernism*, 42. For a general account of the emergence of the private during the early modern period with special reference to printing, reading practices, and literary genre, see Chartier, *History of Private Life*, vol. 3, *Passions of the Renaissance*, esp. chap. 2, "Forms of Privatization."

17. A brilliant account of the market's relation to *representation* in its various senses can be found in Agnew, esp. chap. 3.

18. Foucault, "What Is an Author?" 148.

19. Stallybras and White, 77; see also Loewenstein.

20. Two excellent book-length studies of early modern ideas of "example" have appeared in recent years: Lyons, *Exemplum*; and Hampton, *Writing from History*.

21. *Complete Essays*, 611.

22. It should be pointed out that what is commonly said of the middle class must be reversed in the case of humanism: it is everywhere and always on the decline, yet always with us. Perhaps the most useful terminology for describing this process can be found in the title of Grafton and Jardine's *From Humanism to the Humanities*. The humanities are the ever-present atavism of humanism, sometimes stripped of its faith in the moral possibilities of rhetorical and literary training but always harboring that faith in its methodology and its apologetics.

23. Some exceptions are Whigham and Marotti. For the related topic of literature as encoded political message, see Potter.

PART I

1. For this distinction between the two Greek words, see Pucci, 9. An important element in this distinction not mentioned by Pucci is tense; the aorist infinitive *gerúsasthai* suggests a single, truthful revelation as opposed to the present infinitive *légein*, which indicates an ongoing process that lacks the simple unity of truth.

2. In bk. 1 of *De doctrina christiana*, Augustine elaborates this principle, which he bases on the virtue of charity: "Therefore, when anyone knows the end of the commandments to be charity 'from a pure heart, and good conscience, and an unfeigned faith,' and has related all of his understanding of the Divine Scriptures to these three, he may approach the treatment of these books with security" (1.40.44).

3. As Yarbrough points out with regard to one famous Protestant divine, "The problem is not that communication among men is impossible without its being originated in God, but that it *is* possible" (395). Revelation, Yarbrough goes on to argue, thus becomes a necessary grounding of rhetorical authority for such a thinker. For the connections between Protestantism and literary authority, see also Weimann.

4. On humanism and *copia*, see Cave; for the tradition of imitation and its relation to the "self," see the work of Thomas Greene, in particular, *Light in Troy*.

5. Bouwsma, 232.

6. Calvin, *Institutes*, 31.

7. See Popkin; and Kahn. Also useful in understanding the debate between Erasmus and Luther is Boyle, chap. 3, "Martyrs' Blood."

CHAPTER 2

1. I am thinking primarily of Greenblatt, whose exposition of Tyndale's work articulates this narrative in a manner highly relevant to Lu-

ther's self-fashioning. Just as Luther's "self" emerged at the moment of resistance to the authority of Rome and complete capitulation to God's
Word, so the English martyr Bainham finds identity, according to Greenblatt, "at the intersection of an absolute authority and a demonic Other,
but the authority has shifted from the visible church to the book." Thus
Luther's moment of self-assertion at Worms would represent an early and
outstanding moment in the emergence of the subject as an entity viable
outside and even in opposition to the public sphere. The entity "conscience" arises between an authority that Luther rejects and an authority
to which he feels himself "bound" (Greenblatt, *Renaissance Self-Fashioning*, 76). Luther's moment of defiance also dramatizes the birth of Foucault's "author-function." "Texts," he writes, "really began to have authors . . . to the extent that discourses could be transgressive" (Foucault,
"What Is an Author?" 148). When Luther defies the Diet and admits to
the list of books published in his name, he in effect stands forward as au-
thor-subject through his transgressive proprietorship of his texts. The author-function "Luther" could therefore be seen to have sprung up as a direct effect of the literary (and theological) marketplace. Also relevant
among the numerous studies on the topic of the early modern emergence
of the "subject" are Howard; Montrose; Reiss, *Discourse of Modernism*;
Fineman; and Patterson, *Censorship and Interpretation*.

2. Oberman, 39.

3. For speculation on the authorship of the account, see *LW* 32, 103.

4. One need look no further for this myth than Bainton's magisterial
biography of Luther, *Here I Stand*.

5. For the problem of authority in Paul, see Schütz; Holmberg; and
Munro. Among other "literary" innovations, Paul offered Luther a work-
able model for sacred autobiography: the sporadic anecdotes of a pastor
to his flock rather than systematic exposition. For Paul's knowledge and
use of rhetorical conventions, see George Kennedy, *New Testament Interpretation*, esp. chap. 4, "Judicial Rhetoric: Second Corinthians."

6. The logical difficulties in such a claim are at their clearest in 1 Cor
14.37–38: "If any one thinks that he is a prophet, or spiritual, he should
acknowledge that what I am writing to you is a command of the Lord. If
any one does not recognize this, he is not recognized." Paul was usually
able to avoid such apostolic fiat and the concomitant tautology, but such
a fiat lies behind a good deal of his more subtle rhetoricizing.

7. Paul addresses directly Christianity's dialectical relationship to both
systems in 1 Cor 1.22–24: "For Jews demand signs and Greeks seek wisdom, but we preach Christ crucified, a stumbling block to Jews and folly
to Gentiles, but to those who are called, both Jews and Greeks, Christ the
power of God and the wisdom of God." Peter Brown notes that in Paul's

time certain aspects of Hellenic and Judaic thought begin to appear very similar in the face of the radical ideas put forward by the new sect.

8. The editors of the *New Oxford Annotated Bible* note without comment: "Chapters 10 to 13 constitute a vigorous defense of Paul and his work and are written in a tone so different from that of chapters 1 to 9 that many scholars believe they are a fragment of another letter written to Corinth at some other time" (1398). Schütz, whose reasoning I follow here, argues that "it appears that chs. 10–13 represent a stage of correspondence earlier than much of the rest of the letter" (166*n*).

9. Kennedy, *New Testament Interpretation*, 95.

10. The actual "low" style of the *sermo humilis*, however, developed as the primary vehicle of Christian rhetoric well after Paul's time as a development parallel to the abject rhetoric of late classical prefaces. Auerbach, "*Sermo Humilis*," in *Literary Language*, 43, 41.

11. "At particular moments when there is within a society a crisis of belief—that is, when some central idea or ideology or cultural construct has ceased to elicit a population's belief . . . the sheer material factualness of the human body will be borrowed to lend that cultural construct the aura of 'realness' and 'certainty' " (14).

12. Paul develops his rhetoric of suffering most forcefully and expansively in 1 Thessalonians.

13. Paul's discovery that he could found ethical proof on experience that would heretofore have been considered irrelevant to a public rhetoric is an incipient step toward the view that an author *owns* his words in the same way that he owns the product of his manual labor. Thus Paul's proprietary sense of his discourse, of his "field" to be worked, stems from his paradoxical dialectic of strength produced from weakness, a dialectic that finds its "weakness" in labor and the bodily. First Corinthians develops at length Paul's theology of labor, and it is there that he reveals that he still practices his trade, tent making (9.6). Paul's appropriation and reversal of the classical prejudice against labor may be seen as, among other things, a function of the artisinal origins of Hellenistic Christianity. Paul thus uses his bodily labor to bridge the gap between the classical spheres of public and private, a bridge made possible by the new, somewhat attenuated Christian sense of community, a community founded on the shared "private" experience of the Spirit.

14. Brown's fascinating account in *Body and Society* of the origins of Christian celibacy provides a good basis for understanding the effect Christianity had on Hellenistic and Roman conceptions of the body. "Sexual renunciation," Brown argues, "might lead the Christian to transform the body and, in transforming the body, to break with the discreet discipline of the ancient city" (31). That is, celibacy struck directly at the

social order by removing the body from its position as guarantor of society's continued existence. Brown points out, however, that Paul seemed to be interested in the issue of celibacy only insofar as he was forced to address it by anxious members of his congregations and that his position was far from radical since he depended on the traditional Jewish family to propagate his ministry.

15. In 1 Cor 5.1–5, Paul urges the Corinthians to excommunicate a man for living with his stepmother, and the words of his excommunication carry with them a strong temporal threat: "You are to deliver this man to Satan for the destruction of the flesh, that his spirit may be saved in the day of the Lord Jesus" (5).

16. Luther specifically contrasts his *Vorrede* to obscuring papist *glosen* in the 1546 version of his preface to Romans (*WA* 3: 7, 4; *LW* 35, 365–66). See also his account of the proceedings of the 1518 Diet of Augsburg in which he plays subtly with the extracanonical nature of the bull authorizing indulgences, a bull termed "extravagante" because it was literally outside the canon of canon law, printed in an appendix if printed at all (*WA* 2, 6–26; *LW* 31, 259–92).

17. *Metamorphoses*, 1, 7.

18. Newman points out that Luther's *Testament* was imitated as often as it was attacked, and the authorized Catholic German Bible (1527) relies heavily on Luther's work. It is not surprising, then, that in his treatise on translation, *Sendbrief vom Dolmetschen* (1530), Luther exhibits a proprietary attitude toward his work: "It is my Testament and my translation, and it shall continue to be mine" (*LW* 35, 183). Perhaps more important, as Newman shows, Luther adopted some of the *textual* changes made in the Catholic edition, but "the text itself for the most part seems no longer to be the center of controversy. . . . Rather, it was the marginalia, the poisonous annotations and glosses, that were defiling the 'truth' of the Word" (117). His anger at the deletion of his prefaces and their replacement with Catholic ones stems from the central position of such *parerga* in his work. His exegetical introductions represent the essence of his self-inscription into Scripture, and the battle over *parerga* epitomizes the struggle over Truth itself. In fact, a general analogy exists for Luther between, on the one hand, Scripture and his collected works, entities that exist as it were "above" the need for the "author function" and, on the other hand, the prefaces to his collected works and the scriptural glosses and prefaces, which need to be marked with the name of the author to be both authorized and controlled.

19. Prince John Frederick and especially his uncle Frederick the Wise are important counters in Luther's self-authorization throughout this preface, particularly in his account of the Diet at Augsburg, where he arrived "afoot and poor, supplied with food and letters of commendation from

Prince Frederick" (*LW* 34, 330). The protection of the elector allows Luther this self-presentation as simultaneously impoverished and powerful.

20. I am using *narratio* in the technical sense of classical forensic rhetoric; that is, as the statement of the "facts of the case" that follows the exordium proper of a speech in the law courts. As so often in postclassical prefatory rhetoric, Luther uses topics from the entire forensic oration, not simply the exordium, when he constructs his preface. And while classical theorists often allowed a structural leakage between the *narratio* and the ethical proof of the exordium (see Quintilian, 4.1.26), Luther's extensive expansion of the "facts" constitutes a real attempt to establish a narrative control over the events of his life.

21. Sir Thomas Browne, a much less assertive and self-assured brand of Protestant, provides a classic example of such a rhetorical gesture in the preface to *Religio Medici*: "Therefore there might be many things therein plausible unto my passed apprehension, which are not agreeable unto my present self" (6).

22. Paul comes closest to presenting such a drama in his famous confrontation with Peter in Galatians 2, but stops short of intimating that his vision was informed by Peter's hypocrisy. Acts 15.1–35 relates Peter's important part in overcoming the objections of the Christians in Jerusalem to admitting non-Judaizers to the church. Paul's version of the incident, however, includes Peter's retreat from this stance: "But when Cephas came to Antioch I opposed him to his face, because he stood condemned. For before certain men came from James, he ate with the Gentiles; but when they came he drew back and separated himself, fearing the circumcision party" (Gal 2.11–12). Paul's use of the Aramaic "Cephas" for Peter may be a contemptuous glance at the parochial nature of Peter's backsliding. But this confrontation points to more than Paul's equal-opportunity proselytizing; his ministry to the Gentiles in the face of at best weak support from the church in Jerusalem became the basis for the demotion of Jewish law through typology and the basis for subsequent Christian hermeneutics.

23. The preface does contain one earlier glimpse of this "second narrative." Immediately following his account of the Leipzig debate (1517), Luther notes, "I had then [*iam tunc*] already read and taught the sacred Scriptures most diligently privately and publicly for seven years, so that I knew them nearly all by memory. I had also acquired the beginning of the knowledge of Christ and faith in him, i.e., not by works but by faith in Christ are we made righteous and saved" (*LW* 34, 334; *WA* 1: 54, 183). Like the later *interim*, *iam tunc* occludes any causal relationship between the public and private conversion experiences.

24. See Dillenberger, *Luther: Selections*, xvii–xviii, and Oberman, 153, for the problems of dating this event. Ebeling makes the essential

point when he doubts the ultimate usefulness of the "attempt to fix the date of the so-called Reformation experience," since this experience (despite Lutheran mythology) did not arise out of "a sudden isolated illumination" (41).

CHAPTER 3

1. I am borrowing Helgerson's useful notion that, especially among the Puritans, print began in the seventeenth century to usurp the place of the theater in providing a model for literary authority, authorship, and self-presentation (see "Milton Reads").

2. Wittreich, " 'The Crown of Eloquence,' " 21–22.

3. I use the term *figura* in the fairly strict sense described by Auerbach: "Figural interpretation establishes a connection between two events or persons, the first of which signifies not only itself but also the second, while the second encompasses or fulfills the first. The two poles of the figure are separate in time, but both, being real events or figures, are within time, within the stream of historical life" ("Figura," in *Scenes from Drama*, 53). Although Milton would not have considered himself to "encompass or fulfill" the figure of Christ, he aligns his role with that of Christ in a way that suggests he performs a significant extension of the Christian schema of history. Auerbach adds, in terms significant to my argument, that "figural prophecy relates to an interpretation of history—indeed it is by nature a textual interpretation" (57). Thus Milton places himself at the end of a chain of figural connections beginning with Paul's demotion of Judaism to the "first term" of a Christian figure. Hollander speaks of this figural chain as an example of the revisionary process of transumption: "These ['revisions of revisions'] can be schematized in radical Protestant theology—Luther revises Paul's revision of the Hebrew sect still based on the Law, and Milton and Bunyan revise Luther's revision" (147–48).

4. For Milton on the first set of *figurae*, see *Animadversions*: "In all wise apprehensions the perswasive power in man to win others to goodnesse by instruction is greater, and more divine, then the compulsive power to restraine men from being evil by terrour of the Law; and therefore Christ left *Moses* to be the Law-giver, but himselfe came downe amongst us to bee a teacher" (*YM* 1, 722).

5. Milton's insistence upon his youth—often entirely out of keeping with his actual age—has been much commented upon. As the editor of the *Yale Milton* points out (1, 806*n*37), Milton had a consistent habit (at least until he began *Paradise Lost*) of predating his work, either explicitly or by inference. Webber finds two seemingly different motivations for this habit: the "identification of his own destiny with that of England"

and the need "to assuage his fears and to create sympathy for himself with his audience. The 'elder adversary' with his 'big and blunted fame' is made a kind of Goliath to Milton's David" (188, 214).

6. For some interesting analogues to Milton's young orator, see Curtius, 98–101, on the *puer senex* topos. Curtius fails to mention the most obvious analogue to this Miltonic persona (undoubtedly because the question of age is never specifically broached), the young Christ in the Temple: "And all who heard him were amazed at his understanding and his answers" (Luke 2.47).

7. Emerson, 73. Kranides remarks with regard to *Of Prelatical Episcopy*, "Scripture is the original, the simple, the sufficient. Tradition is, paradoxically, 'new-fangled' 'innovation.' " ("Words, Words," 156). See also Patrides, chap. 6.

8. Milton explicitly states his Marcionite leanings in *De doctrina christiana*; quoting Paul's dictum that "the letter killeth," he adds, "Thus the imperfection of the law was manifested in the person of Moses himself; for Moses, who was a type of the law, could not bring the children of Israel into the land of Canaan, that is, into eternal rest" (*CM* 16, 110–11).

9. Damrosch says of the Puritans: "Their daily experience was of conflict and separation, and they were strongly drawn to the example of biblical prophets who stood out intransigently against their culture" (19). See also Delany.

10. Watkins counts "well over two hundred" spiritual autobiographies before 1725 that can be classified as "Puritan" (2). These narratives, of which Bunyan's *Grace Abounding* and Richard Baxter's *Reliquianae Baxterianae* are the most famous examples, did not really come into vogue until about 1650. Other general studies of Puritan "aesthetics" include Coolidge and Pettit. See also Christopher Hill's biography of Bunyan, *Tinker and a Poor Man*, esp. chap. 6. Two excellent recent studies of more general questions of nonconformist literature are Keeble, *Literary Culture of Nonconformity*; and Smith, *Perfection Proclaimed*.

11. In *De doctrina christiana*, Milton distinguishes the prophetic office from lesser callings, and his distinction (between "extraordinary" and "ordinary" ministers) is couched entirely in terms of the purpose of each office and its "gifts" (*CM* 16, 238).

12. See Horace, *Epode* 2. Røstvig, in her study of the *beatus ille* tradition mentions only *L'Allegro* and *Il Penseroso* in her discussion of Milton.

13. O'Loughlin, esp. chap. 4. O'Loughlin argues that Christian "civic" action always leads to a transcendent contemplation, an argument that points beyond Milton's achievement in the antiprelatical tracts toward *Paradise Lost*. See also Low for a very good overview of Milton's

comments on labor; Low's analysis, however, does not include a discussion of *which kinds* of intellectual activities Milton figures as labor.

14. For example, *Tusculan disputations*, 1.1, *De oratore*, 1.1, and *Orator*, 1.

15. Huntley, 85; C. Hill, *Milton*, 159. Among the other critical works that take up this topic are Kerrigan; J. Hill; Richmond; Wittreich, *Visionary Poetics*; and in a slightly different vein, Helgerson, *Self-Crowned Laureates*.

16. The critic who comes closest to my reading of Milton's antithetical use of the poet in *Church-Government* is Grose, who writes, "In all this reasoning, the would-be poet seems to address us almost reluctantly, as though he were the Attendant Spirit of his own *Masque*, leaving the more congenial neighborhood of Jove's empyreal court" (35).

17. Guillory, 97.

18. For Milton's understanding of the biblical concept of "covenant," see Shawcross.

19. Kranides, in "Milton's *Of Reformation*," 503, cites this passage to support his argument that in *Of Reformation* Milton strives to create a rhetoric and politics of vision that transcends the body.

20. The five men, however, included Thomas Young, Milton's former tutor; Young's involvement in the controversy explains Milton's entrance into the fray as a champion and, not incidently, allows him once more to figure himself as a young hero in an old cause.

21. In his analysis of the *Second Defense*, Hoffman comments on what had by this time become a rhetorical habit for Milton: "The length of this *exordium* is somewhat surprising; it appears at times to assume the functions of the *narratio*" (231). In fact, the *Second Defense* only exhibits in another form what one can already see in the *Apology*: Milton's inability to separate self-presentation from "the facts of the case."

22. See, e.g., Quintilian, 4.1.24–26.

23. In *De oratore*, 2.19, Cicero suggests that a place just before the conclusion is the proper location for a personal digression; it is not entirely clear, however, what the nature of this digression would be.

24. This is not an uncommon use of *neuter* (see *OED*, A2); for its use as a technical term in Puritan polemic, see Kranides, "Words, Words," 157, who quotes John Vicar's *Gods Arke Overtopping the Worlds Wares* (1645): "That unhappy and unholy *Neuter* or ambo-dexter, Dr. Usher." One thinks of that great Anglican "neuter" Sir Thomas Browne, with his great love of "amphibologies."

25. See also *Of Reformation*, "But their [Anglican Ministers'] *devotion* most commonly comes to that queazy temper of luke-warmnesse, that gives a Vomit to God himselfe" (*YM* 1, 537).

26. Milton spends a great deal of space later in the tract compiling biblical precedents for such holy "acrimony" (*YM* 1, 900), citing the words of Christ against the Pharisees. There is a great deal of critical work on Milton's "divine satire." See especially Anselment; Speer; Auski; McGuire; Kranides, "Style and Rectitude"; and Corns, "Obscenity, Slang and Indecorum."

27. Modern scholarship has not settled this issue; see Frederick Lovett Taft's introduction (*YM* 1, 863 and note).

28. *Pro se defensio* was published on Aug. 8, 1655, but over a year earlier, on July 6, 1654, Milton wrote Henry Oldenburg acknowledging his friend's serious doubts about More's authorship of the *Clamor*. Nonetheless, he chose to ignore the intelligence he received from the Continent on the matter of "nomination."

29. Blum, through an enlightening juxtaposition of *Areopagitica* and Milton's work as a licenser, argues convincingly that Milton's career demonstrates not just the author function but the emergence of the notion of authorial property. I would add only that this latter notion can, ironically enough, appear only at the moment when authorial autonomy might be seen to be entering a period of eclipse, when the print marketplace creates the possibility for authorial ownership by subjecting the author to a new system of authority based on public opinion.

30. See, e.g., Quintilian: "My aim, then, is the education of the perfect orator. The first essential for such an one is that he should be a good man" (1.Proem.9).

31. Milton takes his cue in stylistic criticism from Hall himself: "Can nothing then but Episcopacy teach men to speak good English, to pick & order a set of words judiciously?" (*YM* 1, 873). The reference here seems to be to Hall's reply to the Smectymnuans and not to the Confutant.

32. The reference in "this tormentor of semicolons" is to the Senecan trait of short, balanced clauses, as opposed to the longer, more free-flowing sentences of Ciceronian prose. Limouze has challenged the applicability of this traditional rhetorical dichotomy to this tract, arguing that Milton does not write Ciceronian prose but adopts a more flexible "rhetoric of choice."

33. Michael Lieb gives a theological context for this question of inner and outer; in contrast to Hall, Lieb argues, who invoked the concept of "adiaphorism or indifferency" (which has its origin in Pauline relegation of Jewish ritual to nondoctrinal status), Milton believed "that outward conditions are of absolute importance to inward makeup" (88). Milton's ideal of the integral relation of self and text is close to Montaigne's; for Montaigne, each essay is itself a new preface since not only is he the real subject of each essay, but each essay attempts to introduce that subject

anew. Yet Milton's equivalency between inner and outer, between private and public versions of the self, the consistency of a polemicist, is far from Montaigne's detached privacy.

PART II

1. See Grafton and Jardine, chap. 7, "Pragmatic Humanism: Ramism and the Rise of 'the Humanities.' "
2. See Thirsk; and A. Ferguson.
3. For Bacon's influence on his successors, see Webster, *Great Instauration*. For Renaudot and his influential Bureau d'Adresse, see Solomon.

CHAPTER 4

1. All translations of Descartes's letters are mine.
2. In the *Meditations*, Descartes finally has recourse to his own naked body, even if it is only to deny the creatural reality that Montaigne affirms. For a reading of Descartes's use of his nakedness, see Flores.
3. Nancy, 640.
4. Simpson, 97.
5. Lyons, 159.
6. Haldane, 119.
7. See, e.g., his letter of June 18, 1629, to M. Ferrier and that of Apr. 25, 1631, to Jean de Balzac (*A & T* 1, 13–16; 1, 199–201).
8. Strabo, *Geography*, 8.8.1; 16.1.15. Otto Steinmayer, a former colleague in classics, updated the tag for me with a loose translation: "The Big Apple is rotten to the core."
9. Strabo, *De situ orbis*, 75r.
10. *Opera omnia*, 2, 540. Erasmus's commentary on the proverb shows that he understood the original well: "Seleuciam ad Tigrim ait Babylone majorem fuisse, sed pleraque sui parte desertam." Nevertheless, he chose to use the ambiguous word *solitudo* rather than adopt the translation, for instance, of Guarino.
11. "Of Friendship," in *Works*, 6, 437.
12. The topos thus became an ideal tag for Neo-Stoic moralizers; in *Great Prerogative*, the English translator of La Mothe le Vayer's *De la vie privée* writes, "Our minde findes its *Hermitage* every where; and in the most numerous *Assemblies* of men in the greatest Towns and Cities in the world, I very frequently finde my self in a *Desart*. *Magna Civitas magna mihi solitudo*. And I am commonly as much alone as could be *Orpheus in Silvis, inter Delphinas Arion* provided that my Soul may conserve its liberty" (121–22).
13. Many of the details Descartes responds to are from a letter not to

himself but to M. de la Motts Aigron, dated Sept. 26, 1622. The literary nature of Descartes's formulation is thus enhanced by the fact that he is probably reacting to a *published* letter, since the first edition of Balzac's popular familiar letters came out in 1624. The letter in question is 1.15. The actual letter from Balzac to Descartes, dated Apr. 25, 1631, does not mention rural retirement but is full of Stoic reproach for life at court and acknowledges that "Monsieur des Cartes" is more of "le Sage des Stoïques" than Balzac (*A & T* 1, 200). It should also be noted that many of the details of the topos show up in an earlier letter of Descartes, to Ferrier (June 18, 1629): "Nevertheless I dare not invite you to come here; but I'll assure you that had I thought about it when I was in Paris, I would have tried to bring you along. And if you were a brave enough man to make the trip and come to spend some time with me in the wilderness [*le desert*], you would have ample leisure to exercise yourself—no one would distract you—you would be far removed from the things that can disturb you; in short, you'd be subjected to nothing worse than me, and we would live as brothers" (*A & T* 1, 14).

14. I am using *pastoral* and *georgic* in the supraliterary sense developed in recent criticism. The originary moment of this criticism may well be Williams's *City and the Country*, but the most extensive treatment is Low's *Georgic Revolution*. Low argues that the moral and conceptual apparatus of georgic had begun functioning long before Dryden published his translation of Virgil's *Georgics* (prefaced by Addison's laudatory essay) in 1697. Low points to (among other things) the new interest in the study of agriculture, to the "new science" with its emphasis on "use," and Puritanism's insistence on the moral significance of work. See also Fowler's answer to Low, "Beginnings of English Georgic"; Patterson, *Pastoral and Ideology*; O'Loughlin; Turner; Stallybras; Marcus; and Lindenbaum.

15. Balzac's aesthetic appreciation of his laborers, and even Descartes's transposition of that pleasure, are prime examples of what Bourdieu labels the "social picturesque" (58).

16. Descartes's social evaluation of the Dutch merchants and their uniform obsession with trade might be usefully compared with Thomas Sprat's observations that while London "is compos'd of *Gentlemen*, as well as *Traders* . . . , *Amsterdam* is a place of Trade, without the mixture of men of freer thoughts." And even the "Traders" themselves, Sprat thought, differed: "The *Merchants* of *England* live honourably in forein parts; those of *Holland* meanly, minding their gain alone" (87–88). For a more complicated view of the Dutch mentality in the seventeenth century, see Schama.

17. On Bacon and georgic, see Fish's well-known essay "Georgics of the Mind"; Low; and esp. Tillman, "Bacon's Georgics."

18. Descartes's ambivalence toward the choice between retired contemplation and urban activity, however, itself has a tradition; it is as if he were recalling the ironic oppositions of Horace's *Second Epode*, where a vision of the "happy man's" rural retirement is suddenly revealed to be that of the usurer Alfius, a momentary daydream in the ongoing world of moneymaking. By moving his eremite to the city, Descartes does not so much resolve Horace's oppositions as maintain them while laundering out the irony: rather than allowing the vision of the "happy man" to dissolve into the harsh, cynical light of the marketplace, Descartes argues that this glare offers the best protection for a man seeking to avoid the notice of others. In this scheme, the "happy man" and Alfius the businessman can never be the same, not even at the level of fantasy, since only the existence of Alfius provides the glare to make the happy man's urban retirement possible. For discussions of these concepts in antiquity, see Rosenmeyer; and O'Loughlin.

19. "La Cour et la Ville," in *Scenes from Drama*, 170.

20. Sennett, 16. Auerbach examines this public in terms of theater audiences, and Sennett extends this concept to public playacting of all sorts. On the class-specific nature of public and private in the seventeenth and eighteenth centuries, see Nicole Castan, "The Public and the Private," in Chartier, 403–4. Castan argues that the "great" lived an entirely public life, whereas the life of the commoner was, from a contemporary point of view, "exclusively private."

21. Haldane, 104–5.

22. Patterson traces a similar process in England, particularly in the works of Bacon, whom she sees as attempting to reconcile the individual intellectualism of pastoral with the public "practicalities" of georgic. "A pastoralized georgic, or vice versa, as a program for the intellectual development of the seventeenth century could have served his contemporaries very well." Instead of such a synthesis, Patterson argues, a kind of public spirit entered the pastoral through a dialogic engagement with the courtly culture that pastoral represented (*Pastoral and Ideology*, chap. 3, "Going Public," 38).

23. Mumford, 393–94.

24. Benevolo, 706–15.

25. Curtius, 87. Descartes combines this prefatory topos with another, the willingness to be revised.

26. Reiss, *Discourse of Modernism*, esp. chap. 1. Later in pt. VI Descartes argues, "For as experience makes most of these effects quite certain, the causes from which I deduce them serve not so much to prove them as to explain them; indeed, quite to the contrary, it is the causes which are proved by the effects" (*PW* 1, 150). This shift of emphasis to *effects*

changes the entire ground on which philosophical discourse is based. For a detailed study of the gradual ascendance of a language theory in which word and thing were held to be absolutely distinct entities, see Vickers, "Analogy Versus Identity," in *Occult and Scientific Mentalities*, 95–163.

27. As Simpson puts it, "The final resting point of the debate is a surreptitious appeal for the patronage necessary to allow Descartes to carry on with his own work in his own way, undisturbed by having to take account of the attentions of others to different objects" (88).

28. *Works*, 4, 21.

CHAPTER 5

1. Vickers, for instance, notes that Bacon's "detailed exposition of his theories of induction" as well as his "laborious collection of natural data . . . were almost totally ignored in the seventeenth century, and rightly so" (*Bacon and Renaissance Prose*, 1). For the history of the reception of Bacon's scientific works, see also Pérez-Ramos; and Webster, *Great Instauration*.

2. The most complete account of what I am deeming Bacon's bureaucratic sensibility may be found in Martin, *Francis Bacon*.

3. All quotations of Bacon are from *Works of Francis Bacon* and are cited in the text.

4. The Latin original of the *Magna Instauratio* may be found in *Works*, vol. 1.

5. See Whitney's interpretation of these frontispieces in his illuminating study *Bacon and Modernity*. Whitney chooses to emphasize the architectural connection between these "pillars" and the Great Instauration of the Temple of Solomon (33). Although such a connection certainly exists and the architectural metaphor is an important one for my purposes (*frontispiece* originally referred to the facade, and therefore the entrance, of a building), I would prefer to stress the topographic metaphor, which is more ready to hand and corresponds to Bacon's explicit interpretation of the image. "Why should a few received authors," he asks in the *Advancement*, "stand up like Hercules' Columns, beyond which there should be no sailing or discovering?" (3, 321). For Bacon's interpretation of Hercules as an analogue to the laboring man of science, see Tillman, "Pygmalion's Idolatry."

6. Yates, pt. II. See also Strong's two studies, *Cult of Elizabeth* and *Gloriana*.

7. Quoted in Elton, 344.

8. Knapp shows that such a theory gives a new legitimacy to the "trifling" of poets, a legitimacy that explains not only the literary explosion

of the 1580s and 1590s but the "otherworldly" nature of that period's most ambitious work, *The Faerie Queene.*

9. See the preface to *The Wisdom of the Ancients* in which Bacon denies that ancient fables are in any way frivolous: "Now I suppose most people will think I am but entertaining myself with a toy, and using much the same kind of licence in expounding the poets' fables which the poets themselves did in inventing them" (6, 695).

10. The clearest example of this bracketing is in the prayer from the preface to the *Instauratio magna* in which Bacon asks "that things human may not interfere with things divine," with the result that knowledge is "discharged of that venom which the serpent infused into it" (4, 20).

11. Helgerson, *Forms of Nationhood,* 185.

12. His tortuous interpretation of the Atalanta myth highlights the importance he places on this particular facet of the distinction between store and strength. Rather than following what might seem the more "natural" reading of the story—that the wiles of artifice subvert Atalanta's natural strength, causing her to turn aside from the race in pursuit of baubles— he writes, "For Art, which is meant by Atalanta, is in itself . . . far swifter than Nature" (6, 744). Only the corrupting force of Nature, here the temptation to take too quick a profit, diverts Art from her course.

13. Whitney takes the terms *adjacent* and *dynastic* from Said, 10. For the more traditional tropological use of *metalepsis* as a critical term, see Hollander. Whitney's use is based on an application of *translatio* as a technical term in Quintilian's discussion of Hermagoras. The term does, however, prove a useful way to conceptualize Bacon's positioning of himself vis-à-vis the ancients.

14. Whitney, 86. Whitney's discussion of Bacon's humility begins on 84. Cowley's ode "To the Royal Society" provides one of the best retrospectives on Bacon's influence, including these lines on Bacon's banishment of the Orgoglio-like "Autority":

> Autority, which did a Body boast,
> Though 'twas but Air condensed, and stalk'd about,
> Like some old Giants more Gigantic Ghost,
>   To terrifie the Learned Rout
> With the plain Magique of tru Reasons Light,
>   He [Bacon] chac'd out of our sight,
> Nor suffer'd Living Men to be misled
>   By the vain shadows of the Dead.

15. Bacon returns again and again to the metaphor of the machine, and indeed mechanics becomes the model science that geometry will be for Descartes. See *Advancement of Learning* 2: "The use of History Mechanical is of all others the most radical and fundamental towards natur-

al philosophy; such natural philosophy as shall not vanish in the fume of subtile, sublime, or delectable speculation" (3, 332–33). And more forcefully: "There remains but one course for the recovery of a sound and healthy condition,—namely, that the entire work of the understanding be commenced afresh, and the mind itself be from the very outset not left to take its own course, but guided at every step; and the business be done as if by machinery" (4, 40).

16. In *Advancement*, Bacon claims that reading between the lines, one can find great scientific knowledge in Mosaic law, knowledge that Moses acquired among the Egyptians (3, 297). Cowley's ode, already cited, demonstrates that Bacon's Mosaic posture was not lost on his followers. Cowley writes,

> Bacon, like Moses, led us forth at last,
>   The barren Wilderness he past,
>   Did on the very Border stand
>   Of the blest promis'd Land,
> And from the Mountains Top of his Exalted Wit,
>   Saw it himself, and shew'd us it.
> But Life did never to one Man allow
> Time to Discover Worlds, and Conquer too.

17. There must always be quotation marks, at least invisible ones, around the word *method* when one speaks of Bacon since he so often uses the word in the strict older sense of rhetorical methods. For the concept of method in Bacon, see Jardine, but also Ong; Grant; and Gilbert.

18. Fish's essay, "Georgics of the Mind" is the most famous statement of the implications of Bacon's aphoristic method. See also Hattaway, whose argument includes the following formulation of an ideal present in both Bacon and Descartes: "An examination of *philosophia prima* therefore reveals that it is a kind of divine *logos* where there is little distinction between body and method of knowledge" (187). In such a state there would be no distinction between preface and text, but neither philosopher successfully reaches this "first philosophy."

19. Apropos of this belief in the transplantability of knowledge through the recreation of the experience of learning is Bacon's claim that "the truth of being and the truth of knowing are one, differing no more than the direct beam and the beam reflected" (3, 287).

20. *Complete Essays*, 2.

21. For fuller readings of Bacon's gendering of nature, see Keller; and Merchant.

22. Whereas I have been discussing the mysterious privy chambers in terms of Elizabeth, Goldberg argues (conveniently for my purposes) that unlike his predecessor, James I based his rhetoric of rule on a "mystifica-

tion of the body" that shrouded but empowered patriarchal genealogy (85). Elizabeth's virginity made her body a pointedly *public* body, whereas James's production of male heirs emphasized the *private* body as a source of his public power. Whether or not Goldberg overstates the distinction between the two monarchs' styles of bodily self-presentation, it is important to note that Bacon's ideology of masculine generation fits nicely the rhetoric of the monarch under whom it was most fully articulated.

23. Perhaps the most interesting commentary on the hermetic side of Bacon's rhetoric of science is Stephens's *Francis Bacon*. Stephens argues that much of Bacon's method is "acroamatic" in nature, that is, designed to winnow out the unworthy through its difficulty. The aphoristic method, for instance, may reduce the explicit power the teacher has over the student but also requires a student of exceptional abilities to make the leaps of intellect between aphorisms laid out like widely separated stepping-stones.

CHAPTER 6

1. Quoted in Reik, 78–79.

2. *A & T* 3, 354. My translation.

3. *PW* 2, 121.

4. *Leviathan*, ed. C. B. Macpherson, 82. All further references to the *Leviathan* are to this edition.

5. Hobbes's defense of hereditary monarchy in chap. 19 is based only upon his belief that sovereignty must remain in a steady state—i.e., not jump back and forth from one man to the people who would choose a new monarch—in order for the state to avoid chaos.

6. For the importance of such "reading" in the *Leviathan*, see Silver. There is an important analogy between the rhetorical self-evidentiality that Silver notes and the homogeneity of tissue in the political body. Where audience and author share the same "nature," the rules of rhetorical proof have changed.

7. Patterson gives an extensive history of this fable in *Fables of Power*, esp. chap. 4, "Body Fables," which relates the fable directly to *Leviathan* and its frontispiece.

8. See Tricaud.

9. See Corbett and Lightbown, 229–30.

10. Macpherson, 106.

11. For an illuminating account of the relations between the market, concepts of representation, and the theater, see Agnew, esp. chap. 3.

12. Shapiro, 149. Shapiro is answering Missner, who makes the useful observation that Hobbes is vacillating between scientific method and the prudential tradition of humanism in the preface, but he limits the

place of prudential "reading" to very local moments in the *Leviathan*, while Shapiro sees such reading as essential to the method of the book as a whole, particularly to the often neglected final two books, which turn on questions of biblical hermeneutics. For the prudential tradition in Hobbes, see also Kahn's important chapter "Hobbes: A Rhetoric of Logic."

13. Reiss, "Power, Poetry," 219. Patterson also notes the way Hobbes's political vision looks "backward and forward at the same time" (*Fables of Power*, 136).

14. See Pye's reading of the *Leviathan*'s frontispiece. Pye sees the frontispiece as "figuring our sight at once as the sight of the narcissist and the onlooker" (298), thus (in the terms of my argument) revealing the ideological confusions of an authorial claim to sovereignty based on human legibility.

15. Having become associated with Shaftesbury and the Whigs opposed to the accession of James II, in 1683 Locke fled to Amsterdam, where Shaftesbury had died in exile earlier the same year. He did not return to England until 1689, after James had been deposed.

16. I owe this notion about Locke in part to Reiss, who argues, "It will in fact take Locke's discussion about private and public concepts and private and public language before the 'objectivity' of such discourse [a reference to Reiss's concept of the emerging 'analytico-referential discourse'] can be finally and formally 'justified' " (*Discourse of Modernism*, 34). But see also Rohbeck, who argues that Locke is providing, however unconsciously, a theoretical synthesis of the Levellers' idea of natural property rights and the Diggers' notion of property based on labor. The result of the synthesis is much less radical than either of the parts; Locke wishes to show that *present* ownership can be defended as naturally based on *past* labor.

17. Locke, *Two Treatises of Government*, 304–8. Laslett's introduction gives an account of Locke's "abnormal, obsessive" effort to keep secret his authorship of the *Two Treatises*. Locke shelved his copy of the book in his library alongside books by anonymous authors, and late in his life he wrote a younger friend, "Property I have nowhere found more clearly explained, than in a book entitled, Two Treatises of Government" (3). For whatever reasons, Locke was content to allow his book to become public discourse, unappropriated by his labor. Although he would seem to have formulated a theoretical answer to Descartes's conundrum, in this instance Locke is as unable as his predecessor to reconcile public and private discourse. It is perhaps of historical significance, however, that by choosing anonymity, Locke chooses to rest on the public side of dichotomy.

18. The bourgeois individualism behind Locke's theory that govern-

ment arose as a protection for private property elicited a great deal of criticism from conservative theoreticians. Bolingbroke and others objected that there was no ideal, prepolitical state for man, that social behavior (by which these thinkers understood patriarchal groupings) was instinctual rather than necessitated by self-preservation, property, or any other external consideration. This "Tory" viewpoint would have an even higher stake in a common public discourse than the "Whig" interpretation, even if that discourse was dominated by a single class. For a good exposition of these conflicting ideologies, see Kramnick, esp. chap. 4.

19. Locke cites the conditions of the American Indians as an example of how appropriation promotes the public good: the "*Americans*," "who are rich in Land, and poor in all the Comforts of Life; whom Nature having furnished as liberally as any other people . . . yet for want of improving it by labour, have not one hundreth part of the Conveniencies we enjoy" (314–15). Locke is aware that the superiority of Europeans in "use" stems largely from the invention of money, an invention that carries property out of the domain of what can strictly be termed labor. He argues, however, not only that labor indirectly creates these surpluses but that this accretion of property also makes commerce, and therefore "the Comforts of Life," possible. A critique of this position would lead me away from the issues of this book, but suffice it to say that this formulation of the relation between public good and private surplus, when transferred into the realm of discourse, remains an uneasy one throughout the eighteenth century.

20. Thus arises the "essay culture" of the late seventeenth and early eighteenth centuries. No longer the self-dramatization of Montaigne, the essay moved toward the more "public" gossip and criticism of Addison and Steele, personal reflections but with clearly normative claims. For a concise analysis of this essay culture, see Eagleton, 9–27.

21. For a more traditional account of the dispute, see Reik, chap. 7, "Hobbes in the Scientific World of the Restoration."

22. I am quoting from Simon Schaffer's translation, printed as an appendix, 350.

23. Webster argues, however, that this scientific latitudinarianism had already emerged during the interregnum among the "virtuosi" as a means of holding together a scientific community deeply divided on religious issues. See Webster's magisterial and encyclopedic history, *Great Instauration*.

24. Sprat, *History of the Royal Society*, ed. Cope and Jones, 2. All references to Sprat will be to this edition; cited by page number in the text.

25. Although the first meetings of the group that would eventually form the Royal Society took place at Wadham College under the leadership of John Wilkins, then warden of the college, Gresham College had

for over half a century offered a more urban, more bourgeois alternative to the two universities, an alternative that proved very congenial to the group that had gathered at Wadham during the interregnum. It should be noted, however, that this interpretation of the role of Gresham College, put forward by Christopher Hill, is among the issues questioned by H. F. Kearney (and defended by Hill) in a debate published in Webster, *Intellectual Revolution*, 218–61. In general, the proponents of London and the proponents of Oxford as the origin of the Royal Society seem to argue across an ideological divide not dissimilar to that separating the two cities during the Civil War.

26. Cowley, *Essays, Plays*, 248.

27. Corneille composed an *examen* for each of his plays when he collected them in 1660 but wrote none after that for *Sertorius* (1662).

28. The tradition of the critical preface is at least as old as Terence, who regularly addressed the attacks of critics in the prologues to his plays. Dryden's prologues are in this Terentian tradition. A prose tradition also persisted throughout the Renaissance, especially in sixteenth-century France where such prefaces were often the vehicle for articulating a national poetics. See Weinberg for the range of these prefaces. In England, however, despite the prologues of Jonson, the critical preface does not become the norm until Dryden.

29. *Essays of John Dryden*, 2, 246. All further references to the "Preface to the *Fables*" are to the second volume of this edition.

30. Dryden directly connects the roles of critic and translator in the preface to the second part of *Sylvæ*: "Thus it appears necessary that a Man shou'd be a nice Critick in his Mother Tongue, before he attempts to Translate a foreign Language" (*Works*, 3, 5). All further references to Dryden's writings (except the "Preface to the *Fables*") are to this edition.

31. Twenty years earlier, in his preface to *Ovid's Epistles, Translated by Several Hands*, Dryden had suggested the ambiguous familial relationship of poet and translator, claiming that Ovid "gives occasion to his Translators, who dare not Cover him, to blush at the nakedness of their Father" (1, 112).

32. Dryden's genealogical criticism can thus be seen as one more chapter in the history of the topos I noted in my discussion of Milton, a topos that can be thought of as a kind of literary-historical *senex puer*, claiming that the new (Testament-science-poetics) is older than the old since it can appropriate the contributions of its predecessor. The topos has a particular relevance for the preface, because the preface is the usual locus for discussing the author's place in tradition and because the "preposterous" preface is of two ages, coming first but generally composed last.

33. Dryden must perversely refuse (citing, ironically enough, "com-

mon sense") to accept Thomas Speght's correct appraisal of Chaucer's prosody.

34. In the preface to *Ovid's Epistles*, Dryden clearly uses the word in this sense: "It would be unreasonable to limit a Translator to the narrow compass of his Authours words: 'tis enough if he choose out some Expression which does not vitiate the Sense. . . . By this means the Spirit of an Authour may be transfus'd, and yet not lost" (1, 118).

35. Fry connects Dryden's metaphor with Longinus's language of inspiration: "In Dryden, as so often in Longinus, what is happiest in discourse comes from being haunted by an alien voice. What Longinus calls a flooding, or 'effluence,' Dryden with equal vividness describes 'in all transfusion, that is, in all translations' " (112).

36. A good measure of Dryden's development of this voice is a passage from a preface to an earlier anthology of translations, the second part of *Sylvæ* (1685), in which he employs the exact version of the modesty topos that he rejects here:

I am sensible that I have written this too hastily and too loosly . . . and which is worse, it comes out from the first draught, and uncorrected. This I grant is no excuse; for it may be reasonably urg'd, why did he not write with more leisure . . . ? The objection is unanswerable, but in part of recompence, let me assure the Reader, that in hasty productions, he is sure to meet with an Authors present sence, which cooler thoughts wou'd possibly have disguisd. There is undoubtedly more of spirit, though not of judgment in these uncorrect Essays. (3, 18)

This Montaignesque defense contains in its very self-consciousness the seeds of the stance Dryden will adopt in his last preface, but it still partakes of the modesty, however disingenuous, that he will later reject.

37. One might compare Boileau's taunting question to his readers in the preface (1701) to his *Satires*, " 'Jugez-moy?' " (11).

38. Horace the critic and poet is an apt choice since, like Dryden, he is very concerned with evaluating his predecessors. His attitude toward Lucilius is not unlike Dryden's toward Chaucer; Lucilius's problems were technical, Horace says, and if he were alive today with the benefit of modern versification, he would undoubtedly produce polished poetry (*Satires*, 1.10.64–71; see also 1.4).

CHAPTER 7

1. Fielding, *Tom Jones*, ed. Baker, 25. Subsequent quotations are cited from this edition.

2. See, e.g., the preface to bk. 3 of *Joseph Andrews* in which Fielding is at pains to distinguish between his real "biographical" history and

"those Romance-Writers, who intitle their Books, the History of *England*, the History of *France*, of *Spain*, &c." (185).

3. *Robinson Crusoe*, 1.

4. *Moll Flanders*, 1.

5. *Clarissa*, xxi. The interplay between the fiction of history and the more patently fictional in *Clarissa* is fascinating. On the title page to the 1748 edition, one reads beneath the title (in the customary place for the author's name) that the book is "Published by the Editor of Pamela"; beneath the colophon, however, Richardson's name appears as the printer, as was required by law. One cannot help but feel that Richardson's dual role as printer and author made him more comfortable with the fluctuations between the editorial fiction and the admission of authorship that one finds in the 1759 "Author's Preface" from which I have been quoting. I do not have space to detail these fluctuations, but it is worth noting, for instance, how Richardson makes constant use of the passive voice to skirt issues of agency. One feels that Richardson had not even lingering doubts that his work would be read as a fiction but that the power of the historical model in constructing a sphere of public intelligibility was too great to be abandoned.

6. Sterne, *Tristram Shandy*, 154.

7. *Tale of a Tub*.

8. This *parerga*, of course, need not take the exclusive form of prefatory materials. The elaborate set of notes that Pope provides for the *Dunciad* serves the same function.

9. D'Urfey, *An Essay*. This work, a parody of John Norris's *Theory of the Intelligible World*, was published under the name Gabriel John; even the date of "The Archetypally Second Edition" (from which I will be quoting) is parodic: "Printed in the Year One Thousand Seven Hundred, &c."

Bibliography

PRIMARY SOURCES

Addison, Joseph, Richard Steele, et al. *The Spectator*. 4 vols. Ed. Gregory Smith. London: Dent, 1973.

Aristotle. *The "Art" of Rhetoric*. Trans. and ed. John Henry Freese. Cambridge, Mass.: Harvard University Press, 1959.

———. *The Basic Works*. Ed. Richard McKeon. New York: Random House, 1941.

Augustine. *De doctrina christiana*. Trans. D. W. Robertson, Jr. New York: Bobbs-Merrill, 1958.

Bacon, Francis. *The Works of Francis Bacon*. 14 vols. Ed. James Spedding et al. (1857–74). Reprinted—New York: Garrett Press, 1968.

Boileau-Despréaux, Nicolas. *Satires*. Ed. Charles-H. Boudors. Paris: Société les Belles Lettres, 1952.

Browne, Thomas. *Selected Writings*. Ed. Geoffrey Keynes. London: Faber & Faber, 1968.

Burton, Robert. *The Anatomy of Melancholy*. Ed. Holbrook Jackson. New York: Vintage, 1977.

Calvin, Jean. *Commentaries*. 45 vols. Edinburgh: Calvin Translation Society, 1844–56.

———. *Institutes of the Christian Religion*. Ed. John T. McNeill; trans. Ford Lewis Battles. Philadelphia: Westminster Press, 1960.

Cicero. *Brutus, Orator*. Trans. and ed. G. L. Hendrickson and H. M. Hubbell. Cambridge, Mass.: Harvard University Press, 1971.

———. *De inventione, De optimo genere oratorum, Topica*. Trans. and ed. H. M. Hubbell. London: William Heinemann, 1960.

———. *De oratore*. 2 vols. Trans. and ed. E. W. Sutton and H. Rackham. Cambridge, Mass.: Harvard University Press, 1976.

———. *Letters to Atticus*. 3 vols. Trans. and ed. E. O. Winstedt. London: William Heinemann, 1920–25.

———. *The Speeches: Pro archia poeta, et al.* Trans. and ed. N. H. Watts. Cambridge, Mass.: Harvard University Press, 1935.

———. *The Speeches: Pro caelio, De provinciis consularibus, Pro Balbo.* Trans. and ed. R. Gardner. Cambridge, Mass.: Harvard University Press, 1970.

Cowley, Abraham. *Essays, Plays and Sundry Verses.* Ed. A. R. Waller. Cambridge, Eng.: Cambridge University Press, 1906.

Defoe, Daniel. *The Fortunes and Misfortunes of the Famous Moll Flanders, &c.* Ed. G. A. Starr. London: Oxford University Press, 1971.

———. *Robinson Crusoe.* Ed. J. Donald Crowley. London: Oxford University Press, 1972.

Descartes, René. *Oeuvres de Descartes.* 11 vols. Ed. Charles Adam and Paul Tannery. Paris: Librarie Philosophique J. Vrin, 1965.

———. *The Philosophical Writings.* 2 vols. Trans. John Cottingham, Robert Stoothoff, and Dugald Murdoch. Cambridge, Eng.: Cambridge University Press, 1985.

Dryden, John. *Essays of John Dryden.* Ed. W. P. Ker. Oxford: Clarendon Press, 1900.

———. *Works.* 19 vols. General eds. Edward Niles Hooker and H. T. Swedenberg, Jr. Berkeley: University of California Press, 1956– .

D'Urfey, Thomas. *An Essay Towards the Theory of the Intelligible World.* London, 170?.

Erasmus, Desiderius. *Opera omnia.* 10 vols. Hildesheim: G. Olms, 1961.

———. *Opus epistolarum Des. Erasmi Roterodami.* 12 vols. Ed. P. S. Allen. Oxford: Clarendon Press, 1906–58.

Fielding, Henry. *The History of the Adventures of Joseph Andrews.* Ed. Martin C. Battestin. Middletown, Conn.: Wesleyan University Press, 1967.

———. *Tom Jones.* Ed. Sheridan Baker. New York: Norton, 1973.

Hesiod. *The Homeric Hymns and Homerica.* Trans. and ed. Hugh G. Evelyn-White. Cambridge, Mass.: Harvard University Press, 1982.

Hobbes, Thomas. *Leviathan.* Ed. C. B. Macpherson. Harmondsworth, Eng.: Penguin, 1986.

Homer. *The Iliad.* Trans. Richmond Lattimore. Chicago: University of Chicago Press, 1951.

Horace. *Satires, Epistles and Ars poetica.* Trans. H. Rushton Fairclough. Cambridge, Mass.: Harvard University Press, 1966.

La Mothe le Vayer, François de. *The Great Prerogative of a Private Life: By Way of Dialogue* (translation of *De la vie privée*). London, 1678.

Locke, John. *Two Treatises of Government.* 2d ed. Ed. Peter Laslett. Cambridge, Eng.: Cambridge University Press, 1970.

Lucian. [*Works.*] 8 vols. Ed. A. M. Harmon. Cambridge, Mass.: Harvard University Press, 1953–61.

Luther, Martin. *D. Martin Luthers Werke: kritische Gesammtausgabe.* 113 vols. Weimar: H. Böhlau, 1883–1983.

――――. *Martin Luther: Selections from His Writings.* Ed. John Dillenberger. Garden City, N.Y.: Anchor, 1961.

――――. *Works.* 51 vols. Ed. Jaroslav Pelikan. St. Louis: Concordia, 1955–76.

Millhauser, Steven. *Edwin Mullhouse: The Life and Death of an American Writer 1943-1954 by Jeffrey Cartwright.* New York: Viking, Penguin, 1985.

Milton, John. *Complete Prose Works.* 7 vols. General ed. Don M. Wolfe. New Haven: Yale University Press, 1953–74.

――――. *The Works of John Milton.* 21 vols. General ed. Frank Allen Patterson. New York: Columbia University Press, 1931–38.

Montaigne, Michel de. *The Complete Essays of Montaigne.* Trans. Donald M. Frame. Stanford: Stanford University Press, 1965.

――――. *Les Essais.* Ed. Pierre Villey. Paris: Presses Universitaires de France, 1965.

More, St. Thomas. *The Complete Works of St. Thomas More.* 14 vols. New Haven: Yale University Press, 1963– .

Ovid. *Metamorphoses.* Trans. and ed. Frank Justus Miller. Cambridge, Mass.: Harvard University Press, 1971.

Puttenham, George. *The Arte of English Poesie.* Kent, Ohio: Kent State University Press, 1970.

Quintilian. *Institutio oratoria.* 4 vols. Trans. and ed. H. E. Butler. London: William Heinemann, 1969.

Rhetorica ad Herennium. Trans and ed. Harry Caplan. Cambridge, Mass.: Harvard University Press, 1968.

Richardson, Samuel. *Clarissa, or The History of a Young Lady.* Ed. George Sherburn. Boston: Houghton Mifflin, 1962.

Scaliger, Julius Caesar. *Poetices libri septem.* Geneva, 1561.

Sprat, Thomas. *History of the Royal Society.* Ed. Jackson I. Cope and Harold Whitmore Jones. St. Louis: Washington University Studies, 1958.

Sterne, Laurence. *The Life and Opinions of Tristram Shandy, Gentleman.* Ed. Ian Campbell Ross. Oxford: Clarendon Press, 1958.

Strabo. *Geography.* 8 vols. Trans. and ed. Horace Leonard Jones. London: William Heinemann, 1917.

――――. *De situ orbis.* Trans. Gregorius Tifernas and Guarino Veronese. Venice, 1494.

Swift, Jonathan. *A Tale of a Tub.* Ed. A. C. Guthkelch and D. Nichol Smith. Oxford: Oxford University Press, 1958.

Terence. [*Works.*] Trans. and ed. John Sargeaunt. Cambridge, Mass.: Harvard University Press, 1979.

Weinberg, Bernard, ed. *Critical Prefaces of the French Renaissance*. New York: AMS Press, 1970.

Wilson, Thomas. *The Arte of Rhetorique*. Ed. G. H. Mair. Tudor & Stuart Library. Oxford: Clarendon Press, 1909.

SECONDARY SOURCES

Agnew, Jean-Christophe. *Worlds Apart: The Market and the Theater in Anglo-American Thought*. Cambridge, Eng.: Cambridge University Press, 1986.

Anselment, Raymond A. *'Betwixt Jest and Earnest': Marprelate, Milton, Marvell, Swift and the Decorum of Religious Ridicule*. Toronto: University of Toronto Press, 1979.

Appleby, Joyce Oldham. *Economic Thought and Ideology in Seventeenth-Century England*. Princeton: Princeton University Press, 1975.

Auerbach, Erich. *Literary Language and Its Public in Late Latin Antiquity and in the Middle Ages*. Princeton: Princeton University Press, 1965.

———. *Mimesis: The Representation of Reality in Western Literature*. Trans. Willard R. Trask. Princeton: Princeton University Press, 1953.

———. *Scenes from the Drama of European Literature*. Theory and History of Literature, 9. Minneapolis: University of Minnesota Press, 1984.

Auski, Peter. "Milton's 'Sanctif'd Bitternesse': Polemical Technique in the Early Prose." *Texas Studies in Literature and Language* 19 (1976): 363–81.

Bainton, Roland H. *Here I Stand: A Life of Martin Luther*. New York: Abingdon Press, 1950.

Benevolo, Leonardo. *The History of the City*. Trans. Geoffrey Culverwell. London: Scolar Press, 1980.

Betz, Hans Dieter. *Galatians: A Commentary on Paul's Letter to the Churches in Galatia*. Philadelphia: Fortress Press, 1979.

Blum, Abbe. "The Author's Authority: *Areopagitica* and the Labour of Licensing." In *Re-membering Milton: Essays on the Texts and Traditions*, ed. Mary Nyquist and Margaret W. Ferguson. London: Methuen, 1988.

Bourdieu, Pierre. *Distinction: A Social Critique of the Judgement of Taste*. Trans. Richard Nice. London: Routledge & Kegan Paul, 1984.

Bouwsma, William J. *John Calvin: A Sixteenth-Century Portrait*. New York: Oxford University Press, 1988.

Bower, George Spencer. *A Study of the Prologue and Epilogue in English Literature from Shakespeare to Dryden*. London, 1884.

Boyle, Marjorie O'Rourke. *Christening Pagan Mysteries: Erasmus in Pursuit of Wisdom*. Toronto: University of Toronto Press, 1981.

Brown, Peter. *The Body and Society: Men, Women, and Sexual Renunciation in Early Christianity.* New York: Columbia University Press, 1988.

Burke, Kenneth. *A Rhetoric of Motives.* Berkeley: University of California Press, 1969.

Cave, Terence. *The Cornucopian Text: Problems of Writing in the French Renaissance.* Oxford: Clarendon Press, 1979.

Chambers, Bettye Thomas. "Cher Lecteur, Amy Lecteur, Lecteur Fidele: Prefaces to French Protestant Bibles, 1535–1588." Ph.D. diss., George Washington University, 1980.

Chartier, Roger, ed. *Passions of the Renaissance.* Trans. Arthur Goldhammer. Vol. 3 of *A History of Private Life,* general. eds. Philippe Ariès and Georges Duby. Cambridge, Mass.: Harvard University Press, 1989.

Coolidge, John S. *The Pauline Renaissance in England: Puritanism and the Bible.* Oxford: Clarendon Press, 1970.

Corbett, Margery, and Ronald Lightbown. *The Comely Frontispiece: The Emblematic Title-Page in England, 1550–1660.* London: Routledge & Kegan Paul, 1979.

Corns, Thomas N. "Milton's Quest for Respectability." *Modern Language Review* 77, no. 4 (1982): 769–79.

————. "Obscenity, Slang and Indecorum in Milton's English Prose." *Prose Studies* 3, no. 1 (1980): 5–14.

Crewe, Jonathan. *Trials of Authorship: Anterior Forms and Poetic Reconstruction from Wyatt to Shakespeare.* Berkeley: University of California Press, 1990.

Curtius, Ernst Robert. *European Literature in the Latin Middle Ages.* Trans. Willard R. Trask. Bollingen series, 36. Princeton: Princeton University Press, 1953.

Damrosch, Leopold, Jr. *God's Plot & Man's Stories: Studies in the Fictional Imagination from Milton to Fielding.* Chicago: University of Chicago Press, 1985.

Davies, Rupert E. *The Problem of Authority in the Continental Reformers: A Study of Luther, Zwingli, and Calvin.* London: Epworth Press, 1946.

Delany, Paul. *British Autobiography in the Seventeenth Century.* London: Routledge & Kegan Paul, 1969.

Derrida, Jacques. *Dissemination.* Trans. Barbara Johnson. Chicago: University of Chicago Press, 1981.

Diekhoff, John S. *Milton on Himself: Milton's Utterances upon Himself and His Works.* New York: Oxford University Press, 1939.

Eagleton, Terry. *The Function of Criticism: From the "Spectator" to Post-Structuralism.* London: Verso, 1984.

Ebeling, Gerhard. *Luther: An Introduction to His Thought*. Trans. R. A. Wilson. Philadelphia: Fortress Press, 1970.

Elimimian, Isaac I. "The Dedicatory Letter as a Rhetorical Device: The Example of Donne." *Classical and Modern Literature* 6, no. 2 (1986): 127–36.

Elton, G. R. *The Tudor Constitution*. Cambridge, Eng.: Cambridge University Press, 1972.

Emerson, Everett H., ed. *English Puritanism from John Hooper to John Milton*. Durham, N.C.: Duke University Press, 1968.

Ferguson, Arthur B. *The Articulate Citizen and the English Renaissance*. Durham, N.C.: Duke University Press, 1965.

Ferguson, Margaret W. *Trials of Desire: Renaissance Defenses of Poetry*. New Haven: Yale University Press, 1983.

Fineman, Joel. *Shakespeare's Perjured Eye: The Invention of Poetic Subjectivity in the Sonnets*. Berkeley: University of California Press, 1986.

Fish, Stanley E. "Georgics of the Mind: The Experience of Bacon's *Essays*." *Critical Quarterly* 13 (1971): 45–68.

Flores, Ralph. "Cartesian Striptease." *SubStance* 12 (1983): 75–88.

Foucault, Michel. *The History of Sexuality*. 3 vols. Trans. Robert Hurley. New York: Pantheon, 1978–86.

———. *The Order of Things: An Archaeology of the Human Sciences*. New York: Vintage, 1973.

———. "What Is an Author?" In *Textual Strategies: Perspectives in Post-Structuralist Criticism*, ed. Josué Harari, pp. 141–60. Ithaca, N.Y.: Cornell University Press, 1979.

Fowler, Alastair. "The Beginnings of English Georgic." In *Renaissance Genres: Essays on Theory, History, and Interpretation*, ed. Barbara K. Lewalski, pp. 105–25. Cambridge, Mass.: Harvard University Press, 1986.

———. "Georgic and Pastoral: Laws of Genre in the Seventeenth Century." In *Culture and Cultivation in Early Modern England: Writing and the Land*, ed. Michael Leslie and Timothy Raylor, pp. 81–88. Leicester, Eng.: Leicester University Press, 1992.

———. *Kinds of Literature: An Introduction to the Theory of Genres and Modes*. Cambridge, Mass.: Harvard University Press, 1982.

Fry, Paul H. *The Reach of Criticism: Method and Perception in Literary Theory*. New Haven: Yale University Press, 1983.

Gilbert, Neil W. *Renaissance Concepts of Method*. New York: Columbia University Press, 1960.

Goldberg, Jonathan. *James I and the Politics of Literature: Jonson, Shakespeare, Donne, and Their Contemporaries*. Baltimore: Johns Hopkins University Press, 1983.

Grafton, Anthony, and Lisa Jardine. *From Humanism to the Humanities:*

Education and the Liberal Arts in Fifteenth- and Sixteenth-Century Europe. London: Gerald Duckworth, 1986.

Grant, Patrick. *Literature and the Discovery of Method in the English Renaissance.* Athens: University of Georgia Press, 1985.

Greenblatt, Stephen. *Renaissance Self-Fashioning: From More to Shakespeare.* Chicago: University of Chicago Press, 1980.

———, ed. *Representing the English Renaissance.* Berkeley: University of California Press, 1988.

Greene, Thomas M. *The Light in Troy: Imitation and Discovery in Renaissance Poetry.* New Haven: Yale University Press, 1982.

Grose, Christopher. *Milton and the Sense of Tradition.* New Haven: Yale University Press, 1988.

Guillory, John. *Poetic Authority: Spenser, Milton, and Literary History.* New York: Columbia University Press, 1983.

Habermas, Jürgen. *The Structural Transformation of the Public Sphere: An Inquiry into a Category of Bourgeois Society.* Trans. Thomas Burger with the assistance of Frederick Lawrence. Cambridge, Mass.: MIT Press, 1991.

Haldane, Elizabeth S. *Descartes, His Life and Times.* New York: Dutton, 1905.

Hampton, Timothy. *Writing from History: The Rhetoric of Exemplarity in Renaissance Literature.* Ithaca, N.Y.: Cornell University Press, 1990.

Hattaway, Michael. "Bacon and 'Knowledge Broken': Limits for a Scientific Method." *Journal of the History of Ideas* 39 (1978): 183–97.

Helgerson, Richard. *Forms of Nationhood: The Elizabethan Writing of England.* Chicago: University of Chicago Press, 1992.

———. "Milton Reads the King's Book: Print, Performance, and the Making of a Bourgeois Idol." *Criticism* 29 (1987): 1–25.

———. *Self-Crowned Laureates: Spenser, Jonson, Milton and the Literary System.* Berkeley: University of California Press, 1983.

Hill, Christopher. *Milton and the English Revolution.* New York: Viking, 1977.

———. *A Tinker and a Poor Man: John Bunyan and His Church, 1628–1688.* New York: Knopf, 1989.

Hill, John Spencer. *John Milton: Poet, Priest and Prophet.* London: Macmillan, 1979.

Hoffman, Richard L. "The Rhetorical Structure of Milton's *Second Defense of the People of England.*" *Studia Neophilologica* 43 (1971): 227–45.

Hollander, John. *The Figure of Echo: A Mode of Allusion in Milton and After.* Berkeley: University of California Press, 1981.

Holmberg, Bengt. *Paul and Power: The Structure of Authority in the*

Primitive Church as Reflected in the Pauline Epistles. Lund, Sweden: Liber Läromedel/Gleerup, 1978.

Howard, Jean E. "The New Historicism in Renaissance Studies." In *Renaissance Historicism*, ed. Arthur F. Kinney and Dan S. Collins, pp. 3–33. Amherst: University of Massachusetts Press, 1987.

Howell, Wilbur Samuel. *Logic and Rhetoric in England, 1500–1700.* New York: Russell & Russell, 1961.

Huntley, John F. "The Images of Poet and Poetry in Milton's *Reason of Church Government.*" In Lieb and Shawcross, pp. 83–120.

Janson, Tore. *Latin Prose Prefaces: Studies in Literary Conventions.* Stockholm: Almquist & Wiksell, 1964.

Jardine, Lisa. *Francis Bacon: Discovery and the Art of Discourse.* London: Cambridge University Press, 1974.

Johnston, David. *The Rhetoric of "Leviathan": Thomas Hobbes and the Politics of Cultural Transformation.* Princeton: Princeton University Press, 1986.

Kahn, Victoria. *Rhetoric, Prudence, and Skepticism in the Renaissance.* Ithaca, N.Y.: Cornell University Press, 1985.

Keeble, N. H. *The Literary Culture of Nonconformity in Later Seventeenth-Century England.* Athens: University of Georgia Press, 1987.

Keller, Evelyn Fox. *Reflections on Gender and Science.* New Haven: Yale University Press, 1985.

Kendrick, Christopher. *Milton: A Study in Ideology and Form.* London: Methuen, 1986.

Kennedy, George. *The Art of Rhetoric in the Roman World, 300 B.C.–A.D. 300.* Princeton: Princeton University Press, 1972.

———. *New Testament Interpretation Through Rhetorical Criticism.* Chapel Hill: University of North Carolina Press, 1984.

Kennedy, William J. *Rhetorical Norms in Renaissance Literature.* New Haven: Yale University Press, 1978.

Kerrigan, William. *The Prophetic Milton.* Charlottesville: University of Virginia Press, 1974.

Knapp, Jeffrey. *An Empire Nowhere: England, America, and Literature from "Utopia" to "The Tempest."* Berkeley: University of California Press, 1992.

Knapp, Mary E. *Prologues and Epilogues of the Eighteenth Century.* Yale Studies in English, no. 149. New Haven: Yale University Press, 1961.

Kramnick, Isaac. *Bolingbroke and His Circle: The Politics of Nostalgia in the Age of Walpole.* Cambridge, Mass.: Harvard University Press, 1968.

Kranides, Thomas. *The Fierce Equation: A Study of Milton's Decorum.* The Hague: Mouton, 1965.

———. "Milton's *Of Reformation*: The Politics of Vision." *ELH* 49 (1982): 497–513.

———. "Style and Rectitude in Seventeenth-Century Prose: Hall, Smectymnuus, and Milton." *Huntington Library Quarterly: A Journal for the History and Interpretation of English and American Civilization* 46, no. 3 (1983): 237–69.

———. "Words, Words, Words, and The Word: Milton's *Of Prelatical Episcopy*." *Milton Studies* 16 (1982): 153–66.

Lanham, Richard. *The Motives of Eloquence: Literary Rhetoric in the Renaissance*. New Haven: Yale University Press, 1976.

Levy, F. J. "Francis Bacon and the Style of Politics." *English Literary Renaissance* 16, no. 1 (1986): 101–22.

Lieb, Michael. "Milton and the Organicist Polemic." *Milton Studies* 4 (1972): 79–99.

Lieb, Michael, and John T. Shawcross, eds. *Achievements of the Left Hand: Essays on the Prose of John Milton*. Amherst: University of Massachusetts Press, 1974.

Limouze, Henry S. "Joseph Hall and the Prose Style of John Milton." *Milton Studies* 15 (1981): 121–41.

Lindenbaum, Peter. *Changing Landscapes: Anti-Pastoral Sentiment in the English Renaissance*. Athens: University of Georgia Press, 1986.

Loewenstein, Joseph. "The Script in the Marketplace." *Representations* 12 (1985): 101–14.

Low, Anthony. *The Georgic Revolution*. Princeton: Princeton University Press, 1985.

Lyons, John D. *Exemplum: The Rhetoric of Example in Early Modern France and Italy*. Princeton: Princeton University Press, 1989.

McGuire, Mary Ann. " 'A Most Just Vituperation': Milton's Christian Orator in *Pro se defensio*." *Studies in Literary Imagination* 10 (1976): 105–14.

McKeon, Michael. "Politics of Discourses and the Rise of the Aesthetic in Seventeenth-Century England." In *Politics of Discourse: The Literature and History of Seventeenth-Century England*, ed. Kevin Sharpe and Steven N. Zwicker, pp. 35–51. Berkeley: University of California Press, 1987.

Macpherson, C. B. *The Political Theory of Possessive Individualism, Hobbes to Locke*. Oxford: Clarendon Press, 1969.

Marcus, Leah S. *The Politics of Mirth: Jonson, Herrick, Milton, Marvell, and the Defense of Old Holiday Pastimes*. Chicago: University of Chicago Press, 1986.

Marotti, Arthur. *John Donne, Coterie Poet*. Madison: University of Wisconsin Press, 1986.

Martin, Julian. *Francis Bacon, the State, and the Reform of Natural Philosophy.* Cambridge, Eng.: Cambridge University Press, 1992.

Merchant, Carolyn. *The Death of Nature: Women, Ecology and the Scientific Revolution.* San Francisco: Harper & Row, 1983.

Merton, Robert K. *Science, Technology & Society in Seventeenth Century England.* New York: Howard Fertig, 1970.

Miller, Jacqueline. *Poetic License: Authority and Authorship in Medieval and Renaissance Contexts.* New York: Oxford University Press, 1986.

Missner, Marshall. "Hobbes's Method in *Leviathan.*" *Journal of the History of Ideas* 38, no. 4 (1977): 607–21.

Montrose, Louis Adrian. "The Elizabethan Subject and the Spenserian Text." In *Literary Theory / Renaissance Texts,* ed. Patricia Parker and David Quint. Baltimore: Johns Hopkins University Press, 1986. 303–40.

Mumford, Lewis. *The City in History: Its Origins, Its Transformations, and Its Prospects.* New York: Harcourt, Brace & World, 1961.

Munro, W. *Authority in Paul and Peter.* Cambridge, Eng.: Cambridge University Press, 1982.

Nancy, Jean-Luc. "*Mundus est Fabula.*" *Modern Language Notes* 93, no. 4 (1978): 635–53.

Newman, Jane O. "The Word Made Print: Luther's 1522 *New Testament* in an Age of Mechanical Reproduction." *Representations* 11 (1985): 95–103.

Oberman, Heiko A. *Luther: Man Between God and the Devil.* Trans. Eileen Walliser-Swartzbart. New Haven: Yale University Press, 1989.

O'Loughlin, Michael. *The Garlands of Repose: The Literary Celebration of Civic and Retired Leisure.* Chicago: University of Chicago Press, 1978.

Ong, Walter J. *Ramus, Method, and the Decay of Dialogue: From the Art of Discourse to the Art of Reason.* New York: Octagon, 1979.

Patrides, C. A. *Premises and Motifs in Renaissance Thought and Literature.* Princeton: Princeton University Press, 1982.

Patterson, Annabel. *Censorship and Interpretation: The Conditions of Writing and Reading in Early Modern England.* Madison: University of Wisconsin Press, 1984.

———. *Fables of Power: Aesopian Writing and Political History.* Durham, N.C.: Duke University Press, 1991.

———. *Pastoral and Ideology: Virgil to Valéry.* Berkeley: University of California Press, 1987.

Pérez-Ramos, Antonio. *Francis Bacon's Idea of Science and the Maker's Tradition of Knowledge.* Oxford: Clarendon Press, 1988.

Pettit, Norman. *The Heart Prepared: Grace and Conversion in Puritan Spiritual Life.* New Haven: Yale University Press, 1966.

Popkin, Richard H. *The History of Scepticism from Erasmus to Spinoza*. Berkeley: University of California Press, 1979.

Potter, Lois. *Secret Rites and Secret Writing: Royalist Literature, 1641–1660*. Cambridge, Eng.: Cambridge University Press, 1989.

Pucci, Pietro. *Hesiod and the Language of Poetry*. Baltimore: Johns Hopkins University Press, 1977.

Pye, Christopher. "The Sovereign, the Theater, and the Kingdome of Darknesse: Hobbes and the Spectacle of Power." In Greenblatt, *Representing the English Renaissance*, pp. 279–301.

Reik, Miriam M. *The Golden Lands of Thomas Hobbes*. Detroit: Wayne State University Press, 1977.

Reiss, Timothy J. *The Discourse of Modernism*. Ithaca, N.Y.: Cornell University Press, 1982.

———. "Power, Poetry, and the Resemblance of Nature." In *Mimesis: From Mirror to Method, Augustine to Descartes*, ed. John D. Lyons and Stephen G. Nichols, Jr., pp. 215–47. Hanover, N.H.: University Press of New England, 1982.

Richmond, Hugh M. *The Christian Revolutionary: John Milton*. Berkeley: University of California Press, 1974.

Rigolot, François. "L'imaginaire du discours préfaciel: L'exemple de la *Franciade*." *Studi di Letteratura Francese* 199 (1986): 231–48.

Rohbeck, Johannes. "Property and Labour in the Social Philosophy of John Locke." Trans. Leslie Grega. *History of European Ideas* 5, no. 1 (1984): 65–77.

Rosenmeyer, Thomas G. *The Green Cabinet: Theocritus and the European Pastoral Lyric*. Berkeley: University of California Press, 1969.

Røstvig, Maren-Sophie. *The Happy Man: Studies in the Metamorphoses of a Classical Ideal*. Oslo: Norwegian Universities Press, 1962.

Ruch, Michel. *Le préambule dans les oeuvres philosophiques de Cicéron: essai sur la genèse et l'art du dialogue*. Paris: Les Belles Lettres, 1958.

Said, Edward W. *Beginnings: Intentions and Method*. Baltimore: Johns Hopkins University Press, 1975.

Scarry, Elaine. *The Body in Pain: The Making and Unmaking of the World*. New York: Oxford University Press, 1985.

Schama, Simon. *The Embarrassment of Riches: An Interpretation of Dutch Culture in the Golden Age*. Berkeley: University of California Press, 1988.

Schütz, John Howard. *Paul and the Anatomy of Apostolic Authority*. London: Cambridge University Press, 1975.

Sennett, Richard. *The Fall of Public Man: On the Social Psychology of Capitalism*. New York: Vintage, 1978.

Shapin, Steven, and Simon Schaffer. *Leviathan and the Air-pump:*

Hobbes, Boyle, and the Experimental Life. Princeton: Princeton University Press, 1985.

Shapiro, Gary. "Reading and Writing in the Text of Hobbes's *Leviathan.*" *Journal of the History of Philosophy* 18, no. 2 (1980): 147–57.

Shawcross, John T. "Milton and Covenant: The Christian View of Old Testament Theology." In *Milton and Scriptural Tradition: The Bible into Poetry*, ed. James H. Sims and Leland Ryken. Columbia: University of Missouri Press, 1984.

Silver, Victoria. "The Fiction of Self-Evidence in Hobbes's *Leviathan.*" *ELH* 55, no. 2 (1988): 351–79.

Simpson, David. "Putting One's House in Order: The Career of the Self in Descartes's Method." *New Literary History* 9 (1977): 83–101.

Smith, Nigel. *Perfection Proclaimed: Language and Literature in English Radical Religion, 1640–1660.* Oxford: Clarendon Press, 1989.

Solomon, Howard M. *Public Welfare, Science, and Propaganda in Seventeenth Century France: The Innovations of Théophraste Renaudot.* Princeton: Princeton University Press, 1972.

Speer, Diane Parkin. "Milton's *Defensio Prima: Ethos* and Vituperation in a Polemic Engagement." *Quarterly Journal of Speech* 56 (1970): 277–83.

Stallybras, Peter. " 'Wee feaste in our Defense': Patrician Carnival in Early Modern England and Robert Herrick's 'Hesperides.' " *English Literary Renaissance* 16, no. 1 (1986): 234–52.

Stallybras, Peter, and Allon White. *The Politics and Poetics of Transgression.* Ithaca, N.Y.: Cornell University Press, 1986.

Stephens, James. *Francis Bacon and the Style of Science.* Chicago: University of Chicago Press, 1975.

Strong, Roy. *The Cult of Elizabeth: Elizabethan Portraiture and Pageantry.* New York: Thames & Hudson, 1977.

———. *Gloriana: The Portraits of Queen Elizabeth I.* New York: Thames & Hudson, 1987.

Thirsk, Joan. *Economic Policy and Projects: The Development of a Consumer Society in Early Modern England.* Oxford: Clarendon Press, 1978.

Tillman, James S. "Bacon's Georgics of Science." *Papers on Language and Literature* 11, no. 4 (1975): 357–66.

———. "Pygmalion's Idolatry and Hercules' Faith." *South Atlantic Bulletin* 43, no. 1 (1978): 67–77.

Tricaud, François. "An Investigation Concerning the Usage of the Words 'Person' and 'Persona' in the Political Treatises of Hobbes." In *Thomas Hobbes: His View of Man.* ed. J. G. van der Bend. Amsterdam: Rodopi, 1982.

Turner, James G. *The Politics of Landscape: Rural Scenery and Society in English Poetry, 1630–1660*. Oxford: Basil Blackwell, 1979.

Veyne, Paul. *From Pagan Rome to Byzantium*. Vol. 1 of *A History of Private Life*, general eds. Philippe Ariès and Georges Duby. Cambridge, Mass.: Harvard University Press, 1987.

Vickers, Brian. *Francis Bacon and Renaissance Prose*. Cambridge, Eng.: Cambridge University Press, 1968.

———, ed. *Occult and Scientific Mentalities in the Renaissance*. Cambridge, Eng.: Cambridge University Press, 1984.

Watkins, Owen C. *The Puritan Experience: Studies in Spiritual Autobiography*. New York: Schoken, 1972.

Webber, Joan. *The Eloquent "I": Style and Self in Seventeenth-Century Prose*. Madison: University of Wisconsin Press, 1968.

Webster, Charles. *The Great Instauration: Science, Medicine and Reform, 1626–1660*. New York: Holmes & Meier, 1975.

———, ed. *The Intellectual Revolution of the Seventeenth Century*. London: Routledge & Kegan Paul, 1974.

Weimann, Robert. "History and the Issue of Authority in Representation: The Elizabethan Theater and the Reformation." *New Literary History* 17, no. 3 (1986): 449–76.

Weinberg, Bernard. *A History of Literary Criticism in the Italian Renaissance*. 2 vols. Chicago: University of Chicago Press, 1961.

Whigham, Frank. *Ambition and Privilege: The Social Tropes of Elizabethan Courtesy Theory*. Berkeley: University of California Press, 1984.

Whitney, Charles. *Francis Bacon and Modernity*. New Haven: Yale University Press, 1986.

Williams, Raymond. *The City and the Country*. New York: Oxford University Press, 1973.

Wittreich, Joseph Anthony. " 'The Crown of Eloquence': The Figure of the Orator in Milton's Prose Works." In Lieb and Shawcross, pp. 3–54.

———. *Visionary Poetics: Milton's Tradition and His Legacy*. San Marino. Calif.: Huntington Library, 1979.

Yarbrough, Stephen R. "Jonathan Edwards on Rhetorical Authority." *Journal of the History of Ideas* 47 (1986): 395–408.

Yates, Frances A. *Astraea: The Imperial Theme in the Sixteenth Century*. London: Routledge & Kegan Paul, 1975.

Index

In this index an "f" after a number indicates a separate reference on the next page, and an "ff" indicates separate references on the next two pages. A continuous discussion over two or more pages is indicated by a span of page numbers, e.g., "57–59." *Passim* is used for a cluster of references in close but not consecutive sequence.

Freedom of a Christian, 22; *New Testament*, 41, 44, 162; Preface to the 1539 Works, 43; Preface to the 1545 Works, 32–33, 41, 44–50; *Sendbriefe vom Dolmetschen*, 162
Lyons, John D., 88, 158

Machiavelli, Niccolò, 31
McKeon, Michael, 138
Macpherson, C. B., 129
Martin, Julian, 171
Matthew, Sir Tobie, 103f
Melanchthon, Philip, 22, 44
Merchant, Carolyn, 173
Mersenne, Marin, 83, 85, 124f
Milbourne, Luke, 143
Millhauser, Steven, ix–xi
Milton, John, 15, 20, 51–75, 79, 93, 134, 140, 142, 164–68 *passim*, 177
—works: *Animadversions*, 54, 65–66, 164; *Apology Against a Pamphlet*, 53f, 56, 64, 65–75; *Areopagitica*, 64, 167; *De doctrina christiana*, 165; *Defensio secunda*, 52, 74–75; *Doctrine and Discipline of Divorce*, 52, 64; *Of Prelatical Episcopy*, 54; *Of Reformation*, 54, 64; *Paradise Lost*, 54, 62, 164; *Pro se defensio*, 53, 74, 167; *Prolusions*, 51ff, 55; *Reason of Church-Government*, 53–65, 68–74 *passim*
Missner, Marshall, 174–75
Montaigne, Michel de, 11–14, 31, 50, 52f, 64, 75, 85f, 89, 111–15 *passim*, 130, 167–68, 176
More, Alexander, 69, 167
Mumford, Lewis, 95, 99

Nancy, Jean-Luc, 87
Nashe, Thomas, 148
Newman, Jane O., 162
Norris, John, 179

Oberman, Heiko, 29
Oldenburg, Henry, 167
O'Loughlin, Michael, 59, 165

Patterson, Annabel, xi, 170, 174f
Paul, Saint, 14, 24, 31–42 *passim*, 45, 49, 64, 160–65 *passim*
—works: 1 Corinthians, 56, 160ff; 2 Corinthians, 34–41, 161; Galatians, 163; Romans, 36

Peter, Saint, 163
Pettie, George, 148
Picot, Abbé Claude, 84
Plautus, 144
Plutarch, 39–40
Pope, Alexander, 179
Potter, Lois, 159
Prynne, William, x
Pucci, Pietro, 159
Pye, Christopher, 175

Quintilian, 4, 5–6, 38, 66, 167, 172

Rabelais, François, 148
Ramus, Peter, 80
Reik, Miriam M., 176
Reiss, Timothy, 9, 97, 130, 175
Renaudot, Théophraste, 80
Rhetorica ad Herennium, 4–5, 7, 59
Richardson, Samuel, 148, 179
Rohbeck, Johannes, 175

Said, Edward, 172
Scaliger, Julius Ceasar, x
Scarry, Elaine, 39
Schaffer, Simon, 133–34, 176
Schütz, John Howard, 38, 161
Sennett, Richard, 93, 170
Shaftesbury, Antony Ashley Cooper, Earl of, 175
Shakespeare, William, 40
Shapin, Steven, 133–34
Shapiro, Gary, 130, 174–75
Silver, Victoria, 174
Simpson, David, 87–88, 171
Smith, Nigel, 165
Solomon, Howard M., 168
Speght, Thomas, 178
Spenser, Edmund, 108, 172
Sprat, Thomas, 79, 81, 134–37, 169
Stallybras, Peter, 10
Steele, Richard, 176
Steinmayer, Otto, 168
Stephens, James, 174
Sterne, Laurence, 148–49, 152
Strabo, 91, 168
Swift, Jonathan, 72, 149–50

Terence, 3, 177
Tetzel, Johann, 46ff
Tillman, James S., 171

Valla, Lorenzo, 107

Library of Congress Cataloging-in-Publication Data

Dunn, Kevin.
    Pretexts of authority : the rhetoric of authorship in the
Renaissance preface / Kevin Dunn.
        p.   cm.
    Includes bibliographical references (p.   ) and index.
    ISBN 0-8047-2284-6 (cloth : acid-free paper) :
    1. English literature—Early modern, 1500–1700—History and
criticism—Theory, etc.   2. English prose literature—Early modern,
1500–1700—History and criticism.   3. Prefaces—History and
criticism.   4. Renaissance—Great Britain.   5. Authority in
literature.   6. Rhetoric—1500–1800.   7. Authorship—History.
I. Title.
PR428.P67D86 1994
820.9'003—dc20   93–6279
                                                  CIP

∞ This book is printed on acid-free paper.